SECRETS OF
ANCIENT
◆ AND ◆
SACRED
— PLACES —

THE WORLD'S
MYSTERIOUS HERITAGE

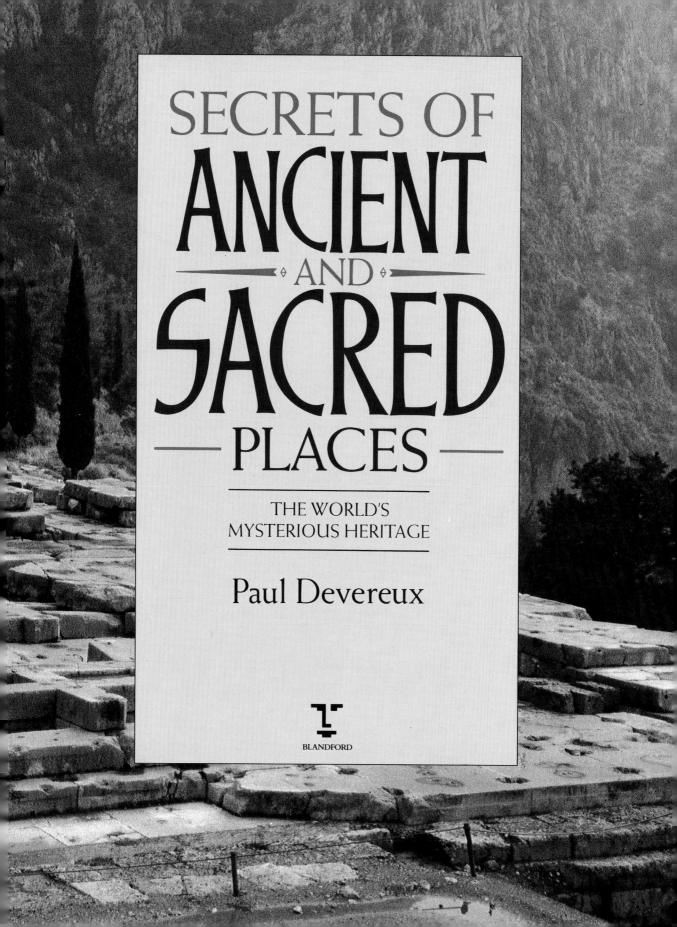

SECRETS OF ANCIENT AND SACRED PLACES

THE WORLD'S MYSTERIOUS HERITAGE

Paul Devereux

BLANDFORD

*For Charla,
fellow traveller . . .*

Paperback first published in the UK 1995
by Cassell plc
Wellington House
125 Strand
London WC2R 0BB

Published in hardback 1992
Reprinted 1993

Distributed in the United States
by Sterling Publishing Co., Inc.
387 Park Avenue South, New York, NY 10016-8810

Distributed in Australia
by Capricorn Link (Australia) Pty Ltd
2/13 Carrington Road, Castle Hill, NSW 2154

British Library Cataloguing in Publication Data
Devereux, Paul, 1945-
Secrets of ancient and sacred places:
the world's mysterious heritage.
I. Title
001.94

ISBN 0-7137-2593-1

Typeset in Great Britain by Litho Link Ltd, Welshpool, Powys, Wales
Printed and bound in Hong Kong by Dah Hua Printing Co., Ltd

CONTENTS

ACKNOWLEDGEMENTS

I always experience unease recording acknowledgements for a book, for if everyone was rightfully recognized for their help with any such work, it would take a chapter's length in itself; thus any short list is going to be inadequate. With that proviso, and keeping to a truly minimum list, in no particular order, I must express my gratitude for the helpful responses from the Cahokia Mounds Museum Society, and particularly William Iseminger, curator of the site, who has been especially generous with his help; to Edward Bakewell III for his fine hospitality during the Cahokia research trip; to Dr Thomas L. Sever of NASA, for his exceptional kindness regarding photographs and information relating to the Chaco roads; to Arthur K. Ireland of the Remote Sensing Division of the National Park Service in the Southwest USA; to Anne Seive of the now sadly-defunct UNESCO Centre in London who gave me much insight into the nature of the World Heritage List; to Martin Wattam of the UN Information Centre in London; to Patrick Horsbrugh for help with pictures and research information; to John Palmer for sharing some of his superb new research on medieval Europe; and to John Blofeld for bothering to answer my enquiring letter some time ago about Mount Taishan.

I am especially thankful to Frances Vargo for guiding me towards sources for rather obscure photograph requirements. Of all the helpful tourist agencies of the various countries containing sites selected in this work, I must single out Anthony M. Cuschieri of the Malta Tourist Office for supplying useful information as well as pictures, and Giovanna Salini of the Peruvian Tourist Board for exceptionally useful help with picture sources. I am also grateful to the Ohio Historical Society for their kind and prompt permission for use of a photograph.

My son Solomon helped smooth the way for the German sites research trip, and shared a grim driving schedule with me; my wife Charla shared with me all the demanding research journeys for this book, and handled most of the logistics. Thanks, too, to Trish and Bob Pfeiffer, Jean and Peter Sheridan, Fran Stockel and our other American friends whose hospitality and logistic help eased many of our US journeys, and to those kind supporters whose efforts in creating lecture and workshop situations made some of those trips financially possible.

Stuart Booth, my editor, always provides the right kind of support, and it is appreciated.

Finally, thanks are due to that motley band of researchers who comb the often unforgiving strand between the rather uncompromising hinterland of mainstream scholarship and the wild shore of speculative fantasy in search of true mysteries that both extremes tend to overlook. Some of these people are my friends, others my acquaintances and many I have never had the chance to meet. But I thank them all for their research, some of which is referred to in these pages.

Photographs – Most of the pictures in this book are my own work; where this is not the case, the appropiate photographer or source is credited in the caption.

PART 1

SACRED SITES
AND THEIR MYSTERIES

The Externsteine, Germany's most sacred site.

CHAPTER 1

SACRED GEOGRAPHY

WE SEEM TO HAVE LOST OUR WAY. New maps need to be drawn, a new geography perceived. We live in the only garden in the solar system, yet we have forgotten how to find our way around it, how to tend it, how to live with it. Even, how to see it. This outer disorientation mirrors that within. We have forgotten our deities, our magic and mysticism, our dreams, the doorways into and out of our minds. These were the means by which we related to nature.

We have thus expelled ourselves from the planetary garden. This process has not been sudden. In the European-based Western culture it has been happening little by little for thousands of years, but it has accelerated dramatically in the last few hundred years since our Industrial Revolution. The materially successful Western-style society has become by far the largest and most influential of all cultures, and as it has spread around the globe it has tended to modify or even eclipse other, traditional societies, and erode the health of Garden Earth itself. Only little pockets of earlier cultural knowledge survive, and those exist in a precarious and decimated manner. At the last minute, as we stare around in alarm, realizing we have become lost, we have noticed these other, disappearing denizens of the garden. We know of the rain forest Indians for example, almost as if by cutting and burning away the trees they have become exposed to our gaze. We know of a tribe here, or an ages-old society there. Anxiously, we try to learn from them: 'How do we find our way?'

We need new maps for another type of geography, another worldview. But where will this fresh cartography of the mind come from?

Guidelines that might help our future may, ironically, lie in the past. We may have gained some worthwhile things in our 'march of progress', but certain vital aspects of being human, conscious and part of nature seem to have slipped from our grasp. If we could learn to graft aspects of forgotten ancient wisdom onto our culture's better achievements, perhaps the future would look more promising.

There are a number of ways we are beginning to learn from the past. Our anthropologists and religious historians glean information on topics such as shamanism, the primary psychospiritual experience underpinning all later religions, passed on by traditional peoples both surviving and extinct; our pharmacologists and ethnobiologists seek the guidance of rain forest Indians in identifying new plants and learning their medicinal and magical (hallucinogenic) properties; our folklorists study the lore of old societies; and, of course, archaeologists probe the material remains of the past. And it is certain of these remains, the cities, temples and sacred sites and artefacts of antiquity, that provide one of the richest opportunities for us to re-learn the old map of a sacred geography which has disappeared from our modern worldview.

RETURNING

The increasing attention these old places are now receiving seems almost instinctive. We see this in modern times particularly in the form of tourism: the visiting of ancient monuments is given in surveys as a key element in people's motives for travel. It is as if there is an inarticulated need to regain contact with something more elemental, at whatever limited level. The mystery of the great monuments of antiquity exert a powerful fascination, as though we were trying to recall an important dream.

Another indication of the raising of general interest in the mysteries of antiquity has been in the plethora of popular literature on ancient sites and societies. The bestseller *Chariots of the Gods?* by Erich von Daniken may seem naïve nowadays, but it touched a deep-seated public fascination when it appeared in the late 1960s, as its serialization by a British tabloid newspaper at the time indicated. The link between UFOs, ancient astronauts and ancient sites was a strange hybrid, emerging out of the post-World War Two mentality, filtered through the psychedelic Sixties. Mysteries merged with mysteries. An endless stream of books and articles on Stonehenge and megalithic sites of all kinds, on ancient astronomy, on 'ley lines' and on the Nazca lines, on alchemy and arcane wisdom, on folklore, on paganism and shamanism, and on studies of the Great Goddess religion of prehistoric Europe have been hungrily received by a worldwide public over the past couple of decades. This reflects a need, however inarticulate, to enquire back into an ancient worldview to see if we left anything useful behind in our rush to some undefined goal of progress.

Out of the interest have come activities. Poorly funded and independent research efforts have developed to investigate leys, hypothesized 'earth energies' at sacred sites, ancient landscapes and peoples, and many aspects of traditional wisdom. Complementing this research movement has been a great rise of interest in neo-paganism, neo-shamanism and practical magical traditions. It is 'neo' because no one today, certainly no Westerner, can quite recover the state of mind, sociological structuring and environmental conditions that occurred in authentic, traditional forms of paganism and shamanism. It is thus largely an act of wish-fulfilment and theatrics, but nevertheless, as with the general interest in ancient sites, it represents our desire to reform our attitudes to mind and nature.

Both the research and religious aspects of this renewed interest in the past have their good and bad sides. Some lines of research are genuinely uncovering new approaches to the past, and fresh facts and perceptions are emerging. Other developments are, however, somewhat fantastical and worthy of the mainstream accusation of 'lunatic fringe'. Because the area is outside the protection of the academic pale, it is open to the predatory attention of journalistic hacks, egocentric would-be gurus and well-intentioned but poorly informed enthusiasts, often from a 'New Age' background, who rush into print with their pet ideas of the past, of ancient

mysteries, before they have done their homework. It makes for a babel of competing claims and ideas, and what is essentially a fictional view of ancient wisdom is created. Fantasies also creep into neo-paganism, and much hype and silliness infect the scene, together with some darker aspects of magical practice (ritually slain dogs and cats have been found at stone circle sites in Britain on occasion, for example). These elements conflict with the serious intent of most modern pagans who wish simply to direct their religious leanings towards nature. They are acting out a primordial impulse, and at this level it is a harmless and, indeed, wholesome pursuit.

Despite the confusion and problems, however, a 'background tone' of alternative but authentic intelligence is beginning to be assembled about ancient worldviews – though there is still a long way to go.

What lessons, then, can ancient sacred sites give us?

ARCHAEOLOGY

An obvious starting point is archaeology. It gives us an idea of the chronology of earlier cultures, something of their material lifestyles and even tantalizing glimpses of their beliefs and rituals. But while it is therefore a useful tool to use in reaching back to earlier worldviews, we must always bear in mind that archaeology is essentially a European invention, a framework developed for the use of the Western mind. Even the term 'prehistory' comes out of this conceptual framework; it means 'prior to documentary record' and to large effect means what happened before the modern European mind got there. So the 'prehistory' in the Americas means prior to the first known European contact.

Other, traditional cultures have startlingly different forms of 'archaeology'. Australian Aborigines, for example, have the Dreamtime, a time of origins, yet also a time of another order contiguous with the everyday world. Places in their landscapes recorded the adventures of the Dreamtime beings and were thus invested with a mythic reality. Tribes moved through mythic time as well as through the physical environment.

The type of archaeology possessed by a society or culture is closely related to its perception or collective image of *time*. Anthro-

Some of the 2,000-year-old Hopewell mounds at the 'Mound City' necropolis, Chillicothe, Ohio. Twenty-three mounds of varied shapes are grouped in an area enclosed by an earthen bank (foreground). In one mound, four cremations were covered with large sheets of mica. This and many ritual artefacts (such as this wooden mushroom 'wand') recovered at the necropolis indicate that the Hopewell culture was concerned with religious, shamanistic practice.

pologist Bronislaw Malinowski observed that the Aborigines 'do not conceive of a past as of a lengthy duration, unrolling itself in successive stages of time. . . . We, in our religious and scientific outlook alike, know that the earth ages and that humanity ages, and we think of both in these terms; for them, both are eternally the same, eternally youthful'.[1] The famous French anthropologist and philosopher Lucien Lévy-Bruhl similarly observed that to us 'the background of time past which we call history is an institution of the mind so familiar, it is almost impossible to imagine any human intelligence lacking it'.[1]

Some traditional societies use 'power plants', botanical hallucinogens, to enter mythic time. This process was often entrusted to the shaman who acted as intermediary between the Other-world and the tribe, seeking lost souls, healing and knowledge. This knowledge was often their form of archaeology. Maria Sabina, a famous Amerindian shaman of Central America, said that when she ate the sacred psilocybe mushroom she could 'look down to the very beginning . . . to where the world is born' (note the use of the present tense). German ethno-psychologist Holger Kalweit noted that it was necessary for a shaman to have 'visions of the mythical past'.[2] The South American Tukano Indians took the hallucinogen yajé (*Banisteriopsis*) to float back down the flow of time to 'the primordial source of all things' where one 're-experiences the beginnings of mankind. . . .' Nor should we in our assumed superiority automatically regard such experiences as being illusory: modern research with psychedelic substances has revealed that subjects

> often obtain access to detailed and relatively esoteric knowledge . . . experiences of collective and racial unconscious . . . and often . . . quite astounding details concerning specific historical events.[3]

So archaeology as we understand it is literally a child of our time, or, more precisely, of our *sense* of time (linear, mechanical, as opposed to the soft, cyclic time of traditional peoples), and worldview, the worldview that nows holds much of the world in its thrall. Indeed, the development of modern archaeology itself mirrored the shift of European consciousness from its own origin myths through the Age of Reason to modern science and rationalism. Archaeology has now become a powerful tool with which the modern mind can study the past. But we must always remember that the ancient sites were not built by the modern mind, and a tool developed by it is bound to miss certain kinds of information present at sacred monuments of antiquity, or at least not to perceive their full significance and implications. It is for this reason that other lessons have to be sought and learned. But how?

GEOMANCY

One of the most potent and comprehensive alternative approaches to ancient sites and landscapes is what is known as 'geomancy'. Strictly speaking, this term refers to an ancient form of divination in which, in its simplest form, handfuls of soil or other materials were scattered on the ground, or markings made in earth or sand, to generate a range of dot configurations which could be 'read' by a seer.

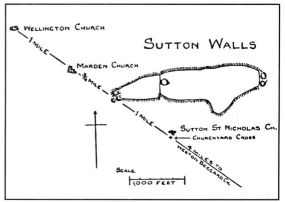

One of Alfred Watkins' own sketches of a 'ley' linking ancient churches and a mound on the corner of a major prehistoric earthwork in his home county of Herefordshire, on the border between England and Wales. Subsequently, the crop mark of an ancient straight track was revealed along part of this alignment.

Victorian missionaries, however, applied the word to a landscape-scale practice they encountered in China called *feng shui*, in which the orientation of houses and tombs was carefully regulated with regard to local topography and conditions. A complex system was employed, in which the feng shui consultant, the geomant, used a magnetic compass surrounded by rings of data relating to astrology, directions, the elements, forms in the landscape, the names of important stars, time of day and so on. The energies or *ch'i* of the land and air had to be harmonized to ensure good luck. Straight features (roads, river courses, ridges, lines of trees, fences and so forth) pointing at the building had to be deflected or masked off, and other landscape engineering was sometimes required.

In the 1960s, a generation of young enthusiasts began to emerge who were interested in ancient sites and old geomantic systems. These 'new geomants' republished Victorian material on feng shui and adopted the Victorian usage of the word 'geomancy', so that today it has become an inclusive term referring to those

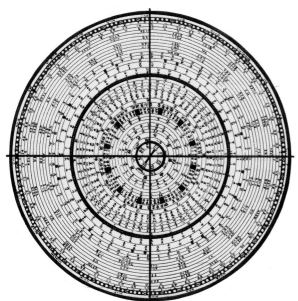

A feng shui geomant's compass or luopan *and ruler.*

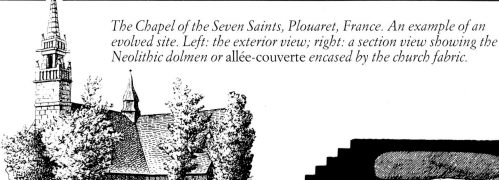

The Chapel of the Seven Saints, Plouaret, France. An example of an evolved site. Left: the exterior view; right: a section view showing the Neolithic dolmen or allée-couverte *encased by the church fabric.*

aspects of a sacred site that concern its placement and orientation in the landscape, and its relationships with natural features and other sites in the area.

One of the pivotal and most mysterious aspects of this modern version of geomancy is concerned with *alignments of sites*, what Alfred Watkins in the 1920s called 'leys'. Such ancient lines had been noted by a number of writers and researchers in Europe and the USA since last century, but it took Watkins' photographs and books, and the Straight Track Club which resulted from them, to really fire the whole subject. To Watkins, the lines were the remnants of old straight traders' tracks, which were laid down in the Neolithic period (roughly 5000–2000 BC in Britain) and which were modified in subsequent ages, only to fall into disuse and virtually disappear from the landscape during the historical era. He saw the lines as initially being sighted from one hilltop to another, using ranging rods and beacon fires, and minimally marked with standing stones, cairns and earthen mounds.[4] Watkins reasoned that some of the sites used to mark these old straight tracks eventually developed into holy and sanctified spots. He further argued that certain pagan locations of particular sanctity tended to be Christianized by having a church or cross superimposed on them. In fact, there is considerable evidence that a minority of churches in Europe, especially France, and, as we shall see, also in South America, were so erected. They therefore 'preserved the pre-

historic pattern in the landscape' as German researcher Joseph Heinsch remarked in the 1930s. (Some strands of modern ley work, however, are showing that there seem to have been various medieval geomantic schemes used in Europe; see Stonehenge and Speyer in Part 2 for differing examples of these. It is probable that until relatively recently ley hunters have unwittingly been noting alignments resulting from this period as well as from prehistoric times.) Another German, Wilhelm Teudt, independently and a little after Watkins, came up with a similar observation of landscape linearity, which he called *heilige linien*, 'holy lines'. He, too, assumed them to have prehistoric origins. Unfortunately, this work became tainted by association with Nazism.

In Britain, the subject of 'ley hunting' or 'archaic tracks' was rejected by orthodox archaeologists, who felt that 'primitive' prehistoric barbarians would not be able to survey lines, and in any case what could the purpose of such a nonsensical activity be? An increasing archaeological appreciation of the sophistication of prehistoric peoples in Europe, however, has now somewhat softened this harsh viewpoint, which was largely based on a chronological prejudice akin to a form of racism. Indeed, while some of what Watkins and other researchers claimed might be questionable, the basic idea of archaic lines on the landscape is now known to be a fact, although their mystery endures. For example, almost invisibly embedded in Watkins' home landscape of the British

One of William Stukeley's eighteenth-century drawings of the Stonehenge cursus, shown from its western end.

Isles are mysterious earthen linear features dating to the third millenium BC. They are known as *cursuses* and were earthen avenues formed by parallel ditches and banks, extending in some cases for miles. They usually link long barrows or other mounds. The eighteenth-century antiquarian William Stukeley was the first to notice one of these features (near Stonehenge, see Part 2), and he used the Latin term *cursus* because he thought it was a Romano-British racecourse. By 1934 six examples of these features were known, but with the advent of aerial photography the number has risen to over 50. This is because there is usually little or nothing to see at ground level, the earthworks having long been eroded away, and it required an air view to reveal their presence by means of crop markings. Apart from being linear in themselves, cursuses often point to distant positions, occasionally marked by a standing stone or other prehistoric site, but more usually now occupied by an ancient church (some churches have been found standing directly on cursuses, too). The present author has found in a study of a large sample of cursuses that about 64 per cent display this extended alignment characteristic.[5] No theory has yet been formulated to suggest what the purpose of cursuses could have been.

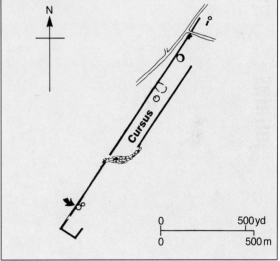

A sketch depicting crop marks near Aston-upon-Trent, England. The crop marks reveal part of a Neolithic cursus and various ring-ditches associated with it. The ring-ditch arrowed was excavated by archaeologists who found it had preceded the cursus. The straight, northwesterly ditch, nearly a mile (1.6km) long, had been aligned on it. (Modified after Gibson & Loveday)

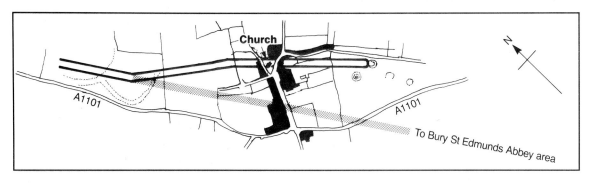

The cursus crop mark at Fornham All Saints, Suffolk. The village church stands on a ditch of one of the three straight segments, while the axis of the northerly section, extended cross country for 3 miles (5km), goes to the ancient and important Abbey of Bury St Edmunds. Note the remains of mounds at the southern end of the cursus. (Redrawn after J. K. St Joseph)

Sacra Via, Marietta, Ohio. This road follows the line of a 2,000-year-old Indian ritual way, which led from the Muskingham River to a group of mounds.

The landscape lines that most match Watkins' criteria for leys, however, are to be found in the Americas. In northern USA, Indian peoples of 2,000 years ago built geometric earthworks on a massive scale, and examples of these were preserved at Marietta, Ohio, where a road called 'Sacra Via' marks the course of a straight Indian sacred way. In the Sierras of California, Miwok Indians built dead straight tracks running for up to 40 miles (65km) from one mountain peak to another, 'airline in their directness', as researchers in the 1930s descri-

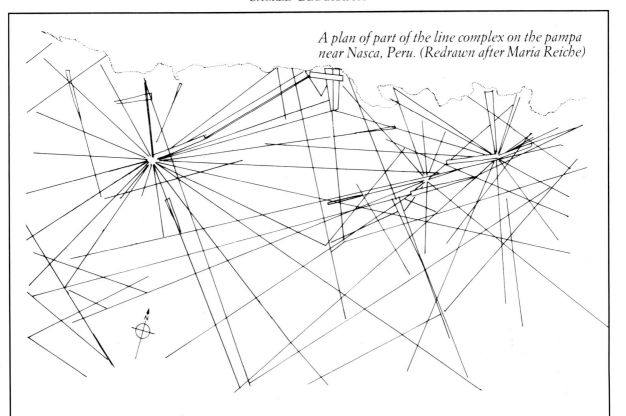

A plan of part of the line complex on the pampa near Nasca, Peru. (Redrawn after Maria Reiche)

bed them.[6] In New Mexico, straight roads radiate for miles around Chaco Canyon, and this site is described in depth in Part 2.

Many Amerindian peoples in pre-Columbian Mesoamerica built straight tracks and engineered roads – over 100 miles (160km) of pre-Hispanic straight roads have been found around La Quemada in Mexico, for instance. The Mayans, too, had straight ritual roads called *sacbeob*, not only within Mayan cities but running out for miles into the landscape linking religious centres. Only segments of these wonderfully engineered features have so far been investigated, as they lie mainly in the choking jungles of the region.

In South America mysterious straight lines are to be found in several Andean regions. The most famous examples are the Nazca lines in Peru, where a thousand or more years ago a multitude of ruler straight lines and curvilinear effigies were engraved onto the desert surface for purposes unknown. Many of the lines meet or diverge at stone mounds called 'ray centres', and detailed checks for astronomical significance among the lines have proved largely negative.[7,8] Further south, on the Altiplano of

western Bolivia, are more extensive networks of dead straight lines. No one knows who built them, and the first white man to record them seems to have been French anthropologist Alfred Métraux in the early 1930s. He found shrine sites, many Christianized, along the lines. The Andean Indian word for the old straight tracks means 'a row of things', whether sacred, such as shrines, or secular, such as a line of people or animals.[9] The lines are thus alignments of sites (the ley concept), with the straight track forming the secondary component. Moreover, Spanish churches stand on some of the lines, in just the way Watkins claimed that old churches did in Britain. The centre of the Inca empire was Cuzco, and this has perhaps the most sophisticated version of the South American lines, as we shall discover in Part 2.

The straight landscape line is found elsewhere in the world: on Java, Indonesia, the famous Buddhist temple of Borobudur falls into alignment with two other temples, Pawon and Mendut. Borobudur stands on an earlier Hindu site, and perhaps prior to that the site was important to the indigenous Earth religion. In

Ireland, the invisible 'fairy paths' from one earthworked hill (rath or 'fairy fort') to another were thought to be straight, and as in China it was considered unwise to build on them. In the Islamic worlds there are alignments of mosques – in Cairo for example, and, as we shall see in Part 2, at Luxor mosques were placed on much earlier alignments, just like the churches on Watkins' leys.

In Europe, the last archaic geomantic system we know anything of came via the Romans, famous for their straight roads, who in turn derived it from the Etruscans, a lost civilization which inhabited Tuscany and western Italy in the first millenium BC. We know little of these people, but they had a profound influence on the Romans, and the Etruscan diviners or *haruspices* were always respected by them. Plutarch described the Etruscan formation of the *omphalos* (the central sacred point or navel): 'A circular trench was dug . . . and in this were deposited first fruits of all things. . . . They call this trench, as they do the heavens, by the name of *mundus*. Then taking this as a centre, they marked out the city in a circle round it.' This pit led directly to the underworld. It was covered by a huge stone, which was lifted up on special days to allow the dead to move among the living or when the first fruits were deposited underneath it as a harvest offering to the gods. This pit was the point from which the two main streets of the town were laid out, dividing the

A diagrammatic depiction of the Borobudur temple alignment on Java, Indonesia.

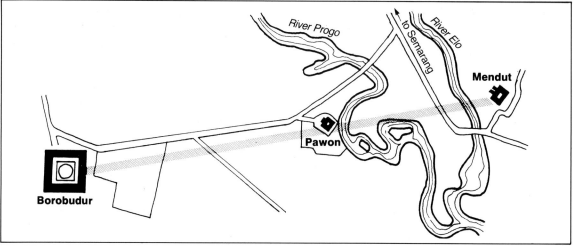

The great, multi-tiered Buddhist temple of Borobudur, Java, Indonesia, is on an alignment with two other temples (see opposite page). (Chris Ashton)

area within the walls into quarters. This grid-iron plan of streets had religious meaning, for the Etruscans believed that the heavens were also divided into quarters, each of which had a special significance. Further divisions into sixteenths were also made, each with its own meaning. The diviners, it has been said, had a 'fundamental doctrine of orientation'. The word *templum*, which gives us our 'temple', was originally a term from the vocabulary of Etruscan divination for a particular area of sky where the diviner collected and interpreted omens (such as bird flight) during which process he faced south. By using geomancy, the Etruscans in effect projected a sacred segment of the sky onto the land.[10,11,12] Surveying was part of a sacred system in Etruria, therefore, whereas the Romans used it primarily for secular purposes. Yet even the Romans would place shrines at intervals along their straight ways.

The concept of the omphalos, the world navel or centre, is fundamental to geomancy. The navel in the human being records the point of origin and sustenance, and so it is symbolically at the foundation point of a building, city or holy site. It is usually marked by a stone but sometimes by a post, tree or, as we have noted, a pit. The concept of the 'World Mountain' is also a version of the omphalos. The standard, classic example of an omphalos is at Delphi, in Greece (see Part 2). At Mecca, Islam's most holy shrine, the Ka'aba, contains a stone, possibly meteoric. From this point paths radiate in the eight directions. The former Temple of Solomon is the ultimate omphalos, being, as one antiquarian scholar put it, 'situated in the centre of the world . . . in the centre of the land of Israel, and the Temple in the centre of Jerusalem, and the Holy of Holies in the centre of the Temple, and the foundation stone on which the world was founded is situated in front of the ark.'[13] The navel stone of Jerusalem was known as the 'Compass of our Lord'. Every temple or holy place in the ancient world would have its centre, omphalos, navel. The idea lingers on in our own foundation stone tradition. The idea of the world centre, the omphalos, existed in totally unconnected cultures. The Zuni Indians of the American southwest, for instance, had a legend in which Water Skate showed the first Zunis the Four Directions by spreading his long legs, his heart and navel marking 'the midmost place of the Earth Mother'.

EARTH MYSTERIES

So geomancy clearly is that 'sacred geography' we need to relearn – or, rather, we need to understand any basic principles that underlie its various manifestations in different societies and ages. In an effort to do this, the 'alternative academy' that has developed around the modern study of geomancy has found it necessary to extend a wider net than anyone could have initially envisaged as necessary. So much so that geomancy has become an extended arena of multi-disciplinary and multi-mode research. In Britain, the somewhat bland term 'Earth Mysteries' was invoked in the early 1970s to refer to this extended scope of geomantic research. We can look only briefly here at some of these further areas of involvement.

CONSCIOUSNESS STUDIES

Where these most obviously come in is in the role of the shaman or priest/ess. The shaman typically used a drum to beat out a trance-inducing rhythm. The instrument acted as a sort of vehicle for him or her to travel to the

This seventeenth-century illustration by J. Schefferus shows two Lapp shamans. One is beating his drum to induce a trance, and the other's spirit has already 'flown' to the Otherworlds. While a shaman was in a trance, his drum was traditionally placed on him, for it was his vehicle or steed into the supramundane planes and warned against sudden disturbance.

Otherworlds of spirit. In myth, the drum was fashioned from a branch of the World Tree – that is to say, it belonged to the world centre, the navel, the omphalos, and it could take the shaman there. Here was the cosmic axis, up or down which the shaman could travel to the spirit domains. In this image, as old as human society, we have the fusion of mind and land; *the geomantic omphalos was simultaneously a physical and a mental location.*

This concept, transcending culture or time, assures us that ancient sacred sites were essentially used for contact with supernatural realms: that is, they were places where human consciousness was moved from the mundane to the supramundane by a variety of mind-changing techniques – rhythmic drumming, dancing, ritual, religious practice, tantric sex, ritual dreaming (see Epidaurus, Part 2) or the use of hallucinogenic plants. Places where the inner nature of humanity met the outer face of nature.

Another way in which consciousness studies have become relevant to geomantic research is in the use of psychics at sites – 'psychic archaeology' as it is sometimes called. The first person we know of in modern times to use psychic means to access information at a site was Frederick Bligh Bond during his excavations early this century at Glastonbury Abbey. Bond made use of mediumistic 'automatic writing' containing information on the Abbey foundations from apparent discarnate entities, or, as Bligh Bond also considered possible, some form of collective memory.[14] Between the World Wars it was a fashion for sites to be visited by psychics sensitive to places or objects (psychometrists).[15] These people allegedly obtained visual glimpses and other information of past happenings at stone circles and henges. The general consensus seemed to be that the stones were erected by wise priesthoods, who conjured with various undefined cosmic energies brought down to earth within the sites and used for ritual and spiritual work in various ways. Ultimately, the original knowledge became lost, the sensitives declared, and degenerate practices began to be carried out at the monuments. In more recent times, American researcher Jeffrey Goodman has used a psychic to help in locating a place where excavation could reveal information about early humans in North America,[16] and the American Moebius group used psychics successfully to identify excavation targets in Egypt. The Dragon Project in Britain has also used a range of psychics to study sites from a psychometric angle.

Modern ley research is also producing evidence to suggest that the function of archaic lines and alignments may have been related to the 'passage of spirit';[17] meaning, essentially, that the ancient landscape lines were various forms of spirit paths. This research links archaeology, etymological evidence, nature mysticism, parapsychological research and anthropology, and it is fully discussed by this writer in a work currently in preparation.[18]

ANCIENT ASTRONOMY

This has been one of the few 'fringe' disciplines to be accommodated within the mainstream academic framework. Its origins were in folk

In 1894 Magnus Spence produced this diagram showing the alignments between key Orkney sites. L. Circle is the Ring of Brogar, and S. Circle is the ruined Ring of Stenness. The Barnhouse and Watchstone monoliths, discussed on the next page, are also shown. Larger distances are shown in chains – a chain being a measure of 100 links or 66 feet (20.12m).

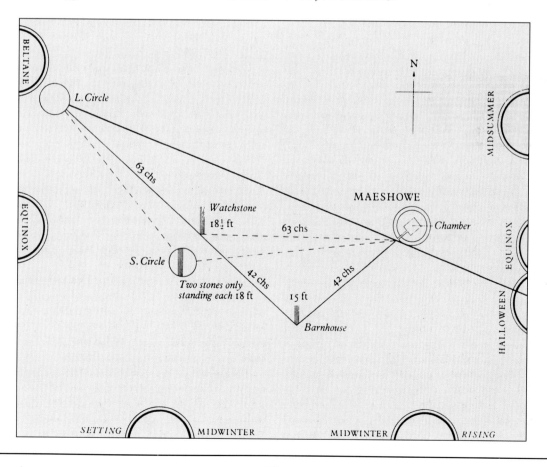

traditions. In Europe there were seasonal fairs and games, often held at sacred places or local landmarks such as prominent hilltops. Such festivities related to the astronomical divisions of the solar year – the solstices, equinoxes and the 'cross-quarter' days between. These latter are recalled in Celtic tradition as Imbolc (February), Beltane (May), Lughnassadh (August) and Samhain (November), and the Christian saints' days of Candlemas, Lammas and All Saints acknowledge three of these. In a sense, then *astronomy was celebrated in the landscape.* This is further emphasized at, for instance, Maes Howe, a Neolithic chambered mound in Orkney, off Scotland's northern coast, where the midwinter setting sun still shines down the entrance passage. The line of that orientation, extended out from the passage into the surrounding countryside, strikes a standing stone called Barnhouse, which itself stands on another alignment involving the Watchstone monolith and the centre of the Ring of Brogar.

Similarly, the dark interiors of many sacred places used to be illuminated at key calendrical times – Neolithic chambers in Ireland (the famous Newgrange, for example, where sunbeams and shadows seem to interact with the rock art[19]) and elsewhere in Europe; at the temple of Karnak (see Part 2), and many more sites, even shamanic caves in California. Many ancient sacred monuments had various astronomical aspects built into their structures or orientations that linked them intimately with the heavens and surrounding landscape, as we shall see particularly well at Avebury, Stonehenge and Cuzco in Part 2.

Such associations between the heavens and the landscape are rather alien to the modern mind, but they were a core element of the former worldview. It was the residuum of this worldview in folk tradition such as festival gatherings and legend that alerted the early European antiquarians to the astronomical aspects of prehistoric sites, and by the end of the nineteenth century ancient astronomy was clearly on the intellectual agenda in France, Germany and the British Isles. The matter was given its major debut as a subject area, however, by the work of F. C. Penrose and Sir Norman Lockyer (editor of *Nature*, the prestigious science journal) around the turn of the century. Both men had noted astronomical orientations in Greek and Egyptian temples, and they went on to study British megalithic sites, particularly Stonehenge, where Lockyer found orientations extending out to landmark hills in the surrounding countryside. Lockyer's findings were resisted by the archaeologists of his day, and it is true he made errors and some dubious claims, but ancient astronomy had nevertheless been put on the map. Over subsequent decades a handful of other researchers conducted astronomical surveys of sites, but it was not until new work at Stonehenge in the 1960s that the subject took on further significance (see Part 2). In 1967, the results of decades of work were published in book form by Alexander Thom, a retired professor of engineering at Oxford. He had undertaken very accurate surveys of hundreds of sites (and went on to study many more in Britain and France) and concluded three things from his findings: many prehistoric megalithic sites could have been used for precise astronomical observation, the groundplans of stone circles where not truly circular were sophisticated geometrical configurations, and the sites had been laid out to a standard of measure he identified as the 'Megalithic Yard' (2.72 feet). The precision Thom felt he saw in megalithic astronomy and measure has subsequently been criticized, and it does appear that relatively few sites can reliably be attributed with high exactitude, but many of Thom's claims remain essentially intact, if now sometimes modified.

Ancient astronomy is usually referred to as 'archaeoastronomy' or, less frequently nowadays, as 'astro-archaeology'. It is maturing into a widespread academic discipline, looking at sites worldwide. For instance, the 1970s saw archaeoastronomy in the Americas develop apace, one of the leading pioneers there being Anthony Aveni. Mayan – and earlier – sites in Mesoamerica, particularly, have become a target for this kind of research, although sites within the USA and South America are also being revealed to have astronomical significance. We will encounter some of this New World archaeoastronomy in Part 2.

There is also no doubt that the early temple architects and megalith builders in both the Old and New Worlds enjoyed producing dramatic lightshows: some of the astronomy at sacred sites seems to have been produced principally

for effect (see the Castillo at Chichen Itza in Part 2, for instance). Nor was the usage of sunlight at holy places simply a prehistoric penchant: it was used in ancient cathedrals (see Aachen and Chartres, Part 2) and Mithraic shrines during Roman times. At the Externsteine, bizarrely weathered sandstone pillars in Germany, an early Christian (or possibly pagan) rock-hewn chapel has a circular window that is

This rock-cut shrine is high on one of the sandstone pinnacles forming the Externsteine, near Detmold, Germany. The circular window is oriented towards the midsummer morning sun. The chapel originally had a roof, and the sunbeam would have penetrated the interior darkness to illuminate a niche on the opposite wall. It is not known for certain whether the chapel was early Christian or pagan.

orientated to the midsummer morning sun.

Overall, ancient astronomy seems to have been more concerned with cosmology than science as we understand it. It was calendrical and *astrological*.

SACRED MEASURES

The possible implications of the dimensions of old sacred sites comprise another area of extended geomantic enquiry. Two of the world's major monuments, the Great Pyramid and Stonehenge, have been found by modern researchers to contain scaled measures of the dimensions of the Earth – *geodetic information*. Such measures, and those of the sun and moon, can quite definitely be deduced from the dimensions of monuments like these, although one has to be alert to much nonsense, particularly with regard to the Great Pyramid – what archaeologist Glyn Daniel called 'pyramidiocy'.

SACRED GEOMETRY

'Sacred' or canonical geometry is the geometry inherent in nature, whether it be the energy dance of atoms and molecules, the formation of a crystal, the growth of a plant or human skeleton, the motion of weather systems or galaxies. Certain patterns and ratios are used by nature in the formation of the manifest universe: the process of becoming is governed by this implied geometry. Such geometry is used in magical invocation for the same reasons. The builders of the ancient sacred monuments observed the ways of nature closely and encoded its architecture into their structures so that the holy places would act as microcosms of the whole universe.

SYMBOLISM

The offspring of 'sacred' pattern and measure is symbolism, for these temple microcosms were for the use of the human mind. Geometry and number were used by initiates in many times

The Great Pyramid of Giza, constructed to the principles of sacred geometry. The measurements of this remarkably precise structure seem to yield information on the dimensions of our planet, and the relative sizes of the Earth and Moon. These are perhaps among the secrets that the mute Sphinx keeps guard over.

Chalice Well, Glastonbury. The wrought iron design on the cover forms the vesica piscis, *an ancient piece of sacred geometry found at places like the Great Pyramid and Stonehenge, which the Christians adopted as a secret symbol.*

and places to encode arcane knowledge. If we take just the example of two interlocking circles, which is found at the base of a good deal of Christian and Islamic architecture, not to mention the elevation or profile of the Great Pyramid and the ground plans of some megalithic sites, a whole vista of symbolism emerges. At Castlerigg stone circle, in northwest England, geometer and architectural researcher Keith Critchlow found that the constructional geometrical circles which were used to produce the final ground plan of the stone ring were defined by solar and lunar axes present at the site, thus, in effect, producing a 'solar' circle interlocking with a 'lunar' one.[20] In Tibetan Buddhist symbology the interlocking solar and lunar circles represent the inner and outer world respectively, with human consciousness being where the two circles overlap. This space is known in Christian symbology as the 'Vessel of the Fish', the *vesica piscis* (the early Christians in the catacombs used the fish sign as a symbol of Christ, for the esoteric meaning of Christ's name was 'Fish'). The design can be seen in the wrought ironwork on the lid of Chalice Well at Glastonbury.

The ancient mode of thought that traced such themes from one level of thought to another was called *correspondence* – the 'as above, so below' principle. In alchemy the sun and moon were used, along with other symbols such as king and queen, sulphur and mercury, or silver and gold, to refer to the masculine and feminine universal principles, the two great forces of creation that emerge from the single godhead and are active at all levels. In Chinese symbology they were known respectively as yang and yin, but they occur in some form in virtually all cosmologies.

In terms of consciousness, the alchemical solar, masculine principle manifests as logical and analytical thought, and the feminine, lunar, principle as creative, intuitive cognition. Both need one another for the optimum balance, what the alchemists called the 'alchemical wedding'. People who have too much solar principle in their mental makeup tend to disregard aesthetic, spiritual and mystical matters, but an excess of the feminine principle results in people who are always 'on cloud nine', who are unable to bring much structure or discriminative faculties into their thinking. In general terms, the sun–moon principles reflect structure and energy, and the two need to go together at any level.

The above is just one slim strand of symbolism that can be found encoded in the geometry and measure of many ancient sacred sites – it can become more complex and profound. But even this brief example shows how the sun and moon can be seen to shine as much in our minds as in our skies.

The alchemical marriage between the cosmic masculine and feminine principles of existence (see text for symbolism). (From Philosophers' Rosegarden *by Arnaldus von Villanova)*

MYTH

Myth and its 'low church' cousin, folklore, also contain symbolism, and this area has also become a topic studied by the modern geomant. Folklore represents the memories and beliefs held by the countryfolk who, for so many generations, knew and observed their local sacred sites.

A specific set of legendary motifs tends to be associated with prehistoric megalithic and earthwork sites. These include lore which states that the stones at a site had healing powers (see Stonehenge in Part 2), could attract lightning if interfered with, could not be counted, were capable of movement (when no one was looking, of course – usually at night), or were people turned to stone, usually for transgressing a local taboo. (This theme of petrifaction is particularly widespread: for example, a set of standing stones south of Morlaix in Britanny is called *An*

Eured Ven, 'The Wedding Party', a group of people turned to stone because they blocked the way of a priest; the Stanton Drew circles in England are likewise said to be a wedding party turned to stone for allowing its revelries to go on into the Sabbath; and exactly the same folklore image is attached to a stone circle near Kaur, in the Senegambian region of West Africa.) Tunnels were said to run beneath some monuments, linking them with other features in the district – Alfred Watkins thought this motif to be a folk mnemonic for alignments. Certain sites are said to be the haunts of the fairyfolk. Fairies are often recorded in lore as *lights*. Within living memory, the Fairy Stone in Shropshire, England, was seen with small balls of light around it. The Irish writer Dermot Mac Manus has recorded a number of eyewitness accounts of light phenomena in Ireland which were automatically assumed to be fairies by witnesses, especially when seen hovering over 'fairy forts' (prehistoric earthworks).[21]

Another major theme in the folklore of prehistoric sites is that the old stones can promote fertility. A typical example of this is recorded at the dolmen of Cruz-Moquen, also known as *La Pierre Chaude*, and which has been Christianized by a cross affixed to the capstone, where women would raise their skirts at full moon in the hope of becoming pregnant. Some stones around the world have been shaped into phalli (in the Soddo area in Ethiopia, for instance), and others into representations of the Earth Goddess, all indicating that themes of fertility and fecundity were associated with megaliths even when they were erected.

Other themes attached to sacred sites include number symbolism, giants, the Devil (seemingly a Christianized version of the giant motif), buried treasure, dragons and divination.

Taken as a whole, a large element of the folk memory attached to the mysterious sites of antiquity tells a tell of places possessing unusual, magical properties, where effects on humans can occur and where strange phenomena can manifest.

ENERGIES

It is not difficult to see, therefore, that folklore is one source of the widespread rumour that ancient sacred sites are places of power; locations where unusual forces can manifest. The

rumour has been augmented over the years by the claims of psychics (see page 18) and by anecdotes from visitors to sites regarding 'electric-shocks' received from standing stones or other strange phenomena or feelings. The possible presence of energies at such places has therefore been of great interest to modern geomantic researchers.

In an attempt to sift fact from fantasy in this rumour, the Dragon Project was set up in Britain in 1977, its field base being the Rollright Stones near Oxford. From 1978 to the time of writing (1991), this informal, multi-disciplinary

The Christianized dolmen of Cruz-Moquen, sometimes known as La Pierre Chaude, *in Carnac-Ville, Brittany, is associated with fertility traditions.*

consortium of researchers has studied a wide variety of sites in the British Isles and, to a lesser extent, in Egypt, the USA and France.

From the outset, the project took a dual approach to the energy problem and looked at the evidence of psychic archaeology and physical – instrumental – monitoring.

Psychics have been used, and the results of

A nineteenth-century drawing by C. Stern of a German miner using a forked twig for dowsing.

sessions at sites have been logged but not fully published, awaiting a time when sufficient work has been done to allow meaningful cross-referencing of accounts from independent sensitives. A similar approach has been applied to dowsers, those people who use dowsing rods (twigs, pendulums, angle rods and so on) to divine for water, mineral deposits, lost objects and, as it is so claimed nowadays, undefined 'earth energies'. This bio-sensing principle has even been extended by the project to seeing how magnetically sensitive organisms such as brine shrimp respond to magnetic fields at stone circles!

The physical monitoring was in many ways more difficult to initiate, considering the lack of previous work in the area and the very limited resources available to the project. The approach finally decided upon was to take anecdotal accounts of phenomena at prehistoric monuments and to study possible physical energy correlates. This work can be only briefly outlined here, but has been described more fully elsewhere.[22]

At first there was a desire to find evidence for exotic energies that might give insight into the ch'i of the Chinese feng shui geomants, the primordial and enigmatic force claimed by many other traditional peoples and which went under many names – *mana, baraka, maxpe, n/um* and dozens more. But, gradually, thinking on this developed somewhat, and it is the feeling of the present author, who is director of the Dragon Project, that such terms covered a whole range of subtle natural energies, most of which are in fact now measurable by modern science, such as magnetic fields, radiation, infra-red, visible light, ultraviolet, gravity variations and so on. We are only just becoming aware of how sensitive we can be to these forces in nature,[23,24,25,26] an awareness that has major implications regarding the emissions of artificially produced energies, which, of course, saturate the environment and were unknown in the times the old holy places were constructed. If a new geomancy comes about, it will have to include modern high-technology within its scheme.

There may well be forces or energies present in the environment that have yet to be discerned by modern science, however, and while scientists *en masse* would reject this possibility, certain brave individual scientists, as well as other non-scientific but informed researchers, have more respect for nature and what it still has to teach us. It is also possible that there is a non-material component to ch'i and its other namesakes: there may exist some kind of *consciousness field*. This has huge implications if true – not least that our brains do not so much produce consciousness as moderate and process it. Although we touch on this again in Part 3, such matters are outside the scope of this present work.[27]

So, eventually, the investigation of possibly significant energy characteristics of sites finally concentrated on what we could *really* expect to find at places where the technology was that of earth and stone, coupled with what was probably a tremendous sensitivity to the environment (the 'missing piece' of modern awareness). This resulted in three basic discoveries: that the locations of stone circles in Britain – and apparently of many sacred monuments around the world – were in close proximity to geological faulting; that magnetic stones were used at certain sites; and that the site builders made use of places and materials that enhanced the

Measuring the Earth's magnetism at the Kermario stone rows, Carnac, Brittany.

presence of natural radioactivity. Let us consider each of these in turn.

The geological term 'faulting' refers to those places where tectonic, seismic, activity has rent or cracked the Earth's crust where different blocks of rock abut one another. At such locales, there tends to be mineral enhancement, where mineral deposits have been raised and pressed close to one another. (That is why mines and quarries are usually in faulted areas.) Because ores have varying magnetic and electrical properties, there are often variations in these forces in fault zones. Moreover, different minerals have different densities, so the value of gravity can change at such places. Ore bodies can also attract lightning, and, possibly, meteoric falls. *Faults, therefore, represent special energy zones in the landscape.* The Dragon Project confirmed that all stone circles in England and Wales occurred within a mile or less of surface faults, with a similar pattern probable in Scotland. Belgian researcher Pierre Méreaux, conducting independent work at the Carnac rows in Brittany, noted that the great megalithic complex there was hemmed in by faulting, it was in an area of significant seismic unrest, and it contained gravity and magnetic anomalies.[28] Looking around the world, it has become obvious that other key sites are related to faulting. The mysterious, 2,000-year-old Serpent Mound in Ohio, for example, is situated over a 'crypto-volcanic' geological feature unique in the whole USA, and sits over a dense cluster of faults. The Icelandic *Althing*, the ceremonial and legal centre of tenth-century Iceland, is situated not on a mere fault, but on the Mid-Atlantic Rift. Numerous other sites are known to have faulting and seismic associations, and some will be noted in Part 2, but detailed geological information is either not available, or the required research has not yet been done, properly to assess this association with sacred sites worldwide.

Another energy aspect of faulted regions is the tendency for such locales to host the appearance of exotic light phenomena. These lights take many forms, though they are usually spherical. Although all colours have been reported, orange, white and red are the most common. They may well be the truly unidentified phenomenon at the heart of the confused area known as 'ufology', and rather than being extra-terrestrial craft, they seem to be *terrain-related*: the present author thus refers to them as 'earth lights'. They haunt faults, bodies of water such as lakes and reservoirs (which often create microquakes in the strata underlying them), and isolated towers, buildings and rock outcrops (all charge collectors). Statistical studies have shown correlations between earth lights outbreaks and seismic activity (usually of low intensity). Research is showing that the lights tend to occur periodically in specific areas such as valleys or hilltops. In some parts of Wales and the Pennines in England, they have recurred at specific spots for generations and

The quarter-mile-long Serpent Mound in Adams Country, Ohio. About two thousand years ago, the Adena Indians constructed this remarkable effigy mound on a site that is geologically unique in the whole USA. (Ohio Historical Society)

have insinuated themselves into local folklore and place-names. In the prairie southwest of Marfa in Texas, just one of over a hundred earth light zones known of in the US, lights have been reported for over a century. There is a great deal of evidence, including photographic, to support the reality of these extraordinary natural phenomena which cannot be presented here, but is available in *Earth Lights Revelation* by the present writer.[29]

In addition to having electromagnetic properties, the lights seem to have characteristics that extend beyond known physics. Not only is there no theory which can explain how luminous energy can maintain itself in coherent, mobile forms in the atmosphere (a problem relating to ball lightning and earthquake lights too), there are also recurring reports from many places and throughout this century of lights that seem to send out luminosity *in only one direction*. There is even tantalizing evidence that earth lights can *respond* to witnesses: are the lights intelligent energy, or are they sensitive to human consciousness in some way? Certainly, such evidence is resisted and ignored by mainstream science, for the implications could lead to a painful reassessment of some currently held scientific dogmas. The study of earth lights will lead us into a whole new area of geophysics, as US geologist John S. Derr has predicted,[30] and perhaps much else besides.

These lights have been known to a great many traditional societies, and many names exist for them. To the Aborigines they are 'min min lights' – ancestor spirits or the result of shamanic activity; to the native peoples of West Africa they are *aku* – devil; to the Malaysians they are *pennangal* – the spectral heads of women who have died in childbirth, and so on. There are also hints of traditions that warn against getting too close to some lights: the Californian Indians referred to the lights as 'spirit eaters' and in the Darjeeling area of India the light phenomena were thought to be the lanterns of little men (*chota-admis*), close encounter with whom could result in illness or in death.

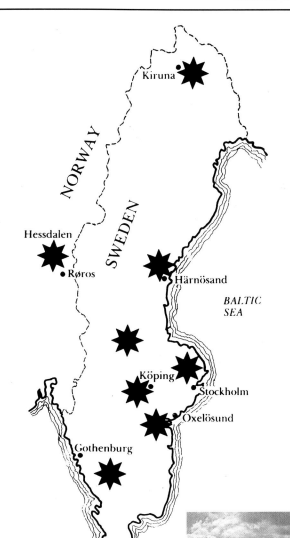

Key 'windows' of light phenomena in Sweden, according to the research of Dan Mattsson. Earth light incidence has been shown to be related to seismic or geological factors in these zones. The lights-infested valley of Hessdalen in neighbouring Norway (see Part 2) is also shown.

Some prehistoric sites, probably because of their occurrence in fault zones, seem to attract earth lights. In 1919, for example, two witnesses saw several 6-foot-wide (2m) balls of white light playing lazily one night over the Castlerigg stone circle, and a number of British stone circles, dolmens, standing stones and earthworks have had lightballs, columns of lights and other forms reported at them. In his autobiographical *The Way of the White Clouds*, the late Lama Anagarika Govinda referred to a temple in the Himalayan foothills that attracted balls of light. The Purnagiri temples situated on a fault in northern India are likewise associated with recurring light phenomena and have traditions woven around them.[31] Similarly, there is a chapel in the Alps which is dedicated to St Mary of the Lights.[32] In Part 2, a spectacular example of a site-lights association is detailed at Mount Taishan, just one example of 'sacred peaks' which have light phenomena associated with them.

It could be that the ancient monument and

The view across Mitchell Flat, near Marfa, Texas. Reports of mysterious lights in this area go back for over a century. The Chinati Mountains on the horizon seem to be the main focus for the lights. The signboard in the foreground marks the 'official' viewing point for the lights on Highway 90 between Marfa and Alpine.

temple builders saw these phenomena recurring at certain spots, and attributed them to spirits or deities, and thus took their appearance as a form of siting divination. Also, there is evidence that such lights may be surrounded by energy fields that cause mind-change effects, and the lights may conceivably have been used for such purposes.

The second basic finding of the Dragon Project relates to site magnetism. Magnetic anomalies have been found at megaliths in at least two forms: (a) magnetometers have picked up so far inexplicable, low-level magnetic fluctuations within individual stones that occur for an hour or two then revert to a stable reading,

and (b) the permanent magnetism found in certain rocks due to iron content – they can 'scramble' a compass held near them, even turning the north end of a compass needle to the south. There is nothing mysterious about this second type of magnetic anomaly, but the presence of such stones at specific sites could possibly be significant. So far, they have been found in stone circles always at key points – a cardinal position or outlying stone (in one case at least, indicating an astronomical direction). It is possible that the magnetism in these special stones was detected directly by the megalith builders – human beings can sense even low-level magnetism – or by use of a piece of

One night in 1919, T. Sington and friend watched awestruck as large balls of light played lazily over the Castlerigg stone circle in England's Lake District. It is now known that other ancient sacred sites around the world attract similar light phenomena. Sington wondered if they were some unknown natural energy effect that ancient peoples thought were spirits. This could explain why temple sites are found in places where such lights manifest. (Main picture: Jerry Hardman-Jones. Inset is a simulation)

This stone is an outlier of the Gors Fawr stone circle in Wales. It indicates the midsummer sunrise when viewed from the circle and is sufficiently magnetic to affect a compass needle held next to it. The stone, the only one at the site that is magnetic, is shaped curiously like a seat. Did Stone Age people have a ritual technology that made use of natural magnetism and radioactivity?

magnetite on a thread. Doubtless, such stones would have been considered to have special 'power', and they may have been used for dreaming purposes, for there is an ancient tradition of sleeping on special stones in order to receive visionary dreams. This may be tied to the fact that those parts of the brain involved in dream and memory are very sensitive to magnetic fields. There may also have been some healing virtue in such stones – again, there is a long-standing idea that magnets can cure maladies, and versions of this are even to be found in modern medical practice.

Magnetic stones are, of course, found not only at British sites. The Dragon Project has

found one Amerinidian 'place of power' on Mount Tamalpais near San Francisco to be very magnetic, and the Namoratunga II site in Kenya is composed of highly magnetic stones. As with faulting, much research needs doing on this aspect.

The third Dragon Project finding relates to another energy property of certain rocks – natural radioactivity. This is especially true of granite. The Dragon Project has identified standing stones at sites that have small areas emitting constant streams of gamma radiation, but, perhaps more significantly, it has been found that enclosed sites such as dolmens – Neolithic sites composed of upright stones supporting a capstone – in Cornwall (see Part 3) have high-radon atmospheres so that the background radiation in them is two to four or more times that of the average, open-air local background (which is in any case above average).

A serpentine outcrop on Mount Tamalpais, near San Francisco. This spot has been identified as an Indian 'power place', and it will 'scramble' a compass. The large rock acts as a snug seat, putting the base of one's spine in contact with the strongly magnetic serpentine.

Again, this is not mysterious in itself, because the granite creating such enclosures itself produces radiation, which builds up in a closed space, but there may have been a *technology* at work here for ritual purposes. It is at least coincidental that underground ritual chambers (souterrains) were built in Brittany, parts of Scotland, Orkney, Cornwall (where they are called *fogous*), Ireland and the American southwest (*kivas*), all locations where there tends to be greater than usual background radiation, due to granite or the presence of uranium. It is also interesting to note that the interior of the King's Chamber in the Great Pyramid, which many argue was a ritual or initiatory chamber rather than a tomb, is clad in Aswan granite and has high natural internal radiation. It may be significant that the ancient Egyptians considered granite to be imbued with, or to represent, spirit.

But what could radiation have to do with ritual? By pure chance, the Dragon Project discovered over the years that some of its participants experienced fleeting but very vivid altered states of consciousness when in enhanced natural radiation zones for certain lengths of time. It may be that this geophysical component of sites was used in the way that the botanical environment was exploited to help create magical states of mind and therefore to augment ritual and shamanistic activity (we will note a hint of this possibility at Machu Picchu in Part 2). As with magnetism, there may also have been a healing potential in such environments: for generations people have frequented naturally radioactive caves and springs for health reasons, and to this day old uranium and gold mines in the US are visited by the sick, and some remarkable healings have been claimed. A few decades ago, even, one could buy canisters of radon gas for supposedly healthful sniffs! While prolonged exposure to radon is harmful, perhaps limited exposure can have a 'homeopathic' beneficial effect?

Another effect that has recently been observed within enclosed granite monuments in Cornwall is curious localized light phenomena, which are described in Part 3.

Apart from these fundamental aspects of site energies, numerous other effects were noted during the Dragon Project's work. Curious radio signals were picked up in highly localized spots near a few megaliths; apparent ultrasonic signals (high frequency sound above normal human hearing) were recorded; odd audible effects were heard from time to time next to standing stones and so on. A variety of other experiments was conducted, but they are outside the scope of this brief, introductory account.

(Another kind of 'energy' work ought to be mentioned here, though, because it has had a lot of publicity. It is the idea that leys, the archaic alignments, are channels of energy of some kind and are dowsable. In fact, this notion has a very tenuous history, it has nothing to do with research into ancient alignments, and its publicity outstrips its substance. Our planet teems with subtle natural energies, and most energy dowsers make precious little attempt to distinguish these, preferring to call on 'spiritual' or 'ch'i' notions to account for the response in their dowsing rods. Even allowing that some of these responses are genuinely the result of an energy reaction, without discriminating among the vast range of natural and artificial energies which are always present to some degree anywhere, such dowsing is meaningless, and any 'pattern' of energy can be read into the results. Certainly, this work is not of the calibre of authentic water or mineral dowsing. Many claims and statements are made about 'ley energies', but they are totally subjective and become somewhat tedious after a time. Much more work would need to be done to make this area in any way accountable and reliable, and for these reasons it is left out of the studies of sites presented in Part 2 of this book. There are enough authentic remarkable aspects to ancient monuments without bringing in what may be little more than fantasy.)

All these areas of research, then, have come within the scope of the modern geomant, and we will encounter them again, as they arise naturally in the study of individual sites in the following section of this work. There are, indeed, even more areas that come within the compass of Earth Mysteries. One the present writer calls simply 'being and seeing': just by being at a site and open to it, without any intellectual agenda or belief system operating, it is possible to experience insight at some level or other, as is demonstrated in the account of Avebury in Part 2. These many disciplines and modes, ranging from the scientific to the visual, aesthetic and spiritual, which are involved in geomantic or Earth Mysteries work, are just now beginning to be considered in a systematic manner.[33]

This broadly-based approach is vital if elements of the sacred geography inherent in the former worldview are to be reclaimed. This archaic, global spiritual geography is defined by its principle features, the ancient sacred monuments, and it is with these waymarkers of the mind that the rest of this book is concerned.

CHAPTER 2

THE WORLD HERITAGE

IN ORDER TO SEE for ourselves the evidence for the mysterious, geomantic worldview of the past as described in the previous chapter, there is no alternative but to study the sacred sites of antiquity that mark out the sacred geography of our planet. There are tens of thousands of them.

Perception of the geomantic and related aspects of a site is dependent upon how well it has survived in something like its original form, how much research has been done at it, what the nature of that research has been (and who did it and how long ago), how its environment has been treated and sometimes when – and even how – a site is visited.

Whole books can be written on just one well-preserved site, and, indeed, some monuments have had many written about them. Our concern here is simply to demonstrate the reality of the topics discussed in Chapter 1 by looking at a selection of sites around the world, concentrating on their lesser known, geomantic or Earth Mysteries aspects. Any selection is bound to be arbitrary to some extent, and in a way that is good: a presentation of geomancy by means of an effectively random sampling of the world's sacred places serves to underscore the universality of the evidence.

For this purpose, we have selected from the major sites of the world which, because of their prominence, also happen to be included in a unique catalogue of monuments of world importance – the World Heritage List. It is worth spending a few moments considering this institution and its symbolic importance.

The 'Convention Concerning the Protection of the World Cultural and Natural Heritage' was adopted by the General Conference of UNESCO (United Nations Educational, Scientific and Cultural Organization) in 1972. By January 1989 108 countries were party to the Convention. Each country which signs it pledges to conserve the sites and monuments within its borders that are 'recognized to be of exceptional universal value'. In effect, these countries present the chosen sites on their territories to the world as the common heritage of all humanity.

The World Heritage List contains not only human structures but also natural landscapes, which is well expressed in the World Heritage logo, which is described by the Convention Committee as symbolizing 'the interdependence of cultural and natural properties: the central square is a form created by man and the circle represents nature, the two being intimately linked. The emblem is round like the world, but at the same time it is a symbol of protection.' To satisfy the criteria for inclusion on the List

The symbol of the World Heritage. (© UNESCO 1978)

established by the Committee, a *cultural* site must for example

> be authentic and have exerted great architectural influence or bear unique witness, or be associated with ideas or beliefs of universal significance, or it may be an outstanding example of a traditional way of life that represents a certain culture.[1]

A *natural* site

> may exemplify a stage of the earth's evolutionary processes, or be representative of biological evolution, or contain the natural habitats of endangered animals. It may be a scene of exceptional beauty, a spectacular view or a reserve for a large number of wild animals.[2]

In order that the List does not become too indiscriminate, the criteria for a site's inclusion are rigorously applied.

The Convention makes a connection that, we may note here, is virtually geomantic in its implications. The World Heritage Committee itself states that for a long time

> nature and culture were perceived as opposing elements in that man was supposed to conquer hostile nature, while culture symbolized spiritual values. However, nature and culture are of course complementary: the cultural identity of different peoples has been forged in the environment in which they live and frequently, the most beautiful man-made works owe part of their beauty to their natural surroundings. Moreover, some of the most spectacular natural sites bear the imprint of centuries of human activity.[3]

The List is still very incomplete, even though it had 315 entries by 1989. Adding to it is an ongoing process; each year new nominations are considered by the committee. There are many reasons why certain world-famous sites have not yet been inscribed on the List, obvious among them being the fact of a country not yet being party to the Convention. So, just for example, none of the important prehistoric sites in Ireland figures on the List at the time of this writing. But there are also many famous sites in countries which are party to the Convention that have not found their way onto the List. (The development of the List, and the aid the

World Heritage committee gives to some countries to enable them to conserve their World Heritage sites, costs money like most things. For those wishing to contribute to the World Heritage Fund the address is: Unesco Account (No. 0330-1/5 – 770,002-4), Société générale, Agency AG, Office FB, 45 avenue Kléber, 75016 – Paris. For further information on the Convention, the address is: World Heritage Secretariat, Division of Ecological Sciences, Unesco, 7 Place de Fontenoy, 75700 – Paris).

So we can see that the List as so far developed is only partial, and we can appreciate that it involves other types of features in addition to key ancient sacred sites. Apart from the natural landscapes of geological or biological value, there are sites of industrial archaeological interest, old towns and important architectural sites – even sites of sombre cultural significance like Auschwitz Concentration Camp.

For our purposes here, while the sites we have selected mainly reflect the archaeological elements in the list, we have also included a few sites of architectural or geological relevance too, because the geomant is specifically looking at the tight-knit association between culture and environment, or, to put that another way, between mind and land.

The selection of sites in Part 2 is, therefore, just a sampler, but, nevertheless, it will be sufficient to confirm that the discussion in Chapter 1 relates to real material and evidence. Because our modern archaeology and other academic disciplines are inevitably framed by the secular attitude of the current worldview, some aspects of sites are literally *invisible* to modern scholarship, and where they are visible they tend to be seen as old superstitions rather than belonging to a coherent former worldview. The reader is urged to remember that the ancient holy places belonged to peoples who had a mindset different from, but not necessarialy inferior to, our own. They made up for a lack of high-tech expertise and scientific knowhow (as we would interpret that) in a greater understanding of the workings of the psyche and knowledge of particular aspects of outer nature than now exist within our mainstream culture. Belief systems, deities, specific rituals and taboos may well be cultural inventions, varying from society to society, but the realities underpinning them could be universal and as 'real' as anything so considered by us today. Indeed, as we move our attention around the world from site to site in the following pages, it is instructive to note just how many underlying themes recur in societies which had no contact with one another or belonged to different chronological periods, even though they may be overlaid by differences of architectural details, belief systems, technological innovation and other cultural variables. *The shared realities of nature and human consciousness are the great constants*, and it is these which can be glimpsed shining through. Only in the last few centuries have some of these principles or ways of looking become obscured or forgotten.

A final note: this book is simply referring to the resource provided by the World Heritage List, and does not in any way officially represent the World Heritage Convention, nor is it to be inferred that the Convention Committee endorses the approach to the material championed here. Nevertheless, the attitude of the Committee as described above is very much in accord with the modern geomant's viewpoint, in particular the way some ancient sites are inscribed on the List in terms of *whole landscapes*, as we shall see.

PART 2

THE
SECRET HERITAGE

Ritual stone stairway descends the north wall of Chaco Canyon.

THE SELECTION OF SITES

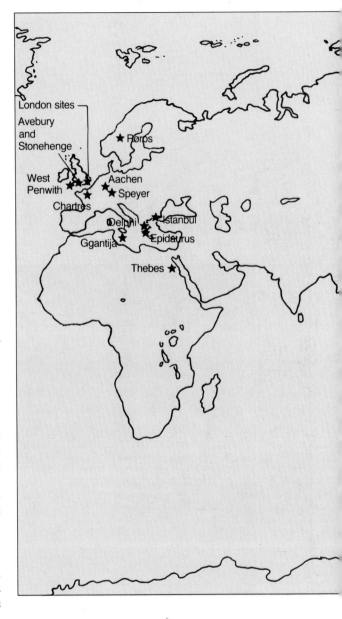

THE MAIN ASPECTS OF THE EARTH MYSTER-
IES or geomantic approach, as discussed in
Chapter 1, are condensed into 10 basic
topic headings for the purposes of the following
selection of major sacred sites worldwide. These
are given, as appropiate, for quick reference at
the beginning of each site entry, and that
site's World Heritage List number is also
mentioned. The topic headings are defined as
follows.

ARCHAEOLOGY

This is involved with most of the sites selected,
almost by definition. However, it is given as a
theme only where archaeological work has been
a key part of a site's story.

ASTRONOMY

This is self-explanatory and is obviously applied
to sites that provide evidence of ancient astronomical usage in their location, orientation or
structure.

CONSCIOUSNESS

This is a shorthand heading to cover a range of
meanings: for sites where there were associations with shamanism, ritual or other mind-
changing usage, including ritual sleep and
dreaming; for sites where modern psychic
information has been claimed; and for sites
where effects on the human mind of any kind
have been noted (i.e., contemporary anecdotal
accounts).

ENERGIES

Another broad heading covering: energy effects
noted at sites; environmental energy characteristics (geological and meteorological); magnetism or radiation in the structural materials of a
monument; strange light phenomena, and so on.

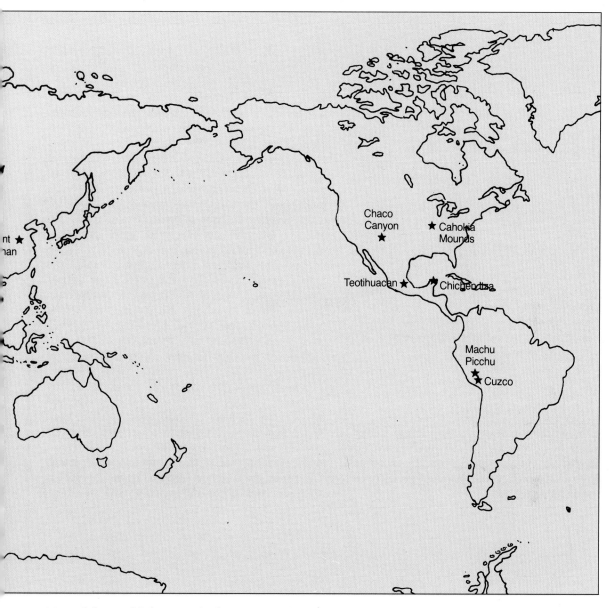

Map of the world showing the locations of the selected World Heritage sites.

EVOLVED

This heading refers to sites that are known to have been superimposed on locations occupied by a holy site of a previous culture or religion, or, conversely, sites that have another religious structure placed on them, thus demonstrating that even if gods came and went, *places* could retain their sanctity for the ancient mind. This site evolution is also known as 'religious conservatism'.

GEODETIC INFORMATION

This heading is used for sites where structural measurements or ratios have been interpreted as yielding scaled numerical information about the dimensions of the Earth.

GEOMANCY

For the purposes of this selection, this heading is used in its specific sense as relating to all forms of 'sacred geography' – any aspects of alignment, orientation, omphalos, topographical relationships or configurations.

MYTH

This heading is included where a site has legendary associations – related to its origins, for example, or some characteristic it possesses – or where it expresses deep, underlying mythic patterns.

SACRED GEOMETRY

This indication is given for sites whose ground plans or structural details contain inherent patterns recognizable as canonical geometry of arcane, cosmological significance. This may relate to ancient wisdom as expressed in astronomy, symbolism and so on.

SACRED MEASURE

This heading is included when the metrology of a site can be interpreted as yielding symbolic information, can generate geometric patterns or can be transliterated by means of gematria into esoteric language.

Where one of these topic headings has a query mark after it, the evidence described in the text entry for the site is dubious, particularly tenuous or only suggestive.

Some of these topic areas of course overlap, and there are other areas of interest to the modern geomant that are outside the requirements of this particular publication, such as aesthetic response, 'being and seeing', modern neo-pagan usage and the like, as indicated in Chapter 1. There is also no attempt here to claim that the described aspects of a site are necessarily the final, total picture of a place – *all* sites require further geomantic research, and even comprehensive archaeological investigation is far from complete in many cases.

The sites selected here do not indicate any particular prejudices on the part of the author nor do they necessarily represent sites of a higher status to those *not* happening to be included on the World Heritage List. They simply provide practical examples of the geomantic or Earth Mysteries topics described in this work.

The information given on the sites in the following pages will open up unsuspected insights for visitors to those places. More than that, however – when the site descriptions presented here are read as an entire narrative, it will be found that *all* the subtle aspects of Earth Mysteries are touched upon. *A complete story is told*, whether or not one actually visits the sites.

CHAPTER 3

CHACO NATIONAL HISTORICAL PARK

USA

WORLD HERITAGE LIST NUMBER 17
ARCHAEOLOGY, ASTRONOMY, GEOMANCY

THE PARK IS SITUATED in semi-arid high mesa country in northwest New Mexico, near the state's junction with Utah, Colorado and Arizona – the so-called Four Corners area. The park lies within the San Juan Basin, a saucer-shaped depression about a hundred miles (160km) in diameter. The core of the park is Chaco Canyon, a broad, shallow sandstone gorge, which is engraved east–west across the Chaco Plateau. The northern wall of the canyon is the most abrupt, rising to about 150 feet (46m).

The Four Corners area saw the appearance of a group of people the relatively recent Navajo called *Anasazi* – 'Ancient Ones'. These emerged in the latter centuries BC out of scattered bands of semi-nomadic hunter-gatherers who had inhabited the southwest for several thousands of years. These people had learned from their southerly neighbours, the now-extinct Mogollon (pronounced mug-ee-yone), about the growing of corn. They gradually developed a more settled, sedentary lifestyle: horticulture and habitations developed. The early Anasazi lived in 'pithouses' – dwellings made of logs, brush and mud set into a circular or rectangular pit – and wove fine baskets, hence the archaeological name of 'Basketmaker' for this stage. Between AD 450 and 700, the 'Basketmaker III' phase, pottery began to make an

appearance, and in the eighth century above-ground, rectangular houses were preferred. Flat-roofed and made of mud, rock and posts, these 'pueblos' marked the beginning of the 'Pueblo Period' of Anasazi development. The pithouse type of structure was adapted into circular subterranean or semi-subterranean ritual chambers (called kivas by today's Hopi Indians).

One of the key Anasazi centres was in and around Chaco Canyon, where the culture reached its height. So distinctive was the Anasazi efflorescence in this area that the term 'Chacoan' is often used. At Chaco the pueblos grew into multi-storeyed and terraced complexes or 'Great Houses', with walls, courtyards, storage pits and many kivas, including Great Kivas – very large ceremonial chambers. The masonry of these pueblo villages is monumental and was skilfully executed. There are nine Great Houses within Chaco Canyon itself, all constructed between AD 900 and 1115. The greatest is Pueblo Bonito. This is a huge complex, covering some three acres (1.2ha) and crescent-shaped in plan, tucked against the north wall of the canyon. It was built over various periods of time and had up to five storeys and contained perhaps 800 rooms. Thirty-seven smaller kivas have been excavated within the complex, in addition to two Great

The crescent-shaped Pueblo Bonito, the largest of the Chacoan ruins, viewed from the northern rim of the canyon. The circular shapes are the site's many kivas. The central wall is accurately aligned north–south. The two Great Kivas are either side of the wall.

Kivas. In the vast landscape stretching out dauntingly around the canyon, some 150 Great Houses have now been identified by archaeologists, along with many other site structures.

Archaeological work over this century at Chaco produces an image of what has come to be called 'The Chaco Phenomenon': 'an integrated group of communities and resource areas in and near Chaco Canyon, appears to have begun functioning as a cohesive system.'[1] At the height of the culture, what archaeologists refer to as the 'Bonito Phase', there was clearly extensive trade and manufacture, with fine turquoise jewellery and high quality pottery being among the items produced by the Chacoans. There was, in addition to the monumental architecture, horticulture, the use of canals

and dams to manage the fitful and limited water supply and rich ceremonial or religious activity. But there are two aspects further to these Chacoan accomplishments that speak of mystery and the geomantic elements we are seeking at sites selected for the World Heritage List: the use of astronomy and the Anasazi geomantic preoccupation indicated by the enigmatic Chacoan roads.

These roads are central to the Chaco phenomenon, and they plunge us directly into consideration of the kind of features we have referred to earlier as 'leys'. Within and for tens of miles around the canyon there is a system of roads of striking linearity. They are not trails, but engineered features, usually as straight as arrows, cutting across country from one point to another, before changing direction then setting off straight again. The Great Houses seem to have been linked to this network, hundreds of miles of which have now been uncovered by aerial and ground study. Today's archaeologists admit that 'the factors that controlled the alignment of the roads and the position of the Great Houses are not understood'.[2] The roads are wide, usually a

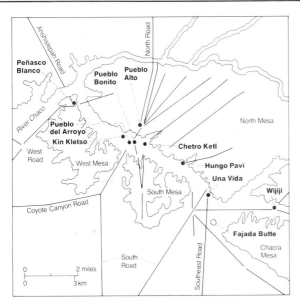

The Great Houses and Anasazi roads in and immediately around the Chaco Canyon.

The mysterious, straight Chaco roads are now almost impossible to see at ground level. This line of stones near Pueblo Alto, however, reveals the edge or berm of one of them.

43

A simplified map of major segments of Anasazi roads in the region around Chaco Canyon. (Modified after Chaco Roads Project)

A pseudocolour composite image from computer-filtered data showing the Anasazi roads converging on Pueblo Alto, as indicated. (NASA)

Examples of pottery fragments found in the midden alongside Pueblo Alto.

fairly constant 9 metres (almost 30 feet), with tributary or spur roads as exactly half that width as can now be determined. They were bordered with earthen 'berms', rows of stones, or, occasionally, drystone walling, and their surfaces were compacted subsoil or sometimes cut to the bedrock. It is mystery enough why a people without the wheel or horse should want such broad and exact roads, yet aerial and infra-red remote sensing has found that some lengths of road had parallel sections running alongside them, and, in at least one case, on the Great North Road, double groupings of parallel roads!

Odd segments of these now almost invisible, thousand-year-old roads were recognized from at least the nineteenth century. An army report of 1879 refers to 'remarkable trails' in New Mexico 'extending as they do in a straight line from one pueblo to another . . .'.[3] A 1901 government agent's report mentions roads at Chaco, and in the 1920s Neil Judd, a pioneer Chaco archaeologist, referred to them in his reports. In 1948 Gordon Vivian, another Chaco archaeologist, discussed the roads with a woman who recalled that 'in the old days' a wide roadway running north from the canyon 'was clearly defined in the spring or early summer because the vegetation on it was different from any other'. But it was not until the 1970s that serious work on the roads began. Existing aerial photographs of the region were minutely studied, and new air pictures were taken. It was found that because of climatic and human action, the roads showed up more clearly in the earlier photographs than in the new ones due to differences in vegetation cover, but the archaeologists were amazed at the extent of the road system that emerged under their gaze, and at the exactitude of the engineering their fieldwork and excavations uncovered on the features. Even more road segments were discovered in the 1980s by state-of-the-art computer image-enhancement and infra-red techniques employed by special NASA research flights.

One of the key sites associated with the roads is Pueblo Alto, which is situated on top of the northern rim of the canyon. It commands a dramatic 360-degree vista of the entire San Juan Basin. Interesting findings were made there during excavations between 1976 and 1979. The Great House had one storey and approximately 85 rooms and had been built in the early eleventh century on top of an earlier site. Only five of the rooms had been used for domestic habitation, yet pottery fragments were recovered that suggested some 150,000 pottery vessels had been discarded over a 60-year period. The midden or trash mound at the site was layered, suggesting intermittent rather than daily domestic deposits. Further, the 'trash' consisted mainly of broken pottery items, suggesting religious or votive activity. (Ceremonial breakage of pottery is often associated with rituals for the dead.) Archaeologists reasoned that perhaps what had happened at Pueblo Alto were seasonal gatherings of large numbers of people, with only a fairly small resident staff occupying the pueblo. The vast majority of rooms were built in rows along the exterior of the building and opened directly onto one of the mysterious roads. They were completely inaccessible from within the pueblo itself. A wall running eastwards from Pueblo Alto has a yard-wide gap or gateway in it where the Great North Road and other roads converge from the mesa to the north. Four roads lead south from the Great House over the rimrock to the canyon edge.

Where roads come to the edge of the canyon, they connect with steps cut out of the living rock of the canyon walls. These stairways can be up to 25 feet (8m) wide, yet they are curiously difficult to see, merging with their backgrounds. The angle and steepness of step of some of these stairways argue against an everyday usage, being more like the ceremonial stairs on the sides of Mesoamerican pyramids. (There are rock stairs at Chaco which are narrower and have handholds, suggesting normal usage.)

What was the purpose of the roads? Clearly, the Chacoans were traders, so goods and raw materials may have been transported large distances by use of the roads. But the roads raise more questions than simple trade and mundane usage can explain. Why the apparent obsession with straightness (there are some slowly curving sections)? Why the exactitude of widths and the width relationships between major and spur roads? Why the parallel and even double parallel sections? The Pueblo Alto findings hint that the roads had a ceremonial, religious function. This is supported by other snippets of evidence. For instance, in the 1920s Neil Judd discussed the roads with Navajo informants. We do not know all he learnt, but Judd began to refer to the roads as 'ceremonial highways'. One Navajo elder, Hosteen Beyal, told Judd that 'they were not really roads, although they looked like them'. A Navajo legend claims that the roads are really 'tunnels' along which the Ancient Ones could pass in

safety.[4] In the 1980s Kendrick Frazier asked a Hopi Indian friend about the roads. The Indian's suggestion was that the features were symbolic, perhaps representing the migration routes of the early Anasazi. The direction of the roads so far discovered match legends in Hopi lore.[5]

Archaeoastronomer Ray A. Williamson also refers to a Hopi tradition in which sunrise or sunset positions along the horizon were marked, and these became sacred places. 'Young Hopi initiates run in as straight a line as possible to the shrines and back in order to plant their prayer sticks. They follow, as it were, literally, the straight road of a beam of sunlight.'[6]

Broken pottery fragments have been found in patches stretched along some of the roads, especially near Great Houses, as at Pueblo Alto. Although some archaeologists have interpreted this as resulting from trade transport, we have already noted that the breaking of pottery vessels was a votive activity in many parts of the world, and it may even be that the roads *themselves* were considered holy. An example of a track being venerated is known of in France as late as the seventeenth century.[7]

There is a mystery, too, about why the roads appeared so 'suddenly' in the eleventh century, and the abruptness with which they fell into disuse in the 1200s (the roads seem to have been little if at all used by post-Bonito Phase occupants of the area).

In addition to the roads, there is another linear mystery in the Chacoan environment. The Great North Road runs for almost 30 miles (48km) virtually due north without deviation, before changing direction a little, and continuing on. About 12 miles (19km) north of Chaco Canyon the road encounters a group of dune pinnacles. It goes directly towards one which archaeologists have dubbed El Faro (The Lighthouse) because on its summit they found a hearth on which many large fires had been lit. A kiva also had possibly existed there. The dune

Broad steps descend the canyon wall at Chaco. Sets of these rock stairways mark the positions where the Chacoan roads connect with the canyon. Their width and steep angle suggest ceremonial rather than utilitarian function.

summit and its hearth aligned with the centre line of Great North Road. Excavations revealed no evidence of the road skirting the feature, yet segments are to be found on either side of the pinnacle. A fire atop El Faro would have been visible from great distances.

This gave further support to findings made shortly before concerning curious structures on mesa tops around the canyon. The first such site, known prosaically as 29SJ423, was a large stone slab, with a carefully worked rectangular stone lid set into it, located by a low, curving wall. Removal of the lid revealed a hole dug to bedrock containing a bowl holding 146 small turquoise beads. Excavation revealed other shell and turquoise items in the hole. This apparent shrine site was so located that it had commanding views, and was in line-of-sight with other similar sites and Great Houses. One of these shrine sites, indeed, was in visual communication not only with Pueblo Alto, but with eight other Great Houses! In some cases, the shrines were intervisible with Great Houses only by the very tops of 'tower kiva' structures to be found at some of those sites.

So it is now pretty certain that in addition to the fantastic straight roads system, there was also a complex line-of-sight communication system surrounding Chaco Canyon. Thomas Sever, a key figure involved with the NASA infra-red work at Chaco, suggests that the roads may have been designed to interface with the shrine communication system. He is sure the roads are ceremonial rather than utilitarian, having methodically dismissed various economic theories for the features. He notes the instances of ritual activity indicated by the ceramic scatters and the Great Houses and other shrine sites associated with the roads, as well as the fact that they linked specific places in the landscape rather than communities. He refers to other places in the New World, such as Cuzco, Peru, Mayan sites and pre-Hispanic Mexican centres such as La Quemada and Xochicalco, 'where cultural and natural features upon the landscape have been endowed with abstract or religious connotations', and where straight road systems occur. Sever also cites curious engraved grooves in some of the Anasazi roads as further evidence of the roads' ritual status. (In Pueblo ritual contact with such grooves is thought to heal a variety of maladies.)

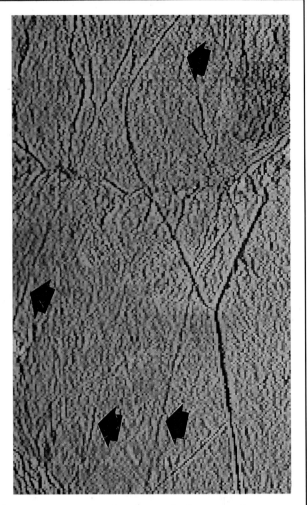

Specialised aerial infra-red photography showing the ancient Chacoan roads as faint straight lines (arrowed). (Dr Thomas Sever NASA)

In addition, he refers to the observations of a number of earlier Chacoan researchers who discovered or heard rumours of stone animal carvings associated with certain shrines and which may have been identification markers for specific roads. Sever warns that 'we should not always perceive roads as always being utilitarian; that, in short, we must not transfer our concept of modern-day roads into the prehistoric past.'[8]

Another aspect of Chacoan geomancy is the probable presence of astronomical knowledge. At points along the canyon walls are rock paintings and carvings, some Navajo and some Anasazi. It is thought that some of these images mark positions for Sun Watchers. In relatively recent times, and still today to some extent, Pueblo Indians such as the Hopi and Zuni have a tradition of Sun Priests who watch the rising sun against the skyline throughout the year. When sunrise occurred at certain horizon features, the Sun Priest would announce that specific ceremonies or the planting of particular crops should be prepared.

Near Wijiji, the easternmost ruin in Chaco Canyon, is a white-painted symbol with rays emanating from four sides. A person standing near this presumed sun symbol can witness the sun rise from behind a natural rock pillar on the skyline at winter solstice. Moreover, on that same day, standing at a nearby carved boulder, an observer can see the sun set in a V-shaped notch in a cliff to the southwest. When the sun is seen to rise behind the rock pillar viewed directly from the apparent sun symbol, midwinter sunrise is 16 days away: the Sun Priests used to give warnings of impending astronomical events to allow preparations for ceremonies to take place.

At the other, western end of Chaco Canyon is a rock overhang below the ruins of Peñasco Blanco, containing a painting of a crescent, a hand and a star or asterisk-type symbol. Some astronomers think this may indicate the supernova which formed the Crab Nebula that

appeared next to the waning moon on 4 July 1054. The hand sign signifies a sacred place, however, and this may have been a sun-watching position as well.

There is other evidence of Chacoan astronomy. The Pueblo Bonito complex was laid out to an astronomical plan: the wall that divides the Great House into eastern and western halves lies on a virtual north–south line, and the western half of the south wall is an almost exact east–west alignment. There are also two unusual third-storey corner apertures inside Pueblo Bonito. As midwinter approaches, a sliver of sunlight enters through one of the apertures and is projected onto the room's wall. As the days progress, this sliver develops in width until by the morning of the solstice it forms a rectangle of light on the wall.

On the south side of the canyon, opposite Pueblo Bonito, is Casa Rinconada, a Great Kiva over 63 feet (19.2km) in diameter. This major ceremonial site is similarly aligned to the

Looking northeast across Casa Rinconada, the major kiva in Chaco Canyon. Like all the kivas in the canyon, it is now roofless. The larger square 'window' (centre of picture) admits the beams of the rising midsummer sun, possibly indicating ceremonial use of astronomy. (See text on page 51.)

cardinal directions and has an opening in its wall to the northeast. It has been observed that the rising midsummer sun casts a beam of light through this aperture onto the opposite wall of the kiva, illuminating one of six irregularly spaced wall niches. Some debate surrounds this dramatic light-play, however; the kiva was partially reconstructed in the 1930s, and it originally had large, roof-supporting posts, which might have blocked the sunbeam.

But the most dramatic evidence of astronomy in the canyon is at Fajada Butte. This isolated 430-foot (130m) sandstone outcrop stands in the southeastern entrance to Chaco Canyon. On a ledge near its summit three slabs have fallen and lean against the rock wall. The Anasazi took advantage of this, for partially behind the slabs are two spiral rock carvings, one about the size of a dinner plate, the other much smaller. Shortly after the summer solstice in 1977, artist Anna Sofaer was on the ledge looking for rock art. It was late morning, and she observed sunlight in the form of a 'dagger' thrown into the shaded area behind the slabs bisecting the larger spiral design.

Further research has confirmed that at noon on midsummer's day a sliver of light does cut precisely through the centre of the spiral. Furthermore, at midwinter, daggers of light exactly frame either side of the carving, and at the equinoxes one slit of light cuts the spiral at a midpoint between edge and centre, while another bisects the smaller carving. There is even evidence that the shadow of one of the slabs cast by the moon onto the larger spiral would also indicate the major and minor standstills in the 18.6-year lunar cycle.[9,10] Despite the difficult location of this feature, thousands of visitors have climbed to it. This pressure of human feet has had the most unfortunate effect of eroding the ground around the base of the stone slabs, and one of them has twisted and slipped, causing the sun dagger to miss its target. The failure of the midsummer event was noted for the first time in 1989, and the place is now closed to visitors.[11]

It is now becoming abundantly clear that the

Fajada Butte. A ledge high on this outcrop contains the stone slabs and rock carvings that accurately display the key solar events in the year.

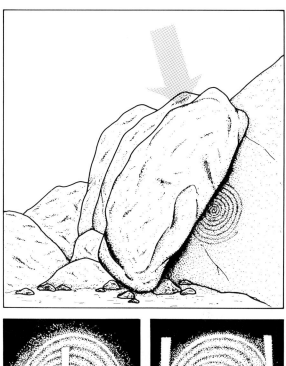

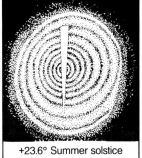
+23.6° Summer solstice

−23.6° Winter solstice

A diagrammatic depiction of the slab arrangements on Fajada Butte and the summer and winter solstitial 'light dagger' effects on the larger carved spiral behind them.

Chacoans developed a highly sophisticated and ordered culture, with exceptional achievements in architecture, trade, the management of a difficult agricultural region and religious life. The astronomy would have linked with both the ceremonial and agricultural activities. The picture now emerging suggests that the canyon must have been a religious focal point for the San Juan Basin, with a relatively modest resident population that was periodically enlarged for seasonal, ceremonial functions. It was, in effect, an Anasazi omphalos site – a sacred centre.

CHAPTER 4

CAHOKIA
MOUNDS

USA

*WORLD HERITAGE LIST NUMBER 18
ARCHAEOLOGY, ASTRONOMY, CONSCIOUSNESS, ENERGIES(?), GEOMANCY*

Mound 55 – a good example of a platform mound.

THIS 2,200-ACRE (890HA) SITE is situated just to the east of St Louis, in southern Illinois, close to Collinsville (not, confusingly, near the town of Cahokia). It is the remains of a large city and ritual complex which was first occupied around AD 700, developed, flowered, declined and was abandoned by AD 1500. At its peak it covered some six square miles (1,550ha) and had a population of about 20,000. It was certainly the largest community in prehistoric times in what is now the USA, and its influence extended for great distances.

The first inhabitants were Indians of what archaeologists call the Late Woodland culture (AD 300–800). Large, permanent villages were established, and cultivation of certain crops supported subsistence off the abundant wildlife. The population grew and social complexity developed during the period AD 800–1000, the 'Emergent Mississippian' period, and corn became an important part of the diet. The full development of Cahokia, however, occurred during the Mississippian period proper (AD 1000–1400). These names for periods of prehistoric Indian culture are invented by archaeologists, because no one knows what the actual people involved called themselves. These Indian peoples based around the Mississippi valleys have also been referred to as 'The Mound Builders'. Whatever one calls them, they are lost to us, except in the remains of their structures and artefacts.

Cahokia at its peak had its central portion surrounded by a defensive palisade enclosing a large D-shaped area. The main mounds and certain dwellings were contained within the palisade, but more mounds, habitations for the ordinary population and the cultivated areas stretched out beyond this boundary. The people lived not in teepees but in pole-frame dwellings that had clay-plastered walls and thatched roofs. Over 120 mounds originally existed on the site, but the locations of only 106 have been recorded. Approximately 68 are preserved within the tract defined by the modern State Historic Site.

There are three basic types of mound at Cahokia – *platform* mounds, which have flat tops and square or rectangular bases, looking like earthen pyramids; round, *conical* mounds, and long, oval-based *ridge-top* mounds. Platform mounds supported buildings on their summits – temples, charnel houses and residencies for the elite. The less common conical mounds (which used to be called 'chocolate drop' mounds because of their shape) seem to have been primarily for burial, and many seem to have been associated with platform mounds.

A conical mound. This is one of the pair known as 'Twin Mounds'.

Cahokia archaeologist Melvin Fowler suggests that the platform mounds 'represent the location of charnel structures and the associated conical mounds were the burial mounds'.[1] The ridge-top mounds also contained burials in a few cases, but their key function seems to have been geomantic: Fowler notes that five of the

Monks Mound from the south. The top two terraces are not visible in this view.

eight ridge mounds mark the extreme limits of the mound area, and three align with Monks Mound to form a north–south line.

A reconstructed view of Monks Mound in its prime. (After William R. Iseminger)

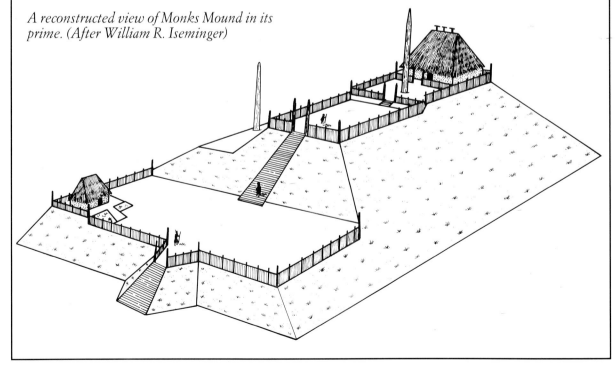

The mounds were placed around open areas or plazas, highly reminiscent of ancient Mesoamerican cities. Most experts now think, however, that these features evolved locally rather than resulting from Mesoamerican influence. Cahokia was laid out to the cardinal directions, and where the east–west and north–south axes crossed stood Monks Mound, a mighty platform mound raised in four terraces, itself orientated close to the cardinal directions. It was not only the largest mound at Cahokia, but the largest in the North American continent. It stands over 100 feet (30m) high, covers more than 14 acres (5.6ha) and contains around 22 million cubic feet (622,600 cubic m) of earth. The depredations of time together with, in recent centuries, building and cultivation on its terraces (by, among others, the French Trappist monks in the nineteenth century after whom the mound was named) has caused Monks Mound to lose some of its shape, and it has slumped in parts. Fortunately, enough survives for its basic form and massive bulk to be still appreciated. (Some idea of its original, pristine appearance is shown in the illustration on page 54, which was drawn by Cahokia's current curator, William R. Iseminger.) So large is it, that even into the beginning of the twentieth century some could still seriously argue that it was a natural feature! This view, Fowler comments, was 'probably influenced by racist attitudes. Many believed that the ancestors of the American Indian did not have the capacity to apply themselves to any task as time consuming and elaborate as the building of Monks Mound.'[2] The site of the mound was occupied in AD 800, but the actual mound was built in various stages and developments from about AD 950 until approximately AD 1200. On the fourth or summit terrace, the Mississippians built a huge building 105 feet long, 48 feet wide and an estimated 50 feet high (32 × 15 × 15.3m). This was presumably the king's or chieftain's dwelling – a palace or even a temple, if we see the leader as a religious figure, as is likely. A great post was erected outside the building, and on the southeastern corner of the third terrace was a small mound.

Quite apart from its size, the central position of Monks Mound, at the hub of the four directions, marks it as Cahokia's omphalos (see Chapter 1), a role no doubt emphasized by the massive pole surmounting it. The late Joseph Campbell noted the significance of the great mound's positioning:

> Since it is in the middle of the site, its symbolic function, as representing the axial height joining earth and sky, is evident. The idea of such a generative center is already represented in the Spiro Mound gorget, which is an unmistakable representation of the mythological archetype of the quartered cosmos: an 'elementary idea' of which the swastika and equal-armed cross are abstractions. The prominence of these symbols [from Spiro Mound, LeFlore County, Oklahoma, and other sites] speaks for the importance of this concept in Mississippian thought.[3]

A crested-bird swastika with sun-swastika at the centre – the design from an engraved shell gorget from Spiro Mound, Oklahoma.

A large ceremonial structure, quite possibly a shrine, was built on the southwest corner of the first terrace of Monks Mound. The first building burnt down around AD 1150, and was replaced by a small platform mound and a new building. In the following century, eight rebuildings took place at this spot. It was clearly a significant location, and it cannot be acciden-

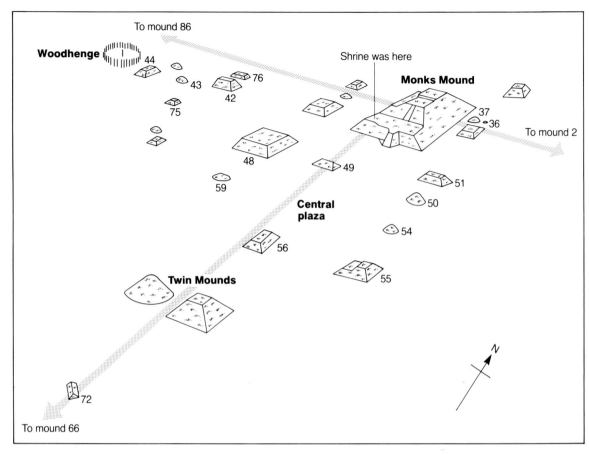

To mound 86

Woodhenge 44

43

76

42

75

48

59

Shrine was here

Monks Mound

37
36

To mound 2

49

51

50

54

Central plaza

56

55

Twin Mounds

N

72

To mound 66

A simplified sketch map (ABOVE) showing some key mounds and the approximate course of axes at Cahokia.
An artist's impression (BELOW) of Cahokia at its height. The view is northwards along the axial alignment through Twin Mounds towards Monks Mound. Note the southwest corner shrine on Monks Mound and the tall pole on the summit. (Painting by L.K. Townsend; © C.M.M.S.)

tal that it is through here that the north–south axis of Cahokia passes. Running south from this point, the meridian passes through a ridge-top mound (number 49 in the archaeological categorization used at Cahokia), between a great platform and conical mound pair nicknamed 'Twin Mounds', across the southeast end of ridge mound 72, and to the southernmost ridge mound, the massive Rattlesnake Mound, number 66.

Mound 72 is most interesting, even though today it seems a fairly insignificant ridge of earth. Excavations revealed that at the precise point where the meridional line passes through the end of the mound, a huge pole – about three feet (1m) in diameter – had been erected. Radiocarbon dating of material in the eight-foot (2.4m) deep pole (the pole had clearly been very tall) gave a date of AD 950 for the time when the pole was placed in the ground. The excavations also showed that the mound had been constructed from a series of earlier submounds that were then reshaped and covered over to give the long ridge form. Beneath these smaller mounds were a series of burials – well over 250 skeletons were found all told. Most were of young women, seemingly sacrificial victims to accompany burials of important individuals. The main burial appears to have been that of a 45-year-old man. He was laid on a bed of 20,000 marine shell beads and accompanied by rich grave goods, including uncut mica sheets, a roll of unworked copper sheeting and several

Mound 56, nearest to camera, is a ploughed-down platform mound. The large platform mound beyond is one of the Twin Mounds.

hundred finely wrought arrowheads. The skeletons of four men with missing heads and hands were also uncovered. Fowler comments that the inclusion of these burials in the mound 'does not mean that the interpretation of this mound form as community marker mounds is incorrect. It is probable that the burials included were also dedicated to the significant point in the community being marked.'[4] As astronomer E. C. Krupp put it: 'Everything about them [the burials] marks their location as a special place. That spot, in turn, was part of the cosmically oriented plan for the entire site. Even without knowing the beliefs of the ancient Cahokians, we can detect their concern for celestial order in the burials of Mound 72.'[5]

Although most of the mounds at Cahokia are approximately oriented to the cardinal points, half of the ridge-top mounds are aligned northwest–southwest or southwest–northeast. Mound 72 has its axial orientation 30 degrees from an east–west axis. Archaeoastronomer Ray A. Williamson sees this as part of the overall significance of the mound:

At sunrise on the winter solstice the shadow of the post would fall right along the axis of the mound. As the sun rose and moved south, the shadow would move north of the

The ridge of earth that marks geomantic mound 72. (See text starting on page 57.)

ridge. On the summer solstice, the setting sun would cause the post to cast its shadow along the axis of the ridge in the opposite direction. Although the present ridgetop shape of mound 72 was not reached until about a hundred years after its construction began, the orientation of the mound seems to merit further examination by archaeologists. The number of high-status burials found there, from several phases of construction, suggests that the mound was known as a sacred, special place for many years. Its orientation along the solstice directions may indicate a conceptual link between burial and the winter solstice direction.[6]

Ridge-top mound 2, at the eastern extremity of the Cahokia site, and the now-destroyed ridge mound 86 at the western limit formed the east–west axis, which crossed the meridian at Monks Mound. Some hundreds of yards westwards from Monks Mound, close to this axis, is the so-called 'Woodhenge', a feature that was possibly instrumental in the laying out of the geomantic orientation of Cahokia. In 1961, while conducting rescue archaeology in advance of road building, Warren Wittry and team uncovered a series of stains in the ground, indicating post holes. On excavating some of these, fragments

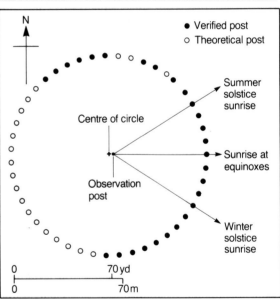

How the partially reconstructed 'Circle 2' at Cahokia's Woodhenge works.

of cedar were found and evidence of earthen ramps within the holes, which would have facilitated the raising of tall poles. Further investigation has revealed that there had been five circles at the site, and radiocarbon dates suggested that they had been created separately over a period bracketing AD 1000. The western end of the site had been destroyed by road

building operations. Studying 'Circle 2' (now known to be the third in the sequence, in fact), Wittry concluded that it had been a Sun Circle (and the others may have had astronomical significance, too). It had been about 410 feet (125m) across, and contained possibly 48 posts. Three of the post positions on the eastern arc of the circle could have marked the equinoctial and solstitial sunrises (spring and autumn equinox sunrises, of course, share the same horizon position). The viewing point could not have been the geometric centre of the circle, however, and would have had to have been slightly off-set. Sure enough, in exactly that position, Wittry found a post hole. In 1978, Wittry set up utility poles to mark the central pole and the three sunrise marker poles, and in 1985, after separate explorations by Wittry and William Iseminger had accurately located 39 post holes, the site was reconstructed using red cedar and black locust logs which had been debarked, trimmed with stone celts and stained with red ochre.

The sight-lines at the site were found to work well at the appropiate times of the year. Most of Monks Mound is visible from the Sun Circle, and to a viewer at the central observation post it would seem as if the equinoctial sun was rising out of the mound itself. Doubtless, this was a ceremonial augmentation of the status of the leader or priest-king who occupied Monks Mound. There is little ethnographic informa-

Looking eastwards across reconstructed 'Circle 2' at Woodhenge. The foreground pole is the observer's post; the post on the circumference marked with white paint is the equinoctial sunrise marker. Monks Mound is visible on the skyline. At the equinoxes (21 March and 21 September) the sun appears to rise out of the mound.

tion regarding sun watching in this region, but a Menomini legend collected many miles north of Cahokia does refer to observing the sun when it 'stands on the treetops'.

The function of much of the circle's posts would seem to have been simply to enclose a sacred space. We must always be aware that to the ancient mind specialized functions, astronomical or geomantic, were not divorced from religious significance, as was noted at mound 72. Also, early travellers in America referred to rings of wooden posts being used by Indians for ritual purposes. This possible ceremonial aspect of Woodhenge seems to be borne out by Wittry's discovery of a piece of pottery close to the midwinter sunrise marker post. It was the fragment of a beaker, probably ritually broken, which had a design on it that Wittry interpreted as representing the Earth and the Four Directions (the encircled crosses in the centre) and the sun (radiating lines) defining a circular path (the sun's passage) opening to the winter

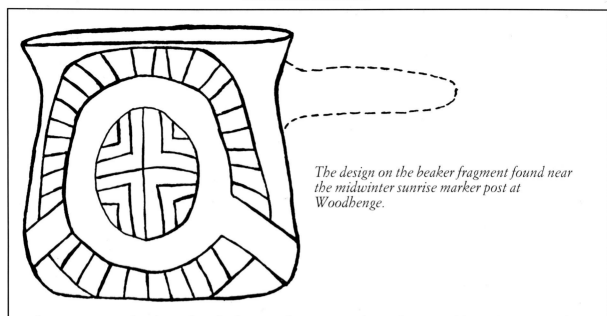

The design on the beaker fragment found near the midwinter sunrise marker post at Woodhenge.

solstice sunrise – the channel in the lower right (see illustration above). The closed channel in the lower left of the design may indicate midwinter sunset.

That the 'Sun King' on Monks Mound may have had a shamanic-priestly role is suggested by a fascinating find on the eastern side of the mound. In 1971 investigators unearthed a small, engraved sandstone tablet. On one side it depicts a winged man, apparently wearing a bird-mask and costume. This echoes a design engraved on a 13-inch-long (33cm) marine shell found at Spiro Mound, Oklahoma, within the immense Mississippian sphere of influence, which shows a man in bird-costume. On the back of the tablet is a criss-cross pattern which,

The engraved designs on both sides of the sandstone tablet found in Monks Mound.

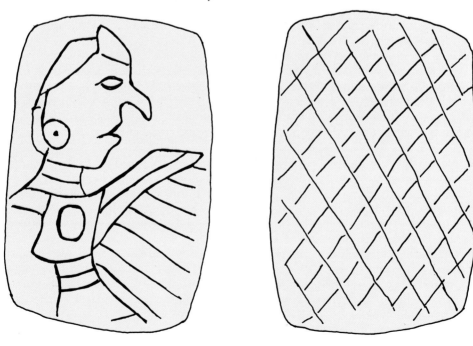

A figure in bird costume, engraved on a shell that was found at Spiro Mound, Oklahoma.

A Mississippian design showing winged rattlesnakes.

it has been suggested, could represent a rattlesnake's skin. This would fit in well with Joseph Campbell's observations that the 'fundamental legend' of the Feathered Serpent, which had appeared in Central America by at least the first millenium BC, seems to have been represented in Mississippian art by the winged rattlesnake.[7] The winged man is a well-known image of the shaman, referring to his 'spirit flight' to the Otherworlds. Elsewhere in the USA there are ancient Indian effigy mounds showing winged humans. Campbell remarks generally with regard to bird masks that they are 'characteristic . . . of the lore of shamanism to this day throughout Siberia and North America.'[8]

Finally, there are tenuous, tantalizing hints – no more – of a possible usage, or awareness, by the Cahokians of natural energies. It was found that seven of the original posts in the southwest sector of Circle 2 had been replaced. The reason for this is not clear, but Williamson notes: 'If the modern experience at Cahokia is any guide to the past, lightning damage appears to have been a particular problem. . . . In 1980, the [reconstructed] observer's post was struck by lightning and shattered. The winter solstice post shows some signs of lightning damage as well.'[9] If the posts of Woodhenge were prone to lightning strikes, how much more so must the great pole on top of Monks Mound have been! And what more dramatic way could the link between heaven and earth be demonstrated to the populace than by a bolt from the sky linking with the sacred omphalos? (Not to mention the enhancement of the 'Sun King's aura of power – he would seem literally to have a hot-line to heaven!) Also, the Cahokia mounds happen to be adjacent to faulting connected with the New Madrid seismic zone, which saw one of the greatest known earthquakes in 1811. A map plotting 488 quake epicentres monitored between 1811 and 1974 shows a modest cluster in the East St Louis – Cahokia mounds region.[10] Such areas tend to have notably varied magnetic and gravity anomalies.

The present State Historic Site containing the core of the mounds area is hemmed in all around by gravel pits, small workshops and sundry other modern features, and a highway cuts through the site immediately at the southern foot of Monks Mound. Nevertheless, within the now protected area, the local authorities have done a remarkable preservation job making the site most accessible. The interpretive centre there (phone 618-346-5160) is the most effective and ambitious of any the author encountered during research visits to World Heritage sites for this book.

CHAPTER 5

TEOTIHUACAN

MEXICO

*WORLD HERITAGE LIST NUMBER 31
ARCHAEOLOGY, ASTRONOMY, ENERGIES(?), EVOLVED,
GEODETIC INFORMATION(?), GEOMANCY, MYTH*

*General view of part of Teotihuacan showing the
Pyramid of the Moon and a section of the Street
of the Dead. (EFI/Patrick Horsbrugh)*

THIS GREAT URBAN and religious centre, 30 miles (48km) northeast of modern Mexico City, was given its present name by the Aztecs who encountered its awesome ruins. In Nahuatl, the language the Aztecs spoke, Teotihuacan means 'place of the gods', or, 'the place of the creation of the gods'. This great site, dominated by two pyramids, was 'regarded by the Aztec as the original source of civilization and government, and the place where cosmic order was established.'[1] In Aztec myth, Teotihuacan was where Nanahuatzin, a dying god, jumped into a ceremonial fire which the four creator gods (representing the Four Directions) were too fearful to enter. Thus turned to flame, Nanahuatzin became the 'Fifth Sun' – the Aztec sun of the present cosmic age. His companion, Tecciztecatl, joined him in the sacrificial fire and became the moon. The Aztecs thus decided that the two pyramids were dedicated to the sun and moon respectively. The Fifth Sun agreed to orient the world by his risings and to organize the passage of time. This legend clearly is a narrative mnemonic for orientation and astronomy, for geomancy, and Teotihuacan is certainly a place where this is demonstrated.

No one knows who the Teotihuacanos were, but they occupied the Valley of Mexico well over a millenium prior to the Aztecs, and even before the Toltecs. Teotihuacan began to be laid out in the first century AD, and at its height (AD 300–650) it had a population of up to 200,000 and extended to around 10 square miles (2,590ha). It was made up of temples, shrines, plazas, dwellings and workshops, was ruled by a priestly elite, and was both a sacred and an economic centre. The influence of this city, the largest in its day in the western hemisphere, spread over vast distances, even as far north as Cahokia or beyond, according to Joseph Campbell.[2] It was burned and abandoned in the eighth century.

The city plan was laid out on a four-fold division scheme, but it was *not* aligned to the cardinal points. The whole layout is skewed 15½ degrees east of north. It took archaeologists and astronomers some time to understand what this odd orientation was all about.

The effective omphalos of the place is the Pyramid of the Sun, which rises well over 200 feet (60m) in tiers, and is composed of 35 million cubic feet (990,500 cubic m) of material. It faces westerly towards Cerro Colorado, though E. C. Krupp states that it actually aligns

The Pyramid of the Sun (EFI/Patrick Horsbrugh)

to Cerro Maravillas, 4½ miles (7km) distant. Either or both may well have been sacred hills to the Teotihuacanos. But the researchers sought a primarily astronomical answer for the curious angle of orientation that the city planners adhered to so rigorously that not only were streets and structures kept to the established axial plan, but even the course of the San Juan River at the site was canalized to conform to it. The skewed north–south central axis is marked by the Street of the Dead, and the Pyramid of the Sun is set just to the east of this with its sides oriented appropiately. The Street of the Dead is about 1½ miles (2.4km) long and aligns to the Pyramid of the Moon at its northerly end. It is really a series of plazas, flanked by platforms and multi-roomed structures which opened out onto it, and was probably a ceremonial way. It ultimately aligns to Cerro Gordo, a major source of the city's water and thus also probably considered holy. But no astronomical target could be identified in the east of north orientation.

The answer came from the study of the other axis. This is believed to intersect the northerly–southerly axis a short distance to the south of

Looking north along the main axis marked by the Street of the Dead towards the Pyramid of the Moon. Note the notch in Cerro Gordo in the background. (EFI/Patrick Horsbrugh)

the Pyramid of the Sun at a point marked by a 'pecked cross'. This feature is in the plaster floor of a ruin complex archaeologists call the Viking Group, on the eastern edge of the Street of the Dead. It measures about a yard (1m) across, and consists of two concentric rings of pecked holes, quartered by two pecked lines crossing at the circles' common centre. Another such circular motif, containing a similar number of pecked holes, was found 2 miles (3.2km) westwards on a boulder on Cerro Colorado. Archaeologists suspect that these symbols are benchmarks left by the early surveyors. Some 70 similar pecked designs occur in ruins from Guatemala to northern Mexico. (These features probably had ritual use as well, as we know the ancients worldwide could combine spirituality and pragmatism at the same place.) The north–east axis seems to have been a perpendicular struck from the line linking the two pecked crosses, which, archaeoastronomer Anthony Aveni verified, aligned to the setting point of the Pleiades in AD 150. At the latitude of Teotihuacan the sun passes directly overhead on two days each year. At noon on those days no shadow is cast and the sun god was said to descend to the Earth briefly. In AD 150 the first annual pre-dawn appearance of the Pleiades heralded the first day of the zenith sun. These conspicuous stars seem to have had great importance not only in ancient Mesoamerica but, indeed, 'are recognized by nearly everyone as something special. Worldwide, they are seasonal heralds.'[3]

So the orientation of Teotihuacan seems ultimately to stem from an astronomical connection with the Pleiades. But the geomancy goes literally deeper than this. In 1971, a heavy rainstorm caused a depression to appear in front of the Pyramid of the Sun. On investigation, ancient steps were revealed descending into a natural cave *beneath* the pyramid. It is a four-lobed cave with a lava tube extension. Archaeoastronomer John B. Carlson described it as 'something like a four-leaf clover with its stem lying flat'.[4] Archaeologist Doris Heyden suggested that the four lobes corresponded to the four-fold cosmos of the Teotihuacanos, with the stem indicating by extraordinary coincidence what was later confirmed as the Pleiades setting point. The Teotihuacanos embellished the cave, and it was clearly a sacred shrine, for many ancient Mesoamericans considered that their final ancestors had emerged from caverns within the Earth. It was also, perhaps, where shamanic initation was conducted. The Pyramid of the Sun and the axial plan of the city seem to have evolved from this holy spot.

It seems, therefore, that the axial arrange-

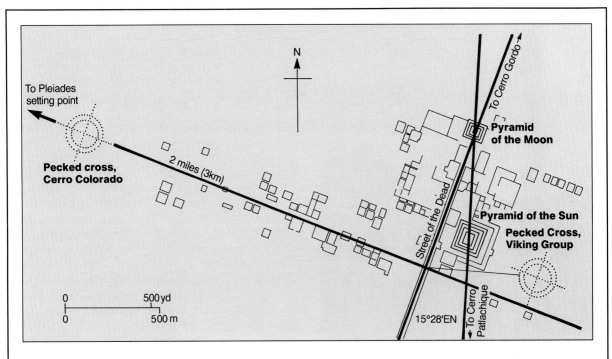

A simplified plan of central Teotihuacan showing the Pyramids of the Sun and of the Moon and the axes.

ment of Teotihuacan echoes both subterranean and celestial configurations at the site. A marriage of heaven and earth.

The cardinal directions are also clearly indicated at Teotihuacan, however, for the Pyramid of the Sun lies due south from the city's other great monument, the Pyramid of the Moon (which had a well penetrating its structure). This alignment extends beyond the southern pyramid to 'pyramid-shaped Cerro Patlachique' visible on the skyline.[5]

It has been suggested that all major solar, and possibly lunar, events are accommodated by alignments extending from the central complex out to other temples and pyramids lying within a 1¼ miles (2km) radius.

At the southern end of the Street of the Dead is a complex called The Citadel, which also marks the course of the main 'east–west' thoroughfare. Within this ritual plaza is a seven-tiered pyramid covered with carvings depicting Quetzalcoatl, the classic expression of the plumed serpent archetype (see Cahokia). American engineer Hugh Harleston claims that the dimensions of the steps on this structure

provide a mathematical basis for a mercator-like projection of the earth.[6] If this is so, then it means the Pyramid of Quetzalcoatl encodes geodetic information.

Taking Teotihuacan as a whole, the sky and topography were welded into a classic geomantic expression. 'Locked within the city's monuments, avenues, and relationships to outlying sites seems to be a complex system of associations,' Krupp observes. 'The order is there.'[7]

Any possible energy aspects of Teotihuacan are uninvestigated, but David Zink notes that:

> In 1906 an archaeologist . . . found a thick sheet of mica covering the top of the fifth level of the pyramid [of the Sun]; this material was lost in the reconstruction. Its presence suggests that perhaps some now unknown energy property of this pyramid may once have been utilized by the priests . . . it would be based, of course, on the electrical insulating properties of mica . . .[8]

A structure like a pyramid is a notable collector of atmospheric electricity, as has been noted at Egypt's Giza Pyramid. The enormous statues which originally adorned the summits of both main pyramids may have been, effectively, instruments in some elemental technology, a technology perhaps echoed in more primitive form at Cahokia.

CHAPTER 6

CHICHEN ITZA

MEXICO

WORLD HERITAGE LIST NUMBER 36
ARCHAEOLOGY, ASTRONOMY, EVOLUTION, GEOMANCY, MYTH

THE RUINED CEREMONIAL CITY of Chichen Itza lies about 75 miles (120km) southeast of Merida in the north of Mexico's Yucatan Peninsula. 'Old Chichen' was built by the Mayans in what archaeologists call the Late Classic Period (AD 600-830) on an earlier site, only traces of which have been found. Buildings in this area include what have become dubbed the Church, the Nunnery, the House of the Three Lintels and the Caracol – a Mayan observatory.

The ancient Maya encompassed a huge area, ranging from western Honduras and Guatemala in the south through to the tip of the Yucatan Peninsula at the north. They emerged from the background of ancient peoples in the second century BC when their first pyramids appeared in what is present-day Guatemala.

By about AD 300 their architecture had developed to remarkable levels of expertise, and the Classic Maya period ran from then to approximately AD 600. Great ceremonial centres were the focus for populations living scattered around them in the jungles. In the Late Classic period these centres were abandoned and northern sites like Chichen Itza came into their own.

The Mayans had advanced their development of architecture, painting and sculpture, and used hieroglyphic writing. They entered records in paintings, in carvings on stelae and in books or 'codices' made from strips of deerskin or paper made from bark, which had been plaster-coated.

They were also 'fascinated by the passage of time', archaeologist Iris Barry tells us:

They developed an advanced arithmetical system and made accurate observations of the heavens which allowed them to compute astronomical events. Their science, however . . . was far more like astrology, being based on a firm belief in the cyclical nature of time and its control by supernatural forces. . . .

The timing of every ritual and ceremonial act, such as sacrifice, marriage or baptism, was dictated by the Maya calendar, which was one of the most complicated ever devised.[1]

The sacred Mayan year (*Tzolkin*) was based on a 260-day cycle in which 20 named days ran serially, with a number from 1 to 13 as a prefix, thus taking the 260-day period for the same combination of number and day-name to recur. No one knows why this system developed, for it does not relate to any apparent astronomical cycle. However, there was also a secular calendar year (*Haab*), with 365 days like our own, running concurrently with the sacred system. It was divided into 18 months of 20 days each, with five days of bad omen added at the end of the year. The months not only had names, but were also numbered from 0 to 19. These two systems of 260 and 365 days were meshed together, and it took 52 years for a date to be repeated in both systems. This period is known as the Calendar Round, the end of each of which caused nervous anticipation among the Maya. The crowning complexity was the Long Count, in which the two cycles of the Calendar Round were combined with lunar months and the 584-day cycle of Venus. The Long Count

commenced in 3113 BC, according to Mayan history or myth, a remote date that mystifies archaeologists. Perhaps there is more to be discovered of an unprecedented early date lying in the jungles of Central America. . . .

Venus was a major player in Mayan cosmology and, indeed, in that of other ancient Mesoamericans. The Mayan codices reveal complex computations regarding Venus – for instance, the Grolier Codex has a 104-year Venus alamanac. John B. Carlson explains that to ancient Mesoamericans

the bright planet was the opposite of ancient Rome's Venus, the goddess of love; it incarnated warfare and blood sacrifice. Therefore one purpose of the Venus almanac was apparently astrological – to determine a propitious time for ritual combat and sacrifice. Although we believe the stylised battles resembled the jousts of medieval Europe, the 'knights' fought for their lives, and the losers were put to death – sacrificed with honor.[2]

The Caracol (the name means 'snail' because of

The Caracol. (Collection EFI)

has been shown by fairly recent research to be wrong, but Anthony Aveni can now claim that Chichen Itza is one of 'the most secure examples of the incorporation of a horizon-based astronomy in architecture':

> Particularly impressive are those sight lines achieved through a set of horizontal shafts that feed into a sealed rectangular chamber at the top of the tower. The extreme northerly and southerly disappearance points of Venus over the western horizon give a nearly perfect match to the measured directions of the azimuth of the shafts. . . .[3]

Additionally, the diagonal of the slightly asymetric upper platform on which the tower stands gives summer solstice sunrise in one direction and winter solstice sunset in the other. There are possibly other astronomical lines embedded in the building.

In AD 987, a breakaway group of the fierce Toltecs arrived at Chichen Itza and took over by force. They began constructing new buildings about a mile northeast of the older city. The Castillo, the Great Ball Court and the Temple of the Jaguars show their influence. 'A complex mix of Mexican and Mayan traditions . . . merged into a system with new artistic and political styles.'[4]

The Castillo is a stepped pyramid, a temple to Kukulcan, the Mayan version of Quetzalcoatl, the Feathered Serpent. It stands on a line connecting the two great cenotes of Chichen Itza. Cenotes are natural wells formed by the collapse of subterranean caverns revealing the groundwater in this arid limestone country. The two at Chichen Itza are probably what attracted the first settlers. One is called the Cenote of Xtoloc, the other the Cenote of Sacrifice, which is nearly 200 feet (60m) across its opening at the top and 60 feet (18m) down to the water, which itself is another 40 feet (12m) deep. This was the sacred well (that of Xtoloc being used as the water supply), and was worked into a circular form at the top. ('Chichen' means mouth of the well.) Votive artefacts were thrown into the water as were, apparently, human sacrifices. A ceremonial way links the cenote with the plaza containing the Castillo, on which its western

the structure's appearance and interior winding staircase) exemplifies this involvement with Venus in particular and the heavens in general. The structure consists of a cylindrical tower on a two-tiered rectangular platform, and it was probably Mayan originally with later Toltec-influenced additions. The upper part of the tower has crumbled, giving an appearance coincidentally reminiscent of modern domed observatories. This probably helped speculation over a long period about possible astronomical aspects to the building. Some of this speculation

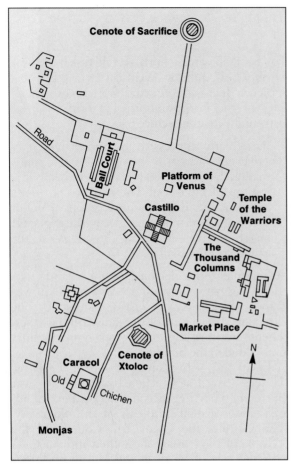

A simplified plan of central Chichen Itza.

edge seems to be aligned (through the Platform of Venus).

An interesting light-and-shadow play is created at the Castillo each equinox. On each side of the pyramid there are cermonial stairs. In the last hour before equinox sunset, the northwest corner of the pyramid throws a serrated shadow onto the west-facing balustrade of the northern staircase. This produces a pattern of sunlight and shadow similar to the markings of Yucatan's indigenous rattlesnake. At the bottom of the balustrade are stone-carved serpents heads to which the shadow 'attaches' itself. This dramatic effect producing the symbol of the 'feathered serpent' was presumably used in a ceremonial capacity by the Mayans or Toltec-Mayans. The spectacle certainly attracts several

thousands onlookers today! It is thought that the Pyramid may also be aligned to sunset on the day of zenith passage. The four stairways plus the platform step give 365 steps in all, possibly representing the days of the year, and each side of the pyramid has nine terraces divided into three segments by its stairway, creating 18 terrace units, the number of months in the Mayan year. Finally, some of the temples at Chichen Itza have remnants of sacbeob aligned to them. These are Mayan sacred ways, and while their existence within ceremonial complexes has long been noted, it has been only relatively recently that awareness has developed that such stone ways linked one centre with another. This system of straight sacred ways is known at present only from fragmentary discoveries, and a full picture is nowhere near being assembled. Certainly northern Yucatan contained systems of sacbeob – the region around Uxmal, another important Mayan centre about 100 miles (160km) southwest of Chichen Itza, for example. One of the earliest accounts of a sacbe was that of Thomas Gann in 1925, who stumbled across one between Coba (about 56 miles (90km) east of Chichen Itza) and Yaxuna. He describes 'a great elevated road or causeway 32 feet wide, and varying, according to the configuration of the ground from 2 to 8 feet in height . . . the sides were built of great blocks of cut stone, many weighing hundreds of pounds; the central part was filled with unhewn blocks of limestone, and the top covered with rubble which . . . was cemented over. It . . . ran as far as we followed it, straight as an arrow, and almost flat as a rule.'[5] This 60-mile long segment of a sacbe is the longest known, and was one of 16 roads which originated at Coba.

Remnants of straight roads linking sacred centres have also been discovered on the island of Cozumal off the east coast of the Yucatan Peninsula. There are doubtless many more Mayan roads to be discovered.

Clearly, the Maya, like so many pre-Columbian Amerindians, had an obsession with old straight tracks that would have done Alfred Watkins and his ley theory (see Chapter 1) proud!

CHAPTER 7

MACHU PICCHU

PERU

WORLD HERITAGE LIST NUMBER 54
ARCHAEOLOGY, ASTRONOMY, CONSCIOUSNESS, ENERGIES, MYTH

MACHU PICCHU was an Inca citadel, located a little over 60 miles (97km) north of Cuzco. Its ruins occupy a topographical saddle about 8,000 feet (2,400km) up in the Andes between the peaks of Machu (old) Picchu and Huayna (new) Picchu. It is a complex of cultivation terraces, stone houses, temples, plazas and residential compounds clinging to the ridge, on three sides of which are vertiginous drops, overhanging the gorge of the Urubamba River about 2,000 feet (600m) below. The city was discovered in 1911 by Hiram Bingham of Yale University, whose reports and photographs captured the public imagination.

The site's importance to archaeologists is that it was never discovered and defaced by the Conquistadores, and so it presents a relatively unspoilt look into Inca life. Otherwise, they do not think it to be anything special. Nevertheless, as the great Inca road explorer Victor von Hagen wrote: 'I wondered just why the Incas had bothered to build these hanging cities . . . these ruins perched midway between the jungle and the clouds?'[1] Apart from the temples, there is other evidence to suggest that Machu Picchu was primarily a religious complex. After bribing their Indian workmen, archaeologists in 1912 were led to natural caves in the slopes below the city containing over one hundred burials. Of 173 skeletons recovered, 150 were those of women, who had the richest graves. In addition, some burials

were found within the city itself, in artificial caves hollowed out beneath huge granite boulders. These were places of religious

importance to the Inca, and Bingham thought that such unusually situated graves were the tombs of the Chosen Women, an Inca religious order dedicated to the worship of the Sun.[2]

The most important, richly furnished grave was found beneath a rock 1,000 feet (300m) above the city. It contained the skeleton of a middle-aged woman whose grave goods included, among other things, a bronze knife with a handle in the form of a flying bird, a concave bronze mirror and painted ceramic ware, including a cooking pot embellished with a modelled snake. It would probably be wise to consider these items as magical, ritualistic artefacts rather than utilitarian objects.

Machu Picchu was, therefore, essentially a women's site. 'It was not a city; it was a temple complex,' avers astronomer Gerald Hawkins. 'The purpose was religious, ritualistic, not secular.'[3] This is further emphasized by the presence of a most curious feature at the site – the Intihuatana. This is a very strange geometric object, a single piece carved out of a granite outcrop atop a natural pyramidal spur. It has an upright, a foot (30cm) high, projecting from a complex platform, containing a variety of planes, facets, recesses and projections. It is asymetrical and oriented so that north–south runs diagonally from one corner to a small facet. It is known that there were other such objects within the Inca empire, but precisely because of their religious significance the Spanish conquerors sought them out and destroyed them. The Intihuatana at Machu Picchu is the only one known to have survived. The name means

A general view of Machu Picchu. (Peruvian Tourist Board)

'hitching post of the sun', and such features are assumed to have been associated with solar observations and ceremony, probably the winter solstice (21 June, as Machu Picchu is in the southern hemisphere), the major Inca festival of Inti Raymi.

'Each year, at the winter solstice the Incas staged a ceremony to "tie the sun", lest it swing even farther north in its daily arc and be lost forever.'[4] It is assumed that the upright is a gnomon, a shadow-throwing device like the centre of a sundial, and Hawkins notes that the shadow cast by the sun or moon could be read to half a centimetre, representing an angular error of a quarter of a degree for the longest shadow line. He further observes that the 'solstice, equinox and the displacements of the moon could be observed. At this altitude Venus would also cast a shadow.'[5] But the truth is that no one knows just how the Intihuatana was used nor whether there were measuring devices employed in conjunction with it.

To the Inca, Inti – the Sun God – was the main servant of Viracocha, the supreme Creator, and the divine ancestor of the Inca royal house – the ruling Inca was 'the Son of the Sun'. It is not surprising, therefore, to find the sun figuring again in at least one other temple at Machu Picchu, although this time with more assured archaeoastronomical understanding. This is the Torreon, a beautifully built structure, rectangular in plan except for the easterly wall which is curved into a semicircle, dividing the interior into an inner sanctum and outer hall. The roof is missing as with all the Machu Picchu buildings (except where reconstructed). In 1980 astrophysicist David Dearborn discovered that the northeastern window of the inner sanctum was centred on the midwinter sunrise. Beneath the window is a sacred altar-like rock, which has been carved so that a very regular cleft divides it in half and lies at right angles to the window. When the solstitial sun rises above the San Gabriel peak to the northeast, its light floods in through the window, falling parallel to the carved cleft.

When he had the opportunity to witness this event, John B. Carlson felt that 'Inti the Sun had again entered his house as he had done silently, without witness, again and again over the centuries since the Inca worshippers had abandoned the site.'[6] Dearborn and Ray White have proposed that a frame may have been hung on carved knobs that protrude from the otherwise featureless wall, supporting a plumb line which would have thrown its shadow along the cut edge on the altar stone at the precise date of the solstice. In addition, this window also aligned to the rising position of the Pleiades – an important star group to many Amerindians – a month before the winter solstice in Inca times.

The Torreon's southeast window may also have had astronomical significance, for it aligned to the rising of the stars in the tail of Scorpius which were called *collca*, the Storehouse, by the Andeans. Anthropologist Gary Urton has found that the Andean Indians today also use that name for the Pleiades, so there may have been some conceptual, mythological link between the two groups of stars.

There are probably energy and consciousness aspects to Machu Picchu, too. David Zink writes that

the site is located on a geological fault. Often what are sometimes extreme magnetic anomalies are found in such locations. My own research has shown a connection between magnetic anomalies and the sensitivity of psychics.[7]

Such associations with sites have been discussed in Chapter 1 and elsewhere.[8] The masonry at Machu Picchu is superb, with massive stones intricately worked and shaped, and locked together so finely that cement was not needed. Moreover, this remarkable drystone technique allowed for some movement thus enabling structures to withstand the frequent earth tremors of the area. In such a seismically sensitive place, one would expect earth light phemonena to occur. Of course, the circumstances at the site today do not encourage much opportunity for comprehensive night-time observation, when such lights are most clearly noticed. Nevertheless, one account is known to

The curious Intihuatana, the 'hitching post of the sun', at Machu Picchu. (Peruvian Tourist Board)

this author. American psychologist Alberto Villoldo was with a group of Americans and Europeans being led by the famed Peruvian shaman Don Eduardo Calderon. They camped overnight by the ruins of the Doorway of the Sun close to and within sight of Machu Picchu. Villoldo states that the whole group saw 'an eerie light shaped like a person, with a large, rounded head' by some bushes only 20 feet (16m) away. He admits that 'the apparition sent shivers through everyone in the group'.[9] The lightform hovered in the bushes, approaching then receding, before finally slipping back into the undergrowth. To Don Eduardo, it was the elemental guardian of Machu Picchu. Such anthropomorphic shapes have been noted in a number of earth lights sightings around the world and over the years. This may be due to witnesses involuntarily imbuing an amorphous lightform with such characteristics, in the way people see figures in clouds or faces in the embers of a fire, but it could also be, as mentioned in Chapter 1 and detailed in *Earth Lights Revelation*,[10] that the lights may have exotic properties, such as some form of rudimentary intelligence of a reflexive ability with regard to the minds of witnesses. These may be 'far out' ideas from the point of view of most mainstream scientists, but the evidence is there, and virtually none of those scientists have examined or checked it.

There is another potential energy factor at the site – it is built from and on granite, a radioactive rock. In Chapter 1 it was noted that granite sites were often of an enclosed nature with a naturally enhanced gamma radiation count inside, and that the Dragon Project had inadvertently found that some people exposed to high natural radiation zones could be spontaneously precipitated into transient but vivid altered states of consciousness (most of which, curiously, had the semblance of what can only be described as some kind of time-slip). If the energetic nature of granite rocks can be used as a geophysical adjunct to the creation of mind-change states, how would this have been effected at Machu Picchu? Obviously the enclosed temple sites could have created geophysically conducive atmospheres for supporting ritual, hallucinogenic and other mind-change activities, but throughout the site there are also individual rocks and boulders which were Inca

huacas or sacred spots.[11] Now, in its study of the British stone circle Long Meg and her Daughters, the Dragon Project found that certain of the granite stones in the ring were exceptionally energetic, with small patches on them emitting constant streams of gamma radiation.[12] In considering how such a feature might have been used, if indeed it was, the present author wondered if head or body contact with the stones had ever formed part of the ritual activity at such places. Interestingly, such an idea is supported by Don Eduardo Calderon at Machu Picchu. Villoldo reports:

> The shamanic legends say that when one touches one's forehead to the stone, the Intihuatana opens one's vision into the spirit world.[13]

Calderon had his charges visit another sacred rock at the site, the Pachamama stone, and *press their backs against it.* The 20-feet (6m) long, 10-foot (3m) high rock represented Mother Earth, according to Calderon. Villoldo recalls that some years earlier Calderon had taken him to the remains of the Great Temple at Machu Picchu, and made him lie on the stone 'bed' in its southwest corner. Villoldo experienced 'great peace and relaxation'. He got up after 10 minutes and walked away from the stone. He looked back and was shocked to see his physical body still on the stone bed. In other words, he had undergone an out-of-the-body experience, which is what is involved in the classic 'magical flight' of shamanic ecstasy. This 'ecsomatic' state of mind is currently the subject of serious research by university-based parapsychologists and dream researchers, after many years of being treated with disdain because of its associations with spiritualistic 'astral projection'.

The Peruvian shaman also claimed that there were tunnels and labyrinths in Huayna Picchu, the peak which towers a thousand feet (300m) above the sacred city, which were known to the local shamans. The legends tell of an old medicine woman who lives within the mountains, to whom the shamans go for their highest initiations. One cannot help but ponder if this is a folk memory of the important woman mentioned on page 71, whose rich grave was found overlooking the site. The flying bird motive forming the handle of her knife is a universal symbol in shamanic cultures for 'magical flight'.

CHAPTER 8

CUZCO

PERU

WORLD HERITAGE LIST NUMBER 56
ASTRONOMY, GEOMANCY, MYTH

MORE THAN MERELY THE CAPITAL of the Inca empire, the very name 'Cuzco' in Quechua, the language of the Incas and still spoken today, means navel. It was the navel of the Inca world, the omphalos of their empire which at its height stretched over 2,000 miles (3,200km) from Chile in the south to Colombia in the north. It was both an administrative centre and holy city, and is said to have been conceived in the shape of a puma, with its head at Sacsahuaman, the great fortress of cyclopean stonework on the northern edge of modern Cuzco.

Around AD 1200 the Incas rose to supremacy over a number of other competing Andean tribal groups. They developed and consolidated their empire and social organization until their cultural destruction by the Spanish in the sixteenth century. The empire was ruled with absolute authority and power by the Sapa Inca, the supreme ruler and a god-king – the Son of the Sun. In Inca society the people had economic security but belonged to a rigid hierarchical scheme in which individual freedom and initiative were in effect planned out. It was, as von Hagen put it, 'a blending of tribal communism and theocracy, a perilously balanced fusion of two antagonistic systems'.[1]

The management of the vast Inca empire from a centralized power base was greatly assisted by a remarkable system of roads which allowed rapid communication and the swift mobilization of armies when required. The basic layout of the system involved two north–south arteries, a mountain route paralleling a coastal one. A secondary road pattern linked these two main lines of communication at various points as well as linking Cuzco with its provinces. Even the rapacious conquistadores had to admit that 'nothing in Christendom' equalled these highways.

Modern study of the Inca roads has been carried out since the early decades of this century, but a great impetus was provided by Victor and Sylvia von Hagen's 1953 Inca Highway Expedition. The expedition succeeded in rediscovering and mapping parts of the road system, and created much public interest in the Incas. More recently, anthropologist John Hyslop has mapped some 14,000 miles (22,540km) of Inca roads, estimating that there are perhaps 25,000 miles (40,250km) in all.

The roads themselves vary between 16 and 33 feet (5–10m) in width. Some sections were paved, while others, particularly in desert areas, were simply marked out by lines of stones edging compressed ground surfaces. Cairns or shrines were placed at certain points along the routes, and wayside stations or *tampu* were located at frequent intervals along them. These were for the *chasquis* or messengers, who would run from one station to the next, where a simple verbal message accompanying special goods or a *quipu* would be handed over to the next relay. Quipus were sets of cords of varying colours having knots at points along their lengths. This clever mnemonic system was capable of transmitting a remarkable amount of information.

Communication between points 1,700 miles (2,730km) apart could be achieved with the messenger system, and fresh seafood could be

An illustration of a quipu from Guaman Poma's 1613 account of life in Inca times. The man depicted is a quipucamayoc – *a quipu keeper.*

brought to Cuzco, even though it is 200 miles (322km) from the coast.

When a new length of road was to be built, surveyors and engineers would go out from Cuzco and use the local community in the region involved to carry out the labour. It was a highly organized procedure. Von Hagen noted that the Inca roads ran 'unerringly straight' between any two points, although Hyslop has commented that the roads tend to be straight where it was the most practical solution, but can deviate to avoid obstacles.

The only truly undeviating lines in the Inca world were *ceques*, which were of a deeply interwoven socio-political and religious nature, and which, like the roads, centred on Cuzco. To begin to understand them, we have to return to the idea of the omphalos, which was the governing concept in the Inca mind.

The great geomantic ordering of Cuzco was instigated by the emperor Pachacuti around 1440. He canalized the Huatanay and Tullumayo rivers through the holy city, and they still run in their Inca conduits today, though covered by concrete slabs. The main buildings of the capital were laid out to a grid pattern, within and around which was strict social ordering. The empire was known as *Tahuantinsuyu*, the 'Land of the Four Quarters', and people coming to Cuzco from the far-flung regions had to stay in certain allotted areas, reflecting where they came from in Tahuantinsuyu. This quartering of the empire which radiated out from Cuzco, was based on an *intercardinal* rather than a cardinal (north–south, east–west) scheme. The northeast quarter was called *antisuyu*, the southeast, *collasuyu*, the southwest, *cuntisuyu*, and the northwest, *chinchasuyu*. This quartering was not a simple X-pattern, however, because the southeast–southwest boundary was splayed at an odd angle, making the southeast segment 37 degrees narrower than a true 90-degree quarter, with the southwest portion being correspondingly wider. The four roads at the hub of the Inca system left Cuzco from the present-day Plaza de Armas – which is in the same place but is a smaller version of the Inca great plaza they called Huacaypata – and went out into their respective quarters. However, the primary centre of the ceque system, also a fundamental element in the four-quarter scheme, was the Coricancha, the Temple of the Sun.

If Cuzco was the centre of the empire, then

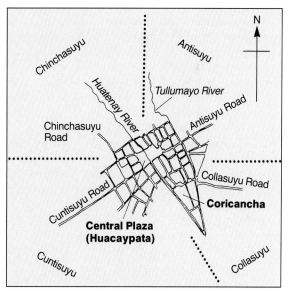

A simplified plan of Inca Cuzco, showing the orientation of the street grid to intercardinal positions and the rivers, roads and key sites. The division of the quarters – the suyus – *is shown schematically.*

the omphalos of Cuzco itself was the Coricancha, the Temple of the Sun. In Inca myth, the spot for this was found by Manco Capac, the first Inca, who was sent to earth to bring civilization. He used a golden rod to test for the correct location, and he knew he had found the spot when the rod disappeared into the ground. Located on a flattened site between and overlooking the point at which two rivers meet, the Coricancha was oriented to the June solstice sunrise – midwinter in Cuzco. Today, only fragmentary ruins of the temple survive, with the church of Santo Domingo superimposed on them. Part of the extant walling, however, still contains the niche or 'tabernacle' that was struck by the rays of the rising solstitial sun. Sixteenth-century Spanish chroniclers claimed that this niche was sheathed with gold plates and set with many precious stones. The emperor, the Inca, would sit in this recess as it glowed and glittered in the sun's rays, a resplendent symbol of his solar lineage. A ceremonial fire would be ignited by a priest using a concave golden mirror on his wrist to focus the sun's beams. (The Coricancha was eventually stripped of its rich, golden cladding and ornamentations by the Spanish conquerors.)

The Spanish historians wrote that radiating out from this place were 41 lines or ceques. Three of the quarters, the suyus, each contained nine of these, conceptually grouped in three sets of three, but the fourth, the wider southwestern cuntisuyu quarter, had 14 ceques. It has taken the work of anthropoligist Gary Urton to find the likely explanation for the asymmetry in the Inca quartering system, which in turn appears to relate to the arrangements of the ceques. Living with the Andean Indians, Urton discovered that the Milky Way is a key image in their cosmology. This band of starlight, which in astronomical terms is caused by the apparent clustering of stars towards the heart of our galaxy, is a brilliant part of the Andean night sky. It arcs through the zenith, and effectively marks the intercardinal directions as its orientation appears to change over a regular period with regard to the Earth's position in space, swinging from southeast–northwest to southwest–northeast. To the Indians, the zenith, overhead, point corresponds to the omphalos on the ground. One can visualize a

pole – or, indeed, a golden rod – running vertically down from the heavens into the landscape: the image of the cosmic axis. A city or village crossroads, or an omphalos point on the ground of any kind, is directly associated with the 'cross' of the zenith. E. C. Krupp summarizes Urton's findings:

> In the Andes the Milky Way is a river. . . . Urton applied the present Andean concepts of the 'cross' at the zenith and the 'river' in the sky to explain the location of the Coricancha – Cuzco's heart. Cuzco's most sacred spot was the intersection of its two rivers. The Inca built the Coricancha at the confluence because that place represented terrestrially the organizing pivot of heaven. Urton believes the unsymmetric division of Cuzco's southern quarters also can be understood in celestial terms. The southeast boundary is set by a ceque that could have been oriented on Alpha Crucis, the brightest star in the Southern Cross. Urton showed this was associated with the 'center' of the Milky Way. . . . Urton believes the Inca expanded the southwest quarter in order to keep the ceques that were aimed at the rising and setting points of Alpha Crucis in the same *suyu*.[2]

Evan Hadingham observes that at the spot on which

> the Temple of the Sun was situated, the directions of the empire, the Milky Way and the sacred rivers were all drawn together in a single focus. Here was an orderly union between earth, sky and mankind.
>
> Since it was believed to be the source of all cosmic forces, the Temple of the Sun was naturally regarded with awe and reverence by the inhabitants of Cuzco. (For instance, anyone approaching within about two hundred paces of the building had to remove his shoes.)
>
> Every social group in the city was assigned its own particular relationship to this radiating source of power. The connection was made along a series of imaginary straight lines that were thought to fan out from the temple like the spokes of a wheel. . . .[3]

Inca stonework of the Coricancha, surmounted by a church. (Peruvian Tourist Board)

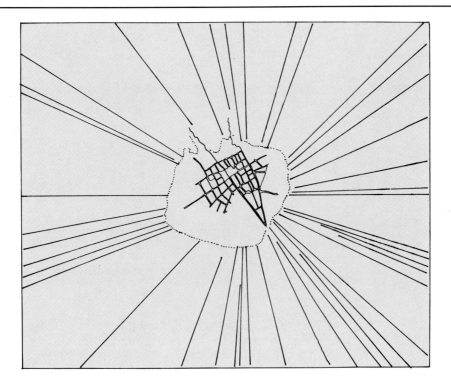

Krupp describes the conceptual framework of the ceque system in a similar way:

> The Coricancha's alignment with the solstice was an umbilical to the sky. Through this conduit the principles of cosmic order flowed into the Coricancha and circulated through the ceques to permeate all aspects of the highly organised life of the Inca.[4]

Each ceque was in the care of a specific social or kinship group.

What exactly *were* ceques? The simplest definition is that they were alignments of sacred places or *huacas*. A huaca could be a standing stone or a natural boulder or outcrop, a waterfall or spring, a temple or shrine, a holy hill or cave, a sacred tree, a topographical feature, or even a bridge or battlefield site. The well-known site of Tambo Machay, a ruined Inca shrine as well as a lodge for the Inca, a short distance out of Cuzco, was a huaca on a ceque, as was the temple of Pukamarka in the city itself, where now a cinema stands on the remains of the site's Inca walling. A sacred rock can be found on Cuzco's outskirts. And so on. There were apparently between three and 13 huacas along any one ceque, and the idea has been likened to that of the knots on the string of

The ceques had a conceptual organization within Inca society, but this diagram approximates the actual arrangement of the 41 lines as they radiated out into the countryside beyond Cuzco. The dotted line indicates the approximate extent of modern Cuzco. (Based on the archive and field research of Dr Tom Zuidema)

a quipu. The Spanish chroniclers identified 328 huacas along the ceques around Cuzco, stating that each represented a day of the year. It was in effect a huge terrestrial calendar, but the Spanish never seemed have bothered to understand it and in addition destroyed a number of the huacas. Dr Tom Zuidema of the University of Illinois suggested that the system was based on the sidereal lunar month of 27.3 days (the time it takes for the moon to pass from a given star in the background firmament back to that same star), for a division of 328 days by the 12 months of the Inca year gives a month of that length. (The 29½-day period the moon takes to complete a full set of phases is the *synodic* lunar month.)

Are ceques therefore astronomical? That is part, but only part, of the answer. The chroniclers relate that the Incas had observatories with

Another illustration from Guaman Poma's 1613 chronicle, showing an inspector of roads. In the background are towers, which may be those that were used for skywatching and which also occurred as huacas on ceque lines.

windows through which they watched points on the horizon, and they also mention sets of towers at various positions along the skyline as viewed from Cuzco, which were used to indicate timings for planting various crops either at Cuzco or at higher elevations up the valley sides at key ceremonial times of year. The Spanish totally destroyed these towers, but years of brilliant archive and field detective work by Zuidema and A. F. Aveni has resulted in the positions of the former towers being identified, and the arrangement of ceques 'on the ground' being clarified to a great extent. Some of the towers were huacas on ceques, but the sixteenth-century reports and the modern research actually make it clear that an astronomical sightline did not necessarily coincide with a ceque. Guaman Poma, himself part Quechua, described a tall 'pillar of well-worked stone' called the Ushnu standing not in the Coricancha, but in the great plaza ¼ mile (400m) away (now Plaza de Armas), as the point from where some observations using the towers as solar foresights were made. How a tower group could be on a ceque and simultaneously on a differently-oriented astronomical sightline is shown on this page in an actual example given by Aveni. He and Zuidema traced back one line, carefully calculated, and found the viewing position to be in the Plaza de Armas. 'This location turned out to correspond to the exact midpoint of the plaza as it was delineated in Inca times,' Aveni recounted. 'Furthermore, the

plaza center was marked shortly after the Spanish Conquest by a "picote" or pillar surmounted by a Christian cross that was said to have been put in place by Pizarro precisely on the site of the Ushnu.'[5] And their research on other lines threw up more confusions: 'When we followed the astronomical directions back into Cuzco . . . we were surprised that only one of them led to the Temple of the Sun, the other terminating at a mountaintop station 2km to the north of the plaza. We are forced to conclude that the horizon-based astronomical system of Cuzco consists of at least three different observing stations overlooking three sets of pillars on

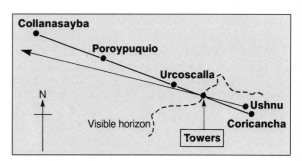

A ceque runs from the Corichancha through four huacas, marked here by dots and named. The first huaca is a set of four towers or pillars on the visible horizon from Cuzco on Cerro Picchu. These towers also form the foresight for an astronomical line (shown arrowed) from the Ushnu position in Cuzco's main plaza. (After A. F. Aveni)

the western horizon, hardly the simple scheme the chroniclers had suggested.'[6]

It is now estimated that perhaps about a quarter of the 41 ceques had astronomical associations, but we know from the early Spanish records that they had other functions, one of which was certainly ritual. Children were brought from various parts of the empire and stayed in the service of the sun god at Cuzco. On certain occasions – the 'crowning' of a new Inca or at times of exceptional concern – children would be sacrificed at selected huacas. This could be in Cuzco, but often the sacrificial children would be sent back under escort to their respective parts of the empire to be put to death. The ceques and not the normal roads were used for this function. So the ceque system clearly served multiple and complex purposes, and there is no easy definition of them. As Hadingham puts it: 'An individual ceque line was never dedicated to any single function, such as fertility rites, ancestor worship or sky-watching. . . .'[7] Zuidema's work has shown that some ceques at least were associated with water in various ways, and indirectly with the ancestors as water comes from underground where the ancestors are.

There has been some disagreement as to whether or not the ceques were simple conceptual lines on which the huacas were laid out like spiritual bustops or physical features. The old chroniclers are quiet about the actual nature of the ceques, yet the impression is that they could have been old straight tracks. Certainly, they fulfill entirely Alfred Watkins' concept of a 'ley' (see Chapter 1), and the markers on them match exactly those type of features the old Englishman had reckoned were on his lines. The matter has now fortunately been settled by brilliant work on the part of the veteran Andean lines researcher, film-maker and author Tony Morrison. Using special infra-red photography techniques, he has been able to photograph some ceques even though invisible to the naked eye. On his false-colour pictures the ceques show up as dark, straight lines marching up the sides of the mountains around Cuzco. As of this writing, these pictures are unpublished.

The chronicler Polo de Ondergardo claimed in 1570 that the ceque system was widely used throughout the Inca empire, and researchers have found other radiating patterns of roads. One has been found at Centinela on the central Peruvian coast, for instance, which John Hyslop has studied closely. He found signs that suggest to him that the complex may date back to pre-Inca times. Such radiating patterns are remarkably like the 'star-centres' of lines on the pampa around Nazca. (There, some lines run in parallel, and this phenomenon has also been noted in parts of the Inca road system, a feature difficult to account for in strictly utilitarian terms.) Hadingham concludes that 'the evidence seems to show that the Incas were not the first to develop the concept of radial pathways . . . the Inca rulers probably drew upon existing practices involving straight-line pathways and elaborated on them until the intricately organized network of Cuzco's huacas and ceques took shape.'[8] There were roads and there were ceques: lines of communication and lines of spirit.

CHAPTER 9

RØROS

NORWAY

WORLD HERITAGE LIST NUMBER 69
ENERGIES

THE TOWN OF RØROS is inscribed on the World Heritage List because of its mining heritage. It owes this, of course, to the mineral resources of the surrounding landscape, and because it is that landscape, the *natural* aspect of the area, that concerns us here, this choice from the List is a little different in kind from the other entries selected for this book.

The valley of Hessdalen is situated about 19 miles (30km) northwest of Røros, reasonably close to the border with Sweden. It is sparsely populated, with fewer than two hundred inhabitants scattered in farms amid the isolated wildness of the place. Despite its remoteness, the Hessdalen area put itself 'on the map' because of an outbreak of extraordinary light phenomena, which commenced in the closing months of 1981 and which were witnessed on and off for a few years thereafter.

The lights appeared in the vicinity of the valley, sometimes high in the sky, at other times hovering below the crests of surrounding mountains. Their shapes included spheres, rectangles, 'bullet' shapes with the pointed end downwards and inverted triangular forms. The colours of the lights were predominantly white or yellow-white, although other colours sometimes were seen, especially small red flashing lights (particularly on larger lightforms). Strong localized white or blue flashes in the sky were also reported.

The lightforms showed a wide range of movement: they could be stationary for up to an hour, move slowly or show sudden acceleration. Sometimes lights would appear in groups. Because the movements of these lights seemed 'choreographed', locals tended to think of them as lights on objects. Most reports of lights occurred during the dark winter months, the phenomena presumably either disappearing in the summer or being less distinguishable because of the long, light days and evenings then. Concurrent with the outbreak of the lights, people also heard curious underground rumblings, discharge sounds like thunder and 'deep booms'. Unusual radio and TV reception was also reported.

In March 1982, Norway's leading UFO group, *UFO-Norge*, held a meeting at nearby Alen to which 130 locals came. From a survey taken at the meeting, it was revealed that 30 people there claimed sightings of all kinds of lights, but mainly yellow globes. At the end of that month the Norwegian defence department sent two air force officers to study the situation. They did not see any lights but took the reports seriously. They also claimed that reports of unusual lights had come to them from the area since 1944. What was happening now, of course, was a greatly increased incidence.

In September of that year, local miner Bjarne Lillevold and a colleague had a typical sighting of a Hessdalen light while returning from work. The two men saw a light against the mountains near Hessdalen, which eventually dropped down towards a forest near Alen. By the time the two witnesses reached Alen they could see the light hovering next to the trees. Then they saw a second light come from the direction of Hessdalen and position itself beneath the first. A short while later, when Lillevold was by himself riding his moped towards Hessdalskjolen, he saw a light alongside a cottage:

> At first I thought the cottage itself was on fire, but then I saw something else, like an inverted Christmas tree, bigger than the cottage beside it. It was about four metres above the hill, and had a red blinking light on it: there seemed also to be a curious 'blanket' over the whole thing. The object moved up and down like a yo-yo for about 20 minutes; when it was close to the ground the light faded, but at the height of the manoeuver it was so bright that I could not look at it for long. When the light was near the ground I could see through it as though it was made of glass.

By 1983 hundreds of reports of light phenomena had been made. In lieu of any further official interest, Project Hessdalen was set up in June of that year by co-operation among Norwegian, Swedish and Finnish UFO groups. They raised interest among ufologists internationally, and obtained various items of equipment on loan. Field operations got under way in February 1984. They had to work in appallingly difficult winter conditions, with temperatures as low as −22°F (−30°C). Their main fieldbase was a trailer equipped with electricity, where most of the equipment was housed, with field observation positions scattered around the area. Up to 40 volunteers in all were mobilized to give as much cover as possible throughout the field research programme.

During the February period of field research, 188 lights were reported. Some of these were definitely identified as aircraft, while others were certainly unknown phenomena. Photographs were taken of the lights, although attempts at spectrum analysis were unsuccessful. The radar picked up 36 signals that were not 'angels', and some of the lights causing these radar returns were watched simultaneously by project members. An intriguing effect was noted in one instance when the light being observed seemed constantly luminous to the witnesses, yet the radar recorded it as going on and off rapidly. On two other occasions, the researchers directed a laser at observably flashing lights. In both cases, the lights repeatedly changed the frequency of their flashing when hit by the laser beam. Leif Havik, one of the project's directors, had one of the most

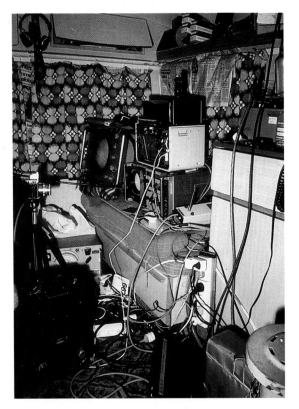

Inside the field headquarters of Project Hessdalen. (Project Hessdalen)

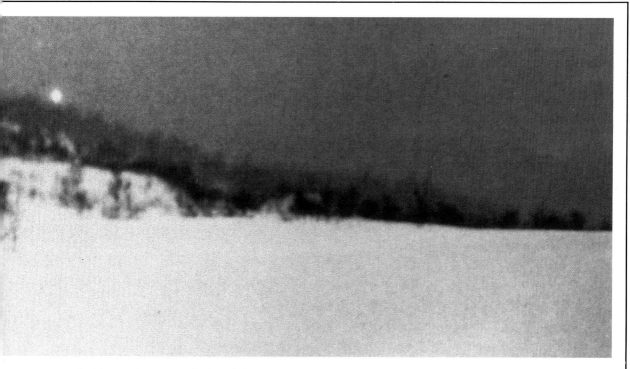

remarkable 'sightings' of the field session: a small red light flashed around his feet when he left the trailer headquarters. This was also witnessed by another group member. Havik went on to see a number of lights at Hessdalen, some of which he managed to photograph.

There seem to be various geological properties that recur frequently in zones that are prone to the appearance of these 'earth lights' (see Chapter 1).[1] Faulting is one of these factors, and faulting occurs around Hessdalen. Mineral deposits are another, and, of course, with Røros being famed for its mining heritage, it is not surprising to find that the area is heavily mineralized with all kinds of ores. Copper mining was once carried out in the Hessdalen region, and the magnetic field there is the strongest in Norway.[2] Seismic stress seems to be another element in the complex matrix that gives birth to these strange lights, and interesting evidence on this aspect was obtained by Project Hessdalen. They are the only researchers so far who have taken seismographic readings when light phenomena were occurring. The histogram on page 86 and its caption describe the present author's findings when he took the raw seismographic data for February 1984 and correlated it with the project's log of lights sightings for the same period, *using only the*

Leif Havik photographed this light during the February 1984 field programme at Hessdalen. The light is seen over the flank of a mountain in eastern Litlfjellet.

most inexplicable lights. It can be seen that there was a dramatic increase of sightings from 12 February, peaking on 15 February, and falling away by 20 February, with the largest seismographic indication 'embedded' in the increase. Researchers such as Professor Michael Persinger of Laurentian University in Canada hypothesize that strain building up to the release of seismic stress can create electromagnetic conditions suitable for producing the lights. The histogram shown here certainly seems to be a classic demonstration of that process. Although Hessdalen is sometimes affected by small-scale quakes (interestingly, the type most associated with earth lights appearances), these seismographic indications were apparently caused by distant epicentres. Nevertheless, the local ground was obviously flexing. If seismic stress is a factor in the manifestation of the lights, however, no one yet understands what the exact mechanism is, what the nature of the light energy is, nor how it forms such distinct, discrete shapes and moves

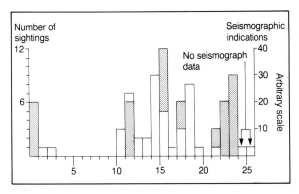

A histogram showing the relationship between observed high strangeness light phemonena and recorded seismograph indications at Hessdalen, Norway, between 1 and 16 February 1984. Sightings of lights are represented by white columns, and seismograph indications by toned columns. Columns are mixed toned and white appropriately for days on which both lights and seismic events occurred. It can be seen that the biggest observed seismograph indication occurred approximately in the middle of a wave of increased light phenomena sightings around mid-February.

around. (These matters are equally problematical with regard to earthquake lights and ball lightning.

Another very strange property the lights sometimes seem to exhibit is *apparent intelligence.* Project Hessdalen field workers felt sure that some lights seemed to sense their presence, and there were occasional dramatic responses from the lights suggesting intelligence, as in the case mentioned on page 84. This disturbing observation has been made even more strongly by the only other field researchers to study an outbreak of lights as it was happening – the team from Southeast Missouri State University led by Dr Harley Rutledge, which investigated the 'flap' around Piedmont, Missouri, in the 1970s.[3] Indeed, there are many reports from around the world by witnesses who felt the lights they saw acted as if having some measure of intelligence. But the idea of there being some kind of intelligent energy haunting localized regions of our planet takes us into areas beyond the brief of this book!

Project Hessdalen carried out further work in the region during the winters of 1985 and 1986, and although lights were reported from time to time, it is now clear that the peak of activity occurred between 1982 and 1984.

We are left with hundreds of reports, the findings of Project Hessdalen and a hundred or so photographs overall testifying to a very mysterious 'visitation' that took place in the Røros district. Such 'UFOs' may not be so much from another planet, as from our own – in this case the mineral-rich geology of the Røros area itself. Every day, in some valley, mountain, moor or desert, such lights are appearing. They represent one of the greatest Earth Mysteries there is.

Part of a sequence of photographs taken by Roar Wister during the February field programme at Hesdalen. An enlargement of the light is inset. (Roar Wister)

CHAPTER 10

AACHEN CATHEDRAL

GERMANY

WORLD HERITAGE LIST NUMBER 72
ASTRONOMY, EVOLVED, GEOMANCY

THE LOCATION NOW OCCUPIED by Aachen, adjacent to the modern borders of France and Holland, was resorted to even in prehistory because hot springs occur there. Exactly how far back into antiquity the place had importance is unknown, but the Celts were certainly established in the area by the time the Romans discovered the springs. The waters were sacred to the Celts and dedicated by them to the healing god, Granus. The Romans called the site Aquis Grani. They built bath complexes and shrines. Some houses edging the Hof, a triangular space a stone's throw northeast of the cathedral, were built on first and second century AD Roman masonry, and part of a well sanctuary was uncovered.

King Pippin, father of Charlemagne, had his court at Aachen and is said to have bathed in a former Roman bath there in the eighth century. Charlemagne decided to build his imperial palace in the city, creating a 'second Rome', where he resided in his later years and where he was buried. The palace chapel is the core of the present cathedral, and in the nineteenth century the remains of Roman baths, their spring dried out, were found beneath it.

Charlemagne regarded himself as the successor of the Roman emperors, and he had visited Ravenna and Rome with an alert eye. The palace he set up occupied the whole area immediately to the north of the present cathedral. His great royal hall was where the town hall (Rathaus) now stands. In front of that location stood a triangular stone which was called 'schildgen' because of its shield-like shape. This was a 'Blue Stone', a medieval geomantic marker, which survived to at least the eighteenth century (see the next entry, on Speyer, for more information on these stones). Researcher John Palmer found a tapestry in the cathedral's treasury which depicted Charlemagne, staff in hand and seated, with one foot on a triangular stone.

The Great Hall stood at the north end of a rectangular courtyard area approximately defined by the present-day city square, the Katschhof, around which other buildings and passageways were grouped. At the southern end, opposite the royal hall, was the palace chapel, an octagonal building now embedded in the cathedral. The whole complex was therefore set to the cardinal (north–south, east–west) directions, which cut across the northeast–southwest orientation of the Roman street grid and is the cause of the several odd-shaped or triangular plazas that are characteristic features

View of Aachen Cathedral from the south. The original Carolingian octagonal palace chapel can be seen beneath its seventeeth-century dome nestling amid later additions.

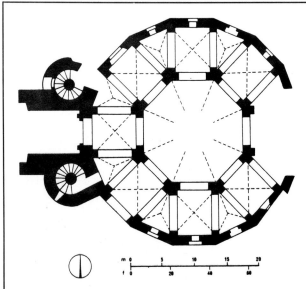

of the ancient city centre. The Holy Roman Emperors were crowned at Aachen between 813 and 1531. The church was also a key European pilgrimage centre.

The foundations of the Carolingian palace chapel were laid in about 768, its massive columns were erected on an octagonal ground plan in 798, and the chapel was inaugurated in 805. The contemporary monk Notker Balbulus wrote that Charlemagne summoned master craftsmen from many countries to work on his church. It seems its octagonal plan was taken from the design of the sixth-century S Vitale in Ravenna, but Charlemagne's chapel had more height and spaciousness in its upper gallery, among other differences. The internal octagon

Plan of the inner octagon and 16-corner surround of the Carolingian palace chapel. There was originally a square, two-storey choir off the east end, its exact form now unknown.

Plan of Aachen Cathedral showing the octagonal palace chapel with its later architectural additions. The star indicates the location of Charlemagne's throne (in the gallery).

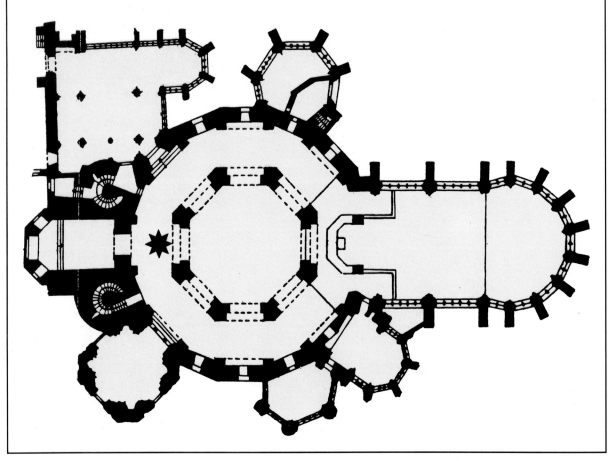

The Carolingian bronze 'wolf doors' at the west entrance to the palace chapel.

was surrounded by a 16-cornered structure, and there was a square, two-storey eastern altar extension, but the exact architectural form of this is unknown, as the surviving Gothic choir with enormous windows replaced it. Indeed, the original octagonal chapel is today only barely visible from the outside, because of several Gothic and later additions. The orientation is due east–west.

Charlemagne gathered a cosmopolitan court dedicated to the revival of the arts and sciences of antiquity (although, ironically, he was responsible for the suppression of numerous pagan traditions). Because Alcuin, a Briton, had acquired such a reputation for his knowledge ... the emperor invited him to Aachen and entrusted to him the task of reviving art and the sciences. His role in the organization of the schools, the Academy and the palace chapel, where manuscripts were copied, was of crucial importance. ... There were goldsmiths and builders – and all the different traditions had to merge together.[1]

One of the wolf heads on the bronze western doors.

The second-century AD bronze she-bear, now in the western entry porch. Often thought to be a 'Roman wolf', Charlemagne brought this Gallo-Roman feature to his church.

Among the classical texts translated at Aachen was the highly influential treatise by the first-century BC Roman architect Vitruvius Pollio, in which the principles and traditions of earlier architecture, secular and sacred, were incorporated. The palace chapel can be seen to be essentially Vitruvian in nature. It followed Vitruvius' octagonal scheme (which involved geomantic consideration of the 'eight winds'). It was located near springs, which conformed to the Vitruvian principle of *propriety*, which was 'attainable by the erection of temples in healthy neighbourhoods where suitable springs existed. At these springs, the shrines were to be built, one of the fundamental principles for temples underlying what is now known as geomancy.'[2] The true east–west alignment of the palace chapel also follows the Vitruvian dictum on the orientation of temples.

The writings of Vitruvius also relate to other astronomical aspects of architecture, 'particularly his Analemma, the theoretical basis for sundials'.[3] The Roman architect described the use of the gnomon, a shadow-throwing device, in dividing the circle to determine the directions of the eight winds. The use of sunlight by the builders of the octagon chapel was rediscovered accidentally in the late 1970s by German photographer Hermann Weisweiler.[4] While waiting for the right sunlight in order to take interior shots of the church, he was surprised to observe a sudden flash of sunlight enter the inner octagon through one of the windows at exactly 90 degrees. This inspired Weisweiler to investigate further the entry of sunlight into the church. He was encouraged in this investigation when he noted that the biography of Charlemagne by his contemporary Einhard mentioned the Emperor's interest in astronomy. Weisweiler found that at noon on 21 June the sun's rays illuminate the golden ball at the end of a chain hanging from the centre of the octagon's dome, from which, in turn, is suspended the 'Barbarossa chandelier', which represents the heavenly Jerusalem, the City of Revelation. The midwinter noon sun shines on a mosaic, above the north window of the 16-corner outer rim of the building, which depicts the PX-symbol of Christ between the letters Alpha and Omega. These features were added a few centuries after the building of the chapel, however, so it seems, as Horst Hartung notes, that 'the astronomical tradition of the octagon was not forgotten.'[5] But Weisweiler's most intriguing discoveries revolve around the position of Charlemagne's throne, situated in the gallery at the west end of the octagonal chapel, facing the altar. The throne is a simply designed oak chair clad with four marble slabs and placed atop six marble steps made from ancient pillars. From this throne, which was used for imperial coronations throughout the Middle Ages, the ruler 'could see everything and be seen by everyone'. The early light at the equinoxes would have entered horizontally through the upper window of the original eastern section, and the Emperor standing at his throne would have been the only person to see the sun. On 21 June sunlight would enter at 30.5 degrees through the eastern octagon window, illuminating the head of the Emperor seated on this throne. An additional possibility noted by Weisweiler is that if an appropiate window existed in the original eastern extension, a sunbeam would have entered the octagon at about 12 degrees and shone on the enthroned Emperor on 16 April, which is thought to have been the date of Charlemagne's birthday.

It therefore seems the palace chapel is a form of sundial. But the discoveries extend further than this. Weisweiler drew attention to other calendric devices of antiquity, particularly the Solarium Augusti in Rome, which had an Egyptian obelisk for its gnomon (now found on the Piazza Montecherino). The diameter of Augustus' mausoleum near the sundial differs by only 10¼in (26cm) from that of the ring of Aubrey Holes at Stonehenge. Weisweiler looked more closely at the possible connections between Stonehenge and Aachen. Not only was the megalithic monument the most famous calendric device of remote antiquity, the German researcher also knew that ancient knowledge had probably been introduced into Charlemagne's court from the British Isles. He noted that both Stonehenge and Aachen lie close to the latitude 51°N (0.12° above and 0.16° below, respectively). Then he made a truly startling finding: the plan of the sarsen stones at Stonehenge – the inner trilithon horsehoe setting and the surrounding lintelled ring – was of the same dimensions as the palace chapel ground plan and fitted its features remarkably, as illustrated on page 89.

The next step was to look at the placing of the cathedral in its surroundings. Investigation of the 'sunrise line' in what is the Heelstone direction at Stonehenge, superimposed on Aachen, shows an alignment running northeast that passes through 'megalithic tombs, ancient springs, churches'.[6] In the immediate vicinity of the cathedral the line would appear to graze the northwest corner of St Foillan's church and to pass along the building line on the southerly

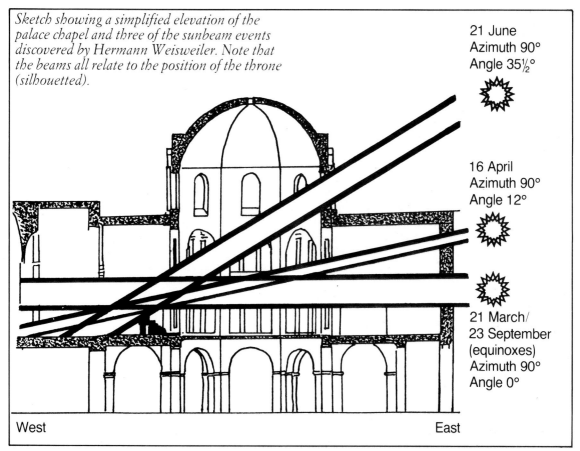

Sketch showing a simplified elevation of the palace chapel and three of the sunbeam events discovered by Hermann Weisweiler. Note that the beams all relate to the position of the throne (silhouetted).

21 June
Azimuth 90°
Angle 35½°

16 April
Azimuth 90°
Angle 12°

21 March/
23 September
(equinoxes)
Azimuth 90°
Angle 0°

West

East

side of the Hof, which covers the remains of the Roman holy sanctuary.

It seems that many of the old secrets of geomancy were resurrected at Aachen. Did this knowledge find its way through the craftsmen's guilds and monastic orders into the secret associations like the Freemasons of later centuries? At Speyer, the next site of this selection, we will find possible evidence of this, ranging from the medieval period to the eighteenth century, and similar hints at Chartres, Salisbury and London, which are described in later pages.

The Barbarossa chandelier hanging within the octagonal chapel. It depicts the heavenly Jerusalem, and the ball from which it is suspended is illuminated by the sun at noon on midsummer's day.

The sarsen stone settings of Stonehenge (shown in black) superimposed at the same scale onto the

plan of the palace chapel. Hermann Weisweiler's brilliant discovery leaves little doubt that ancient knowledge was at the heart of Charlemagne's church. (After Hermann Weisweiler)

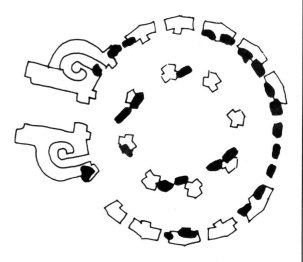

CHAPTER 11

SPEYER CATHEDRAL

GERMANY

WORLD HERITAGE LIST NUMBER 73
EVOLVED, GEOMANCY

SITUATED IN RHINELAND-PALATINATE, this extensively rebuilt Romanesque structure is the largest cathedral in Germany. Although it dates from the eleventh century, the origins of the site are much older. To the Celts it was known as *Noviomagus*, and the Romans called it *Civitas Nemetum.* The cathedral has evolved on a former pagan holy place, for the site was occupied by a Roman temple dedicated to the Celtic goddess Nantosvelta. It is even thought 'probable that buildings from the Roman period were converted to construct the church'.[1] It is likely that the site was considered sacred 'even before the Roman temple was built'.[2]

There is archaeological evidence of Christian worship on the site as early as 342, and a continuous list of bishops has come down from the sixth century. The first cathedral church was released from all rates and taxes by the Merovingian King Childerich II in 665. The original structure of the present cathedral was commenced in 1025 by Conrad II of the Salien dynasty: Speyer was chosen as royal burial place, and so its status was raised to that of an important dynastic and ecclesiastical centre of the Empire.

The cathedral was the largest building of its age in the West, and there were various stages of building over the years. It became a centre of pilgrimage in the Middle Ages because it possessed what was venerated as a miracle-working image of the Madonna. It was at Speyer in 1529 that the name 'Protestants' was first given to the followers of Martin Luther.

The French set fire to the city in 1689, when the cathedral was accidentally set alight. The cathedral was rebuilt in it original form, and a new west end was constructed using the existing Romanesque basement as a foundation. The structure was further extensively damaged around 1794, when the French took the city in the campaigns following the French Revolution. New interior and exterior additions were made in the nineteenth century. The west end, for example, was executed as a richly ornamented neo-Romanesque façade. This and the west towers, which were rebuilt at the same time, give the flavour of the original appearance of the cathedral 'when seen from a distance'.[3] Between 1957 and 1966 renovation took place with the aim of recovering the original Salien

The Domnapf in front of the west end of Speyer Cathedral. This spot marks the omphalos of Speyer, the point from which the street plan was struck. It also marks the boundary between the spheres of influence of Church and city, and lies on the alignment discussed on page 98. The great stone base may occupy the site of a 'Blue Stone', a class of medieval geomantic markers.

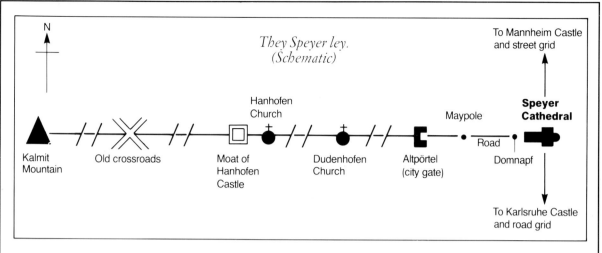

N

They Speyer ley.
(Schematic)

To Mannheim Castle
and street grid

Hanhofen
Church

Maypole

**Speyer
Cathedral**

Road

Kalmit
Mountain

Old crossroads

Moat of
Hanhofen
Castle

Dudenhofen
Church

Altpörtel
(city gate)

Domnapf

To Karlsruhe Castle
and road grid

architecture. The floor level was reduced to that of the medieval period, alterations were made to windows to restore Romanesque proportions, the roofs were reconstructed and other modifications were carried out.

It is claimed that the structuring of the vaulting in the aisles of the cathedral shows the ratio 2:1, 'the first example of a proportional system in medieval architecture'.[4]

The visitor to Speyer can hardly fail to notice that the main street of the city, Maximilianstrasse, aligns on the cathedral and forms a westwards continuation of the cathedral's axis. German geomantic researcher Ulrich Magin has noted that this line is directed westwards to Kalmit Mountain, the highest peak in the Palatinate.[5] This could be the indication of a 'holy hill' line, a type of alignment onto a local hill or peak noted by 'ley hunters' in Britain in the 1980s and alignment researchers in Germany in the 1930s. Indeed, Magin has found evidence of a ley-type alignment at Speyer to which Dutch-based geomant John Palmer and the present author have been able to add features.

Starting at its eastern end, the ley or alignment crosses the Rhine at the point where, according to tradition, the bodies of the German Emperors of the Middle Ages were ferried across the river. The line passed down the axis of the cathedral, and in the forecourt or atrium in front of the west façade stands a sandstone basin on a plinth known as the *Domnapf* ('Cathedral cup'). This is situated on the alignment, and it marks the boundary between the secular and religious areas of influence in Speyer and thus represented the limits of episcopal immunity. The Domnapf was first mentioned in 1314 and received its present form when it was replaced around 1490. New bishops were expected to fill the basin with wine after their consecration, and this was then distributed among the citizens. John Palmer claims that this point is in fact the location of a 'Blue Stone'. These features were geometrically shaped stones that were sited in the centre of medieval towns and were of considerable importance. These stones, according to Palmer, seems to be 'a degeneration of the older markstones and the holy stones of the Germanic and Gallic peoples' and were where 'judgement was pronounced . . . involving lengthy proc-

edures bound up with the sacred number three. . . . There are definite relationships to be found with the four quarters according to which many towns were divided and organized during the early Middle Ages'.[6,7] The Domnapf was the judicial stone of the bishops of Speyer. There may have 'originally . . . have been an ancient megalith with a circular depression at the spring in the atrium of the basilica, dating from the time of the Merovingian king, Dagobert.'[8] The Blue Stones were omphaloi (see Chapter 1) and were common in medieval founded towns of continental Europe such as Leiden (where the hexagonal Blue Stone was removed due to road works in 1991, hopefully to be replaced) and Delft in Holland, Lier and Ghent in Belgium, and Zurich in Switzerland. Researcher Nigel Pennick has noted the 'Blue Stane' of St Andrews (the home of golf) in Scotland: 'a geomantic marker which was touched by each soldier on the way to Culloden in the '45 rebellion'.[9] Palmer, who has prepared a major study of Blue Stones, regards them as 'true geomantic features', and has discovered 'Red' and 'White' stones, which also existed as part of the medieval geomantic system. From what evidence of original stones Palmer has been able to trace, it seems the stones very often did have a hue appropiate to their name. In fact, in the Low Countries there seemed to have been a preference for Blue Stones to be a very specific type of stone, perhaps harking back to ritual associations of remote antiquity.

These geomantic stones had associations with certain alignments and the axial centres of towns. The Domnapf location not only had typical Blue Stone connotations with ancient judicial rules, as indicated above, but also expresses this geomantic role as its presence on this alignment attests. Furthermore, it was from this spot that the layout of the streets of Speyer was arranged. The omphalos point.

The great maypole or Maibaum on Maximilianstrasse. Maypoles are pagan surivals, symbolizing fertility and the World Tree or cosmic axis, the link between the world of humans and the Otherworlds of spirit. The Speyer Maibaum falls on the alignment discussed on page 100, as can be seen in this view looking eastwards down part of aligned Maximilianstrasse towards the cathedral.

Maximilianstrasse was created at the time of the cathedral in the eleventh century as a *Via Triumphalis*, linking the west gate – the Old Gate or Altpörtel – and the west porch of the cathedral. The German Emperors and the newly appointed Bishops of Speyer used it for their ceremonial entrances into the city. (This is a medieval continuation of the link between kingship and straight alignments.[10])

Between the cathedral and the Altpörtel, the line of the ley passes through the great maypole or *Maibaum* situated on Maximilianstrasse. As mentioned in Chapter 1, maypoles are a pagan survival, representing the cosmic axis or World Tree linking this world and the Otherworlds of spirit. It is also a phallic symbol of regeneration. The Speyer Maibaum therefore is a pagan element linked by the line of Maximilianstrasse with the Christian manifestation of spirituality embodied by the cathedral. Its position on this line may, of course, be fortuitous.

Ulrich Magin has noted that the axis of the cathedral and the course of Maximilianstrasse continue beyond the Altpörtel, which marks the ancient city limits and dates from 1246 (upper storey 1512), to pass through sites in the countryside to the west. The line strikes the church of St Gangolf at Dudenhofen, passes through the church at Hanhofen a few kilometres further west, through the moat of the no longer extant castle at Hanhofen where once existed a chapel on this site as well, bisects an old crossroads, one of the arms of which is marked *Hohlweg* (hollow road), indicating antiquity, before reaching the ridge from which rises Kalmit (Bald Mountain).

This strong alignment is under 15½ miles (25km) in length. Magin states that the features on the line point to it being 'both ancient and deliberate', and notes that the strict east–west direction supports the 'holy hill' pattern (page 98). It seems as if the basic line may date from prehistory, with elements on it being evolved up to the medieval period. As this book

Looking westwards over Hanhofen to the distant ridge, which contains Kalmit Mountain.

An airview of Karlsruhe. (EFI Collection)

One of the Karlsruhe ley-like road alignments. (Solomon Devereux)

goes to press, Magin reports the finding of further sites on this line.

But, as we noted at Aachen, it is also possible that ancient knowledge became fed back into arcane threads of knowledge in medieval Europe, surviving perhaps as late as the eighteenth century in 'secret' groups such as the Freemasons, resulting in alignments and other geomantic patterns belonging solely to the historic era. This clearly is an element in the medieval evolution of this line, and must be certain in the case of another curious geomantic 'coincidence' affecting the site of Speyer Cathedral – it lies on a line that links the castle (now *Landesmuseum*) at Karlsruhe with the castle at Mannheim.

Karlsruhe was laid out on a linear system in the eighteenth century, and 29 straight roads radiate out from the Landemuseum. The city plan was based on a regular 32-fold division of the circle. The line from Speyer not only goes

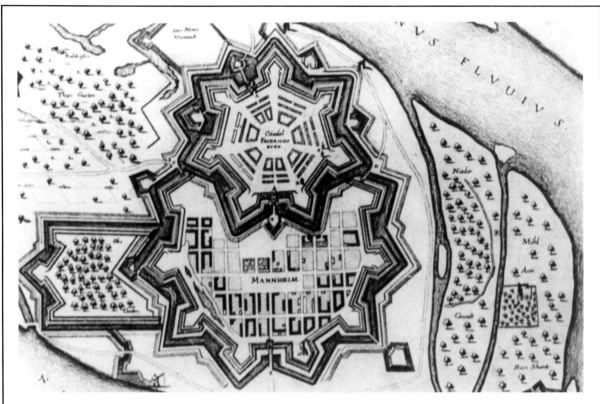

An old print showing the layout of Mannheim. (EFI Collection)

through the fulcrum of the city plan, the Landesmuseum, but continues through to the main city church. As Pennick comments, at Karlsruhe we have 'a perfect example of the linear layout of a city, incorporating sacred and secular places of power within the alignment framework, laid out with reference to earlier sacred places, in this example, the cathedral at Speyer'.[11] The German researcher Jens Möller has noted that Masonic symbolism occurs along the street alignment.[12]

The Karlsruhe – Speyer line continues northerly from Speyer to Mannheim. It passes through the corner of the castle there, and cuts diagonally across the city's street grid. So not only does a line link Speyer with specific, central features in Karlsruhe and Mannheim, it also relates to the street plans in both these places. This is powerful evidence of some kind of continuity of geomantic awareness into relatively modern times – a factor we will note again when looking at an alignment connecting Stonehenge and the medieval city of Salisbury in later pages.

CHAPTER 12

WESTMINSTER
PALACE AND ABBEY &
ST MARGARET'S CHURCH

UK

WORLD HERITAGE LIST NUMBER 93
ENERGIES(?), EVOLVED, GEOMANCY, MYTH

IT IS AT FIRST SIGHT difficult to imagine any ancient, geomantic mysteries to be present in the teeming modern metropolis that is London. There is no doubt that what may be there is well submerged both actually, beneath accretions of buildings and earth, and metaphorically, beneath layers of time. We have to look to legend, history, archaeological glimpses and the barely discernible lineaments that have survived in the present layout of streets, sites and place-names.

That the area now covered by the sprawl of central London had a prehistory is indicated by numerous if fragmentary archaeological finds of all periods back to the Bronze Age, and even the Neolithic, especially along the Thames. London as a specific community probably emerged only in the late Iron Age, however, and really began as a town with the Romans (the walled area known as 'The City' covers the Roman town) and developed intermittently thereafter in the Romano-British and Anglo-Saxon periods.

Westminster Abbey was built on Thorney Island, a small gravel spur formed next to the Thames by a fork in the River Tyburn. The supposed meaning of the name was 'Isle of Thorns', but Nigel Pennick speculates that 'it was so-called because the Saxons recognized that it was shaped like the protective rune *thorn'*.[1] Further, Thorney 'may have been a pagan sanctuary of the Anglo-Saxon god Thunor (Thor)'.[2] The area was marshy, and so firm islets had great importance; the earliest crossing place along this section of the Thames was probably located at Thorney. E. O. Gordon claimed that there was traditional evidence for a stone circle to have existed on Thorney Island.[3] Roman buildings stood on the island, apparently destroyed by an earthquake in the fifth century. It is reputed that one of these structures was dedicated to Apollo, and it is interesting to note that the fifteenth-century monk-historian John Flete, referring to the partial return to paganism in the fifth century, claimed that then 'were *restored* the whole abominations. . . . London worships Diana, and the suburbs of Thorney offer incense to Apollo'[4] (this writer's emphasis). Westminster is the West Minster as distinct from the East Minster of St Paul's, and if Flete's inference is correct, we can look upon Westminster as marking a pre-Christian solar (Apollo) site, and St Paul's as commemorating a lunar (Diana) location, for the remnants of a

Looking down Tothill Street towards Westminster Abbey (one of the towers was encased in scaffolding and sheeting when this picture was taken).

Roman temple to Diana were found on Ludgate Hill next to the location of St Paul's Cathedral (see next entry). What is more certain is that an ancient mound existed on Thorney. It is recalled in the name of Tothill Street, which aligns to the northern transept of Westminster Abbey, paralleling its axis, and the former Tothill Fields, which was a medieval tournament ground, only a fragment of which now survives as the playing field of Westminster School in Vincent Square. 'Tot' or 'toot' hills were beacon hills and places of assembly, and were a key feature in Alfred Watkins' 'ley system' (see Chapter 1 and elsewhere). The Thorney Mound may thus have been prehistoric. It was recorded in a late Saxon charter as existing on Thorney, and it was apparently still extant as late as the eighteenth century, for it seems to be depicted on John Rocque's map of 1746 standing by the bend of Horseferry Road approximately where Regency Place now is.

The first church on the site of Westminster Abbey was erected in the seventh century, 'possibly attracted there by the ruins of Roman buildings which offered a good source of materials.'[5] The earliest historical account of the foundation was written between 1076 and 1085 by the Westminster monk Sulcard. It seems that after the founding of St Paul's Cathedral in 604, King Aethelberht, the first Christian king of Kent, wanted to found a church dedicated to St Peter. An anonymous person offered to build this church, and it was sited on Thorney Island. After Sucard's time, the tradition grew up that the anonymous individual had been King Saeberht (or Sebert, Segbert) of the East Saxons, Aethelberht's vassal.

A remarkable legend is attached to the dedication of this Saxon church: the night before it was due to be consecrated by Bishop Mellitus, the building was filled with 'a multitude of shining lights'. There were angelic singing and 'celestial odours'. A fisherman, Edric, who had witnessed the strange events, reported them to Bishop Mellitus, along with his belief that he had encountered St Peter himself. This story was given credit as late as the fourteenth century, but it was dismissed as rank superstition at the time of the Reformation. In Chapter 1 it was observed that legends might contain authentic memory elements if they are not taken too literally. If we remove the St Peter associations with the claimed heavenly consecration, we may be dealing with a genuine recall of odd light phenomena on the site of Westminster Abbey, for, as Nigel Pennick has noted,

> more modern thought on 'earth energies' interprets the illuminated building in terms of 'earth lights'. These terrestrial light phenomena have been seen in more recent times in connection with sacred buildings constructed on sites of intense geological activity. The reputed earthquake of the fifth century may indicate this. Other London earthquakes, in 1580, 1692, 1750 and 1884, have been felt at Westminster.[6]

Westminster Abbey towers over the rooftops of Dean's Yard.

Sounds and smells are frequently reported to accompany earth light phenomena, not to mention phantasmagoria apparently induced in witnesses' brains by the energy fields surrounding the lights.[7]

After Aethelberht's death in 616, there was a restoration of paganism, and a bishopric in London was not established again until the late seventh century.

London continued to develop as a wealthy trading centre, and a new port was established on the Thames between the old Roman city and Thorney Island. But in the ninth century, marauding Danish Vikings sailed up the Thames and succeeded in taking control of London. The city was wrested back under English control by Alfred the Great in 886. After this, the old Roman-walled city became once more the focus of urban development, giving pre-eminence to St Paul's Cathedral. Westminster was thus literally 'outside the pale' of London, a suburb to the west, and its buildings, which had been damaged, were left in a largely forlorn condition. In 957, however, St Dunstan arranged for the refounding of Westminster as a Benedictine abbey. In the eleventh century, the abbey was completely rebuilt, marginally to the east of its original spot, by King Edward, the son of Aethelred the Unready and the last king of the old Anglo-Saxon dynasty. It was dedicated in 1065, shortly prior to Edward's death. He was buried in the Abbey. Edward left no direct successor, and the dispute between his brother-in-law, Earl Harold, and his cousin, Duke William of Normandy, led to the Norman Conquest. William was crowned at Westminster Abbey in 1066, thus starting the great and continuing tradition of coronations there. William went ahead with the completion of the new buildings but only fragments of these survive, as the church was demolished in the thirteenth and fourteenth centuries to make way for the Gothic edifice, which structure, with later additions, survives today.

A cult developed around Edward. There were accounts of him healing the sick while he was alive, and rumours of cures at his tomb continued. In 1102 it was opened and his body found incorrupt. After a campaign lasting for decades, Edward the Confessor was canonized in 1161. His body was raised from the tomb before the high altar and replaced in a richly ornamented shrine, the key, sacred focal point of the Abbey.

The other principle element of the Abbey, its setting for coronations, could be thought to be essentially secular, but this, too, has it esoteric aspects. This is revealed by two other key features within the Abbey – the Cosmati Pavement and the Stone of Scone set in the Coronation Chair.

In the thirteenth century, Henry III had the Italian School of Cosmati create mosaics on the floors of the Sanctuary and the Confessor's Chapel, the base of his shrine and various tomb bases, including that of Henry III himself. The design on the Sanctuary floor was completed in 1268. It is of prime significance because it is on this spot that the annointing, consecration and crowning of monarchs takes place, with a throne in the centre of the design (which, for much of the rest of the time, is covered with a carpet). This Cosmati Pavement is a little over 28 feet (8.5m) square with a wide border, and it contains another square set diamond-wise, with four circles in the four angles between the inner and outer squares and five more within the inner square (see the illustration below). The four corner circles in the inner square mark the four compass points. Inside the border of the outer square, fragments of words in brass-lettered Lombardic script tell that Henry III comissioned the design. Lettering that was carried in the quatrefoil formed by the four circles exterior to the inner square has dis-

A diagrammatic depiction of the Cosmati Pavement, Westminster Abbey.

appeared, but it described a method of calculating the end of the world. Parts of the innermost inscription, around the central circle, survive and can be translated as: 'Here the sphere points to the microcosm, the globe to the archetype.' This 'alludes to the cosmic significance of the pavement and the coronation ritual performed upon it'.[8] It may possibly be the case that the mosaic also has some greater geomantic significance – hinted at by the cardinal arrangement of the inner circles – yet to be discovered, for a similar design, in the German Xanten Cathedral, was found by Josef Heinsch to relate to the geographical layout of ancient sacred sites around the cathedral.[9]

There are two parts to the Coronation Service: the secret, Sacremental Coronation, described above, conducted by the Lords Spiritual, and the Enthronement and Homage, witnessed by the Lords Temporal. The throne used for this second, more public part of the ritual is *not* the Coronation Chair, however, which is to be found between the High Altar and the Confessor's Shrine when not in use. The Coronation Chair is the 'magical' throne that is placed in the centre of the Cosmati Pavement during the sacred aspect of the ritual.

This oak Chair was made in 1300 at the request of Edward I, to house the Stone of Scone. This four-hundredweight (200kg) block of Old Red Sandstone was captured from the Scots by Edward in 1296. The stone is a 'king stone', part of a tradition of utmost antiquity which associates certain stones with the special power of conferring kingship. Further up the Thames, for example, at Kingston-upon-Thames, a stone, now standing enclosed by iron railings, was once used for the inauguration of Saxon kings. Sometimes a king stone was fashioned into a seat, as at Castlereagh, Ireland, for instance, or had the shape of footprints carved into it, in which the new king stood, as was the tradition on the Scottish island of Islay. The concept of the king stone is closely related to the ancient idea of kings being divine or semi-divine, and being literal symbols of the land – 'the king and the land are one'. This image is presented in the story of the Grail, in which, also, Arthur proves his kingship by being the only one able to pull the sword Excalibur from a block of stone. Ireland had several king stones, perhaps the most famous

The Coronation Chair and Stone of Scone, placed beneath the seat. (Mansell Collection)

being the *Lia Fail* on Tara, the original residence of the high kings of Ireland. This stone was said to cry out when the correct king was crowned. Such traditions seem to go back to at least Druidic, Iron Age, times, and they in turn most probably emerged from even older themes – the idea of a stone as the omphalos (see Chapter 1 and Delphi) probably pre-dated the king stone concept.

It was from Ireland that the Stone of Scone was said to have been brought to Scotland, but legend claims the stone to have come originally from Solomon's Temple, or to have been the stone on which Jacob slept when he had his visionary dream of angels ascending a ladder to heaven. At Scone, in Perthshire (where Old Red Sandstone is to be found!), 34 Scottish kings were inaugurated on the stone, and it can be inferred that Edward I took the 'Stone of Destiny', as it is also known, in order to break that power in Scotland and centre it in London. The stone was reshaped somewhat to fit into the ledge beneath the seat of the Coronation Chair, and all but one of the monarchs of Britain have been inaugurated above it since 1308. It was reclaimed by Scottish Nationalists in 1950, but returned in time for Queen Elizabeth II's coronation.

Finally, the old ley hunter Alfred Watkins noted geomantic aspects of the siting of Westminster Abbey. In plotting a line from the Tower of London to Southwark Cathedral, he made the interesting observation that the line goes on to Westminster. As we shall see in the next entry, the site of the Tower is likely to be prehistoric, and recent archaeological work beneath Southwark Cathedral shows it to have been built on a pagan shrine.[10] Watkins' line therefore links three key pre-Christian, and possibly prehistoric, sites in London. He further noted that the alignment

converges with a line down the middle of Tothill Street, to a point in Wellington Barracks. Lines on the exact orientation of Westminster Abbey and the adjacent St Margaret's Church were then laid down, and

they too converge to the above point. Here, then, are four indications (one of them Tothill Street) of convergence to one point. . . .[11]

St Margaret's stands immediately to the north of the Abbey, and three churches are known to have stood on the site. No one knows when the first foundation was made, but the present church is essentially medieval. It is the parish church of the House of Commons. Its axis is slewed slightly southwards to that of the Abbey, so the two axial lines do converge as Watkins claimed. Wellington Barracks is on Buckingham Gate, and Watkins supposed the convergence point there to have been the site of the old Tot Hill, but this does not agree with Rocque's map, if that does in fact show the mound.

St Margaret's Church, with Big Ben in the background.

CHAPTER 13

THE TOWER OF LONDON

UK

WORLD HERITAGE LIST NUMBER 94
ASTRONOMY(?), EVOLVED, GEOMANCY, MYTH

MOST PEOPLE TODAY think of the Tower as the sinister place built by William the Conqueror where prisoners were kept and tortured, and where illustrious heads rolled, including those of Sir Thomas More, Sir Walter Raleigh, Anne Boleyn and Lady Jane Grey. Over the centuries, in addition to being such a notorious place of confinement, the Tower has served as a garrison, a palace, a zoo, a mint and an observatory. The Tower continues to house the Crown Jewels and other royal regalia, but this important spot in London's geography goes back much further, and is referred to in the medieval Welsh texts known collectively as *The Mabinogion*, which record themes much older. To the Celtic Britons, the site on which the Tower stands was *Bryn Gwyn*, the White Mount, 'White' meaning holy. The White Tower, the central keep of the site and the original part of the structure to be built, recalls this appellation.

The sanctity of Bryn Gwyn is established in the story from *The Mabinogion* called 'Branwen Daughter of Llyr'. It tells how, in a disastrous adventure in Ireland in which the sovereignty of Britain is jeopardized, the legendary god-king Bran is mortally wounded. He instructs the surviving seven men of his army to cut off his head, which he predicts will remain incorrupt, and to transport it from Ireland 'to the White Mount in London, and bury it with its face

towards France' and 'no plague would ever come across the sea to this Island' as long as the head was there interred.[1] The group, who, with Branwen (Bran's sister), formed the 'Assembly of the Head', was on the road for many years, being distracted and enchanted *en route*. Branwen died early on from a broken heart. Eventually, however, they made it to the White Mount and buried Bran's head. Much is encoded in this multi-layered story – relics of the Celtic head cult, the matter of sovereignty and other themes – that is outside the brief of this account. (It is perhaps just curious coincidence that the Tower is so associated with beheading.) A tradition that is an echo of this legend states that if the ravens of the Tower should ever leave, Britain will be at risk of invasion. To guard against this the ravens' wings are clipped! The connection is that 'Bran' means raven in Welsh.

Other legends establishing the importance of the mound in mythic memory tell that Brutus, the legendary founder of London ('New Troy'), and the road-building King Molmutius were buried there. And King Arthur, wishing to be solely responsible for defending Britain, had Bran's head dug up – not a good idea, as history turned out! As Caitlin Matthews puts it, the precincts of the Tower are 'redolent with the overwhelming potency of sovereignty'.[2]

There is a well deep within the foundations of

the White Tower. It is stone lined and thought to date to at least Roman times. In her *Prehistoric London* E. O. Gordon noted that a similar well 'of unknown antiquity under Sadlers Wells Theatre' may have been a 'telescope well'.[3] Such shafts were used in many parts of the world to assist the observation of the heavens by cutting out the ambient glare of the moon or other illumination. It is thought that the Iron Age Druidic priesthood used such devices for their astronomy. If the Tower shaft was a telescope well, then, as Janet and Colin Bord point out, the 'tradition was continued, for the north-east pinnacle of the White Tower ... was an observatory until the seventeenth century when the Royal Observatory was built further down the river at Greenwich.'[4] Further astronomical ruminations were propounded by John Griffith. Writing in the appendices to *Prehistoric London*, he suggested that the legend of Bran's head encoded an astronomical mes-

sage, and calculated that an alignment from the Tower to Parliament Hill (or 'Llandin' according to Gordon, a prominent height on Hampstead Heath topped by a prehistoric mound) gave a summer solstice azimuth. Griffith went further and suggested that these two mounds plus the Tot Hill at Westminster and Penton ('Pen', head, 'ton', sacred mound) were observatories, with various astronomical alignments associated with them. The landscape configuration of the mounds according to Griffith's measurements is shown on page 112, and includes Gospel Oak, a place-name that hints at a sacred tree location, and Primrose Hill, another prominent spot which formerly had at least one mound associated with it.

The geomantic significance of the White Mount is shown in its association with other key ancient locations of London. We have already noted that it falls in line with Southwark Cathedral and Westminster (see previous

Looking north across the Thames to the Tower of London. The White Tower is the keep in the centre of the picture and the 'Traitor's Gate' water-gate is at the extreme lower left.

entry), and another alignment links it to other major ancient sites of the city. This runs from the precincts of the Tower to Ludgate Hill, as can be seen from the illustration on page 113.

Starting at the Tower, the line passes across Tower Hill, where a scaffold stood until the eighteenth century, and through All Hallows by the Tower. Beneath the present church are remnants of Roman flooring and fragments of a seventh-century Saxon church. Pieces of Saxon and medieval crosses have also been uncovered. This was evidently an ancient sacred site of some importance.

After a short distance, the course of the line connects with the axis of Cannon Street, passing through the former position of the London Stone. The remnants of this undoubtedly ancient feature are to be found today behind an iron grill set into the wall of the Bank of China on the north side of Cannon Street, opposite Cannon Street Tube (subway) station, more or less in the position it formerly occupied against the wall of St Swithin's church, until that was demolished in the 1960s. Up until 1742, however, it was located on what was then the south side of Cannon Street in a position that would now be in the middle of the modern roadway, as it was subsequently widened. No one really knows the origins of the stone. Only a fragment now, it was described in the sixteenth century as 'a great stone' set into the ground. It was an established landmark by the twelfth century, and pacts and proclamations were made at it, suggesting that it may have been, or used as, a Blue Stone, a geomantic feature we have encountered elsewhere (see the Speyer entry). The rebel Jack Cade struck it with his sword in 1450, an act that was meant to symbolize his possession of the city. Ralph Merrifield concedes that 'the veneration of it [the stone] in the Middle Ages may have stemmed from an earlier tradition'.[5] Alfred Watkins exclaimed that it was 'surely a mark stone!' on a ley – which we are demonstrating here to be the case. E.O. Gordon felt it was an outlier stone to the circle she presumed to have once existed at the St Paul's Cathedral and churchyard site.[6]

Cannon (formerly Candlewick) Street lies parallel with, and a furlong (220 yards/200m) to the south of, Cheapside, factors that reveal underlying Saxon street-grid patterns. In fact, the eastern length of Cannon Street also marks a Roman street line, so it has retained its basic course from the very beginnings of London. This is an ancient line indeed.

It goes on to cut across the southwest corner of St Paul's churchyard and cathedral. Writing of St Paul's around 1600, the historian Camden stated:

Some have imagined a temple of Diana formerly stood here, and their conjectures are not unsupported. The neighbouring old buildings are called in the church records *Camera Dianae*, and in the reign of Edward I were dug up in the churchyard . . . an

All Hallows by the Tower stands on a site that goes back to at least Roman times.

incredible number of ox heads, which were beheld by the multitude with astonishment as the remains of heathen sacrifices: and it is well known to the learned that Taurobolia were celebrated in honour of Diana. When I was a boy I have seen the head of a buck, fixed on a spear (which seems to agree with the sacrifices of Diana) carried about with great pomp and blowing of horns within the church . . . the custom certainly savours more of the worship of Diana and heathenism than of Christianity.

Nigel Pennick considers that this ceremony 'appears to have been the continuation of pagan hunting rights associated with Diana, or her Northen Tradition counterpart, Frigga or Freya . . . This association is reinforced by the names of two streets close to the cathedral in medieval times: Friday Street and Distaff Lane. Friday is the sacred day of Frigga, and one of her sacred attributes is the distaff.'[7]

E. O. Gordon fancied that on the highest ground of what has become known as Ludgate Hill

where St Paul's now stands, might have been silhouetted against the sky, the mighty unhewn monoliths of the druidic circle, the seat of the Arch-Druid of Caer Troia. It is an interesting link with the pre-Christian religion, that St Paul's has always been the Metropolitan Cathedral of the City of London, a National Church, never at any time a religious corporation ruled by Abbot or Prior.

No trace of the circle remains. . . .[8]

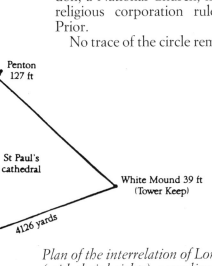

Plan of the interrelation of London mounds (with their heights), according to John Griffith in Prehistoric London. *(After Standford)*

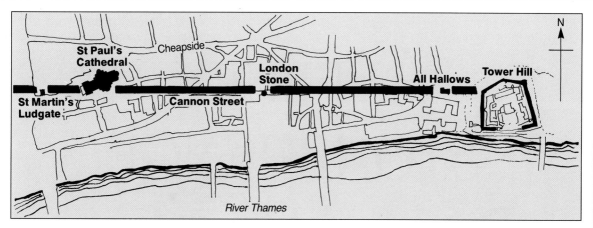

The 'kingship line' linking sites between Tower Hill and Ludgate Hill.

The present cathedral is, of course, Wren's masterpiece, completed in 1708, but it stands on the site of at least four earlier churches. The marriage of Prince Charles and the (then) Lady Diana Spencer took place at the cathedral, rather than at the more customary Westminster Abbey. This led some to speculate than an esoteric tradition was being observed, with the future Queen of England, Diana, being married at the supposed site of the goddess Diana.[9] 'In mystical terms, Charles can be envisaged as the solar king, and Diana as representative of the virgin moon goddess, whose union would symbolise an alchemical bonding.'[10]

The alignment continues to St Martin-within-Ludgate. It seems a church stood here from at least the sixth century, built, legend states, by Cadwallader, King of the Britons. In medieval times the church was immediately against the inside of the wall of the old City, touching the Ludgate. The present church was built by Wren.

Like Tower Hill, Ludgate Hill is a 'holy hill'. Not only was Cadwallader buried at St Martin's, but the hill is supposed to be the resting place of the legendary King Lud, and Aethelred the Unready was buried at St Paul's. This line, a little over a mile in length, thus traverses a mythic as well as a topographical landscape. Indeed, it can be seen to be a mythic 'kingship line', including as it does locations associated with so many kings of the British 'dreamtime'.

A study of pre-Fire of London churches by Nigel Pennick[11] has revealed a very similar version of this line, incorporating some now destroyed churches. It runs: All Hallows – St Leonard Milk Church – London Stone – St John-upon-Walbrook – St Thomas-the-Apostle. The City of London has alignment patterns from different periods superimposed one on another, relating variously to church deployment, parish boundaries and street gids. Cannon Street is just one example of a street's course being in itself a remnant of an underlying alignment pattern.

The various alignments referred to here demonstrate that the Tower of London marks a site that is a major geomantic feature of the ancient, secret face of Britain's capital city.

The London Stone as it appeared early in the nineteenth century. As can be seen, the housing for it had an opening so that the remaining stump of stone within could be touched. (From an engraving by J. Shury, published in 1832. Collection of John Palmer)

CHAPTER 14

AVEBURY, STONEHENGE & RELATED MEGALITHIC SITES

UK

WORLD HERITAGE LIST NUMBER 96
ARCHAEOLOGY, ASTRONOMY, ENERGIES (?), EVOLVED, GEODETIC
INFORMATION, GEOMANCY, MYTH, SACRED GEOMETRY, SACRED MEASURE

THE TWO GREAT HENGE MONUMENTS of Stonehenge and Avebury are only about 20 miles (32km) apart in Wiltshire, yet each has its own surrounding ceremonial landscape containing many other monuments. All are entered as site number 96 on the World Heritage List, but here we will describe each of these major monuments and landscapes in turn.

AVEBURY

Avebury is often thought of as being just the great 28-acre (11.5ha) henge and stone circle. This is probably because the village of Avebury, with pub, restaurants and bookshops, has sprawled within the henge enclosure. But this remarkable monument of the third millenium BC, the era of the Neolithic or New Stone Age in Britain, is surrounded by other sites contemporary with it or even older, and 'Avebury' must be considered as a *complex* of sites. Indeed, the local area is effectively a surviving Neolithic landscape, with sites and natural topography blending together.

The actual henge is the huge ditch and bank enclosure, excavated with antler picks out of the solid Wiltshire chalk. The ditch was originally up to 33 feet (10m) deep but is now silted to more than half that depth. The bank is on the outer rim of the ditch, meaning that it was not for defensive purposes. Around the inner lip of the ditch stand the survivors of a great stone ring, which in turn contains the remnants of two inner circles. The northern one of these had a central stone grouping now partly surviving as The Cove; the southern circle had a curious setting of low stones (the 'Z Feature') and a giant standing stone at its centre. This stone, referred to as the Obelisk, had already fallen when antiquarian William Stukeley drew it in the eighteenth century. He described it as

The southwest sector of Avebury henge, showing banking, ditch and part of the main stone ring.

having been the tallest stone at the site, in excess of 20 feet (6m) in length. It no longer exists, but its original hole is now marked by a large concrete plinth erected by Alexander Keiller during his excavation and restoration of part of the complex in the 1930s. Keiller's work revealed much about the site, but large parts remain uninvestigated. The chronology of the henge and its stones is thus poorly understood, although the monument is thought to date in general to about 2600 BC.

The site experienced its greatest destruction in historical times. In the early fourteenth century at least 40 stones were buried, probably as a result of Christian anti-pagan encouragement. Many of these stones still remain underground.[1] Then from the seventeenth century up until the early nineteenth century the interior of the henge was built upon and many stones were broken up.

Long before the henge existed, the natural eminence of Windmill Hill, about a mile north-north-west from the henge, was being used as some kind of gathering place. The nature of these meetings is unclear, possibly being a mix of religious and secular activity. The beginning of regular human activity on the hill is thought to date to around 3700 BC. At about the same time, the earlier phases of construction of the West Kennet long barrow occurred. This barrow, at over 300 feet (100m) in length, is the longest in Wiltshire, and is oriented east–west. It started life as a smaller, linear mound of rocks. This was later covered with chalk quarried from side ditches, creating what would have been a striking white feature. Later still came the stone passage and chambers that occupy the eastern end of the mound. Human bones were uncovered, with each chamber apparently having been given over to a specific group – adult males, old people, women, children. The barrow was not simply a grave, for the skeletons of the dead were regularly rearranged and, it would seem, only particular bones kept, skulls and long bones being removed. Room was made for fresh internments. Activity took place at West Kennet barrow up until about 2200 BC. The original entrance had been crescent-shaped, but at the end of the barrow's use, great standing stones

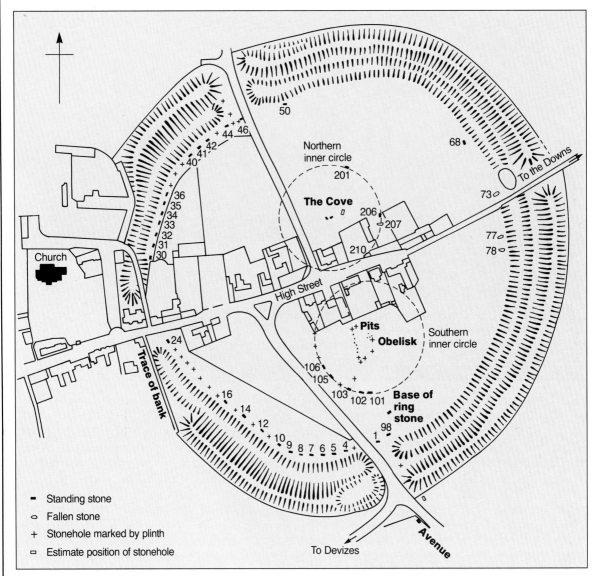

Ground plan of Avebury henge. Note the position of the Obelisk and stone 102. (After I. F. Smith)

were placed across this as if to seal it off. The bulk of the final mound is earthen, and as the inner chambers comprise such a small part of the barrow, other explanations have to be found to explain its length. That explanation is now forthcoming as a result of research by the present author, as will be shown.

Other surviving long barrows in the Avebury landscape include, notably, East Kennet and Beckhampton barrows.

Around 3000 BC work began on the Sanctuary, which evolved into a double stone circle on the site of six concentric timber rings atop Overton Hill, which forms the eastern ridge containing the sacred geography surrounding Avebury henge. Both stone and post holes are now marked by concrete blocks – Stukeley saw the final destruction of this site in the eighteenth century. Excavational evidence suggests

The eastern façade of West Kennet long barrow. Some of these megaliths seem to have been placed to 'close off' the site when its ancient, ritual use came to an end.

William Stukeley's 1723 drawing of the fallen Obelisk stone at Avebury henge.

that great feasts took place here, and some form of mortuary ritual was carried out. The site stands at one end of the Kennet Avenue, which ran between here and the henge. Most of this is no longer visible, but sets of stones were re-erected by Keiller at the henge end of the Avenue. Although this restored section looks sinuous at first glance, archaeologists have discovered that it is comprised of straight alignments of stones articulated together.

There were other Neolithic structures of stone, earth and timber in the landscape around Avebury henge, all now vanished, as well as later Bronze Age monuments, but all the Neolithic sites described above are the surviv-ing ones that have line-of-sight communication with Silbury Hill, around which they form a ragged circuit (see the illustration on this page). Silbury, an artificial mound some 130 feet (40m) high, containing over 12 million cubic feet (339,600 cubic m) of chalk and covering over 5 acres (2ha), was the tallest Neolithic structure in all Europe. *It is the geomantic hub of the Avebury complex.* It was built in three stages over a period of time, the first phase taking place sometime around 2700 BC. The culminating phase resulted in a cone-shaped mound of six concentric steps built from chalk. Chalk blocks created a honeycomb lattice, and the cells so formed by this method were infilled with chalk rubble and silt. The whole was covered with soil, each step of the chalk cone being filled and smoothed into the overall profile of the hill *except the top one*, which was left as a terrace or ledge running about 17 feet

A simplified map of the Neolithic landscape around Avebury. All the sites are intervisible with Silbury Hill.

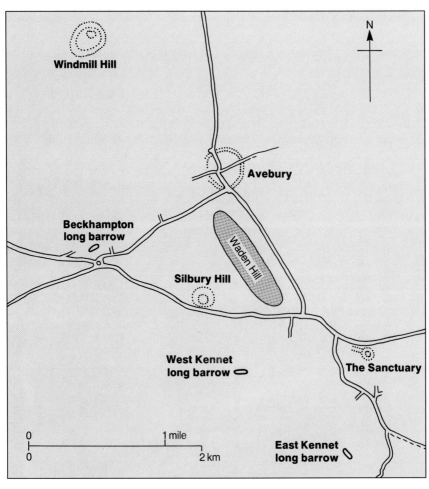

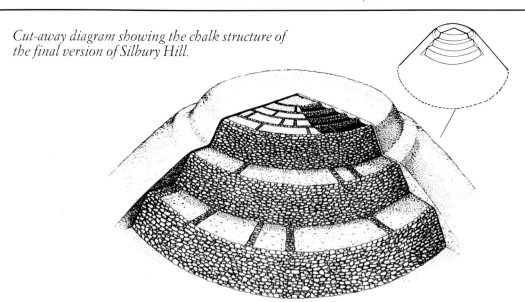

Cut-away diagram showing the chalk structure of the final version of Silbury Hill.

(5m) below the flat summit. Today this terrace is clearly visible on the eastern side of the mound, although the western part of the circuit is less distinct. Whether this was deliberate, or due to erosion by the prevailing southwest winds, is unclear. But the segment of the hill between terrace and summit is significant, as we shall see.

Silbury Hill is located in the lowest part of the Kennet Valley immediately to the west of Waden Hill, a natural, hog-back ridge. Why did the builders expend such effort and engineering skill making a great mound that is set so low in the landscape and is partially obscured by an adjacent hill? Grandiose effect cannot have been the motive for its creation.

Silbury was thought for a long time by archaeologists to have been a Bronze Age burial mound. Legends of a buried king, in golden armour, fuelled ideas of a particularly rich burial. But excavations in the late 1960s revealed that Silbury was much older than the Bronze Age, and no burial was found. But something remarkable was nevertheless encountered. The archaeologists had tunnelled into the heart of the mound, and sections of its base and the original ground level were uncovered. The organic material there was stunningly well-preserved: *grass still had its greenish colour after almost 5,000 years, and insects had been preserved with it.* From this material it proved possible to establish that the first turves in the construction of Silbury had been turned

in late July or early August!

It has been assumed that the purpose of Silbury Hill will never be known or understood. However, recent investigations by the present author have begun to reveal new insights into the monument. This new evidence has been an open secret, but has previously remained unnoticed.

Part of this open secret can be confirmed by any visitor to the complex who takes the trouble to look. Beckhampton, West Kennet and East Kennet barrows, the Sanctuary and the henge all have line-of-sight contact with Silbury. The nature of this intervisibility is interesting. Take West Kennet, for instance. The viewing position there is on the very western tip of the long mound. Archaeologist Richard Bradley feels that some long barrows may have had earthen 'tails' added to them to turn them into extra long mounds, and cites West Kennet as one example.[2] But what were such extensions for? In this case, at least, it allows a remarkable sight-line. Standing at the western extremity of the barrow, therefore at a point in the landscape indicated from Neolithic times, the observer sees Silbury sitting like a great Christmas pudding to the north. *The skyline beyond cuts Silbury's profile almost precisely at the point where the exposed terrace makes a notch on the easterly slope of the great mound.* That skyline is formed by Windmill Hill 3 miles (5km) from West Kennet. This alignment of West Kennet, Silbury Hill and Windmill Hill must have been

Telephotograph of Silbury Hill from the western end of West Kennet long barrow. Note how the skyline, formed by Windhill Hill, intersects Silbury's profile at the level of the terrace (the slight notch in Silbury's profile).

The relationship of Silbury Hill (depicted in silhouette) with skylines viewed from key Neolithic locations: (a) from East Kennet long barrow; (b) from the Sanctuary; (c) from Beckhampton long barrow; and (d) from West Kennet long barrow. In this last instance the skyline is formed by Windmill Hill. It can be seen that the far horizon always intersects the profile of Silbury Hill between the monument's summit and terrace. These views are derived from telephotographs. Broken lines indicate foliage.

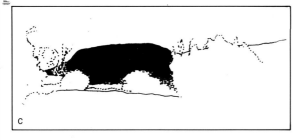

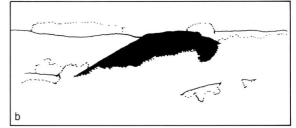

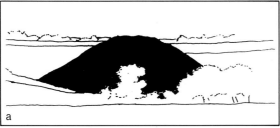

important and obvious to the builders of Silbury, for there is no way they could have built the mound without noticing that they were on the line between Windmill Hill and the already constructed long barrow. The fact that the *elevation* of the sites also fits so precisely is further evidence of the deliberate nature of this alignment.

But there is more. When viewed from East Kennet barrow, the Sanctuary and Beckhampton barrow, the far horizon in each case likewise intersects Silbury's profile somewhere between the summit and the terrace, as shown in the illustration above.

From the henge, the sight-line is exceptional. The chosen observation point has to be the

Telephotograph of Silbury Hill from East Kennet long barrow. Note how the skyline is level with the summit of Silbury. The ledge can be clearly seen on the righthand slope of the mound.

position of the Obelisk, which, because of its great size, must have been the ceremonial focal point. From this position, looking south past what is called stone 102 (part of the ruined southern inner ring), Silbury can just be perceived. In the foreground beyond the bank of the henge, the northern end of Waden Hill slopes down, and the distant horizon dips sharply behind that slope. At this precise point of intersection, the careful observer can just discern the top segment of Silbury Hill (see the illustration on page 122). Such geomantic precision can only be marvelled at.

This Obelisk–Silbury sight-line is most difficult to observe in the summer when the cereal crop on Waden Hill is high; after harvest the view is clearer. This must have been even more of a factor in the Late Neolithic period, when we know that cereal crops were grown on Waden and corn grew taller than modern strains, which have been developed for mechanical harvesting. Perhaps the crop obscuring the view of Silbury from the Obelisk was taken as the signal that harvest-time was at hand. The sight-line could therefore have been *harvest dependent.*

From the centre position of the Obelisk stone hole, stone 102 would have blocked the view of Silbury. The Obelisk was, however, much wider than even the present-day plinth, so views from either side of the great monolith would always have been possible. The top of the Obelisk would also have been visible from the top of Silbury, as it towered above stone 102. Why the ground level central position view from the Obelisk should have been blocked, though, remains a secret of the Neolithic mind.

One way or another, therefore, it seems that the summit-terrace segment of Silbury had great significance. But what could that be? Patient research has revealed that it almost certainly relates to an astronomical effect that can be observed from Silbury.

Looking eastwards from the top of Silbury one can see the nearby ridge of Waden Hill, and, several miles beyond, the far skyline formed by the Marlborough Downs. In 1987, in early May (the Celtic Beltane, see Chapter 1) the author observed that the sun rose in a slight dip in this far horizon. Later, it was noticed that the distant horizon closely mimics the contours of Waden Hill when viewed from Silbury's

summit. When the observer scrambles down to the terrace on the slope of the mound, however, the far skyline appears to drop with eye-level so that visually it only just skims the Waden ridge, and at the slight dip it actually disappears behind the bulk of Waden for a short distance. In early August (the Christian Lammas or Celtic Lughnassadh, see Chapter 1) in 1989 it was confirmed that the sun, by rising out of this dip – this 'horizon window' – seemingly *rises twice* as viewed from Silbury. The first sunrise occurs, as viewed from Silbury's *summit*, over the far horizon of the Marlborough Downs. If the viewer than moves down to the *terrace*, the sun is seen to rise again a couple of minutes later, this time over nearby Waden Hill. The summit-

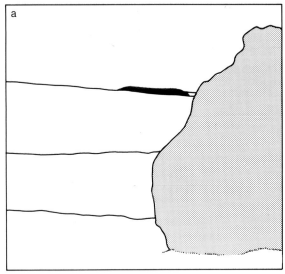

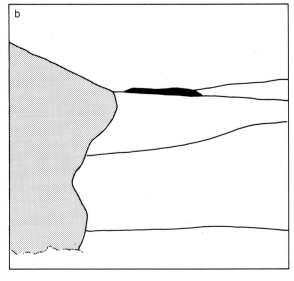

The first gleam of Beltane sunrise over the far skyline (left), viewed from Silbury's summit. The bulk of Waden Hill looms darker in the lower foreground, and it can be seen how the fainter, misty far skyline echoes the ridge of Waden. Note the dip in the horizon where the sun is rising. On the right, the 'second sunrise' as the sun clears the top of Waden Hill as viewed from Silbury's terrace.

Looking southwards towards Silbury Hill (depicted in silhouette) from the Obelisk stone position inside Avebury henge: (a) from alongside the eastern side of the Obelisk marker plinth looking past stone 102 (shaded); and (b) from the western side of the Obelisk marker plinth looking past stone 102. Most of Silbury Hill is concealed behind the lower slope of Waden Hill, and the distant horizon curves down to intersect Silbury at summit level. This view was obtained immediately after the harvest of crops on Waden Hill; when the crop is high Silbury can be only barely perceived, which suggests that this sight-line was 'harvest dependent'. Again, it is the summit-terrace segment of Silbury that seems involved with skyline coincidence.

terrace segment of Silbury can thus be seen to be a product of astronomy being combined with the topography; the heavens united with the land.

It is as if the double-sunrise effect was engineered to celebrate the sowing and harvest times of year, which were traditionally regarded in a festive and joyous manner. In particular, Silbury can be seen as a harvest hill. This is further supported by the harvest-dependent sight-line from the Obelisk, and the fact that the building of Silbury commenced at that time of year. But the Great Goddess has three aspects – virgin, mother and hag. The Beltane double-sunrise therefore also recognizes the young, bridal aspect of the land, bedecked in blossom and harbouring the seed from which the harvest birth will ensue. Silbury is certainly a joyous monument.

The alignment between Windmill Hill and West Kennet determined the east–west positioning of Silbury, and the double-sunrise horizon configuration meant that it had to occupy a particular location north–south for the effect to occur. In its location, height and shape, therefore, Silbury Hill monumentalizes the

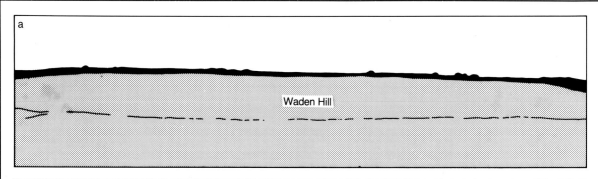

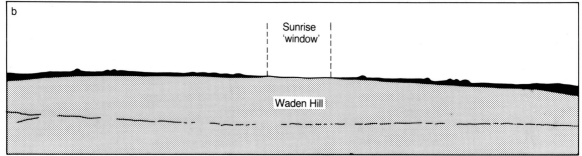

The eastwards view from Silbury Hill: (a) the view from Silbury top across Waden Hill (shaded) to the far skyline (depicted in silhouette), showing the 'double horizon' effect; and (b) the view from Silbury terrace showing how the far skyline 'dips' behind the bulk of Waden Hill forming a 'window' in which Waden's crest provides the only horizon. This 'window' coincides with the sunrise position at Beltane and Lammas; changing viewing positions between Silbury top and terrace allows a 'double sunrise' to be seen at those times.

relevant elements of land and sky within the sacred landscape of the Avebury complex. Silbury Hill is the expression of geomancy, of sacred geography, *par excellence.*

The Neolithic builders included one further piece of celebratory showmanship into their structure. In the moments as the sun rises, the shadow of the mound is thrown far and long onto fields to the west. An observer on top of Silbury sees a dramatic flare of light radiating off the tip of the shadow. This is an optical effect called a 'glory', and it is caused by refraction in dew drops on the grass or crop in the field – the Silbury Glory.

A modern mystery that is occurring around Silbury at the time of this writing have been *crop circles*. Throughout southern England, and occasionally elsewhere, these geometrically precise circles and rings have appeared overnight in large cornfields to the confusion of experts and researchers. Although these circles occur regularly at a number of locations, the fields immediately to the north and south of Silbury Hill have been particularly affected. Although there can be no doubt that hoax is a considerable element in the crop circles affair, some, particularly the simple circles and rings, may have had a genuine geophysical cause. Local people have reported mysterious lights playing around the Avebury monuments since at least 1983.[3] A very dramatic light phenomenon was observed next to Silbury Hill on the night of 28 June 1989. The occupier of the roadside house next to the footpath which leads up to West Kennet barrow, saw a ball of light 30–40 feet (10–13m) in diameter descending over the field to the south of Silbury, immediately across the main road from the monument. The lightball was orange in colour, with greater brilliance around its periphery. When the phenomenon made contact with the crop the bottom part of the sphere flattened. The ball gave 'a little bounce', then disappeared. The next day the witness found a crop circle where the light had been, and this was further confirmed by a pilot flying over the site later that day. He also

reported that the circle had a ring round it.[4]

The mysteries ancient and modern of the Avebury complex spreak in their different ways of the great sanctity of this exceptional World Heritage site.

The Silbury Glory – a remarkable optical effect that issues from the shadow of the great mound at sunrise during Beltane or Lammas periods. The photographer's shadow can be seen thrown across the flat top of Silbury in the foreground.

STONEHENGE

South across the Wiltshire landscape from Avebury is the famed Stonehenge. The monument as we now see it was not built all at the same time. The first feature on the site, at around 3300 BC, seems to have been a wooden building about 100 feet (30m) long. It had an entrance at the northeast and a narrower opening at the south. Prehistorian Aubrey Burl thinks that it was a charnel house and may also have been a centre for astronomer-priests making the first prolonged lunar observations at the site.

About 100 years after this, *Stonehenge I*, as it is known in archaeological parlance, was built: a circular ditch-and-bank enclosure (the actual henge), a ring of 56 infilled pits known as the Aubrey Holes inside the inner bank, and the Heel Stone, outlying to the northeast. The entrance to the henge was on the northeast, on the axis of the original timber building. Numerous small post holes were found in the entrance causeway, and these probably belong to this phase of the monument or even preceded the earthen henge. There was another set of larger post holes in a line near the Heel Stone.

In *Stonehenge II*, about a thousand years later, the axis was shifted a little, and on this an earthen avenue was built, approaching the henge entrance. Either during this phase or at sometime in Phase I, the Station Stones were put in place, forming what is virtually a rectangular setting. These stone positions, located on the circumference of the Aubrey Holes circle, are known as 91, 92, 93 and 94 on plans of Stonehenge, and they are crucial to the site's astronomical role, as we shall see; more so, in fact than the famous Heel Stone midsummer sunrise. Only two Station Stones survive today. Also during this phase the first setting of blue stones was arranged within the henge. (The blue stones are the smaller, darker stones the visitor sees at Stonehenge today.)

Stonehenge III dates to about 2000 BC and involved the erection of the huge, lintelled sarsen stones that most people identify with Stonehenge. The blue stones were carefully removed and stored no one knows where. In their stead, five huge, free-standing 'trilithons' were arranged in a horseshoe configuration. A surrounding circle was formed with 30 slightly

Stonehenge viewed from Station Stone 91.

smaller sarsen uprights topped with lintels which formed a uniform ring of stone 16 feet (5m) above the ground. The centre of this outer sarsen ring differed slightly from that of the original henge and Aubrey Hole circle. Two stones were erected by the entrance, one

survives today as the fallen 'Slaughter Stone'. Archaeologists divide Phase III into a series of subdivisions stretching over the following centuries, when various changes were made to the monument: the blue stones reappeared, a large stone, the Altar Stone, which may have also been present in Phase II, was erected within the trilithon horseshoe, and, around 1100 BC, the avenue had a longer addition made to it but on a sharply different axis to the east.

Probably the best-known 'mysterious' aspect of Stonehenge is its association with ancient astronomy. That this characteristic of the monument was anciently recognized is implicit in the fact that traditional midsummer festivities were held there. In 1223 the Bishop of Salisbury referred to them as 'vile and indecorous games' – they smacked too much of their pagan origins

One of the great trilithons of the 'inner horseshoe' of trilithons at Stonehenge.

The 'classic' view from the centre of the sarsen circle looking northeast towards the outlying Heel Stone. The large stones with the lintels are sarsens, belonging to Phase III of the site, and the shorter standing stones in front of them are the blue stones. The central gap in the sarsen uprights frame the midsummer sunrise, and the gaps on either side frame lunar events as viewed from the centre position.

for his liking, no doubt. Sports were held at Stonehenge even as late as the eighteenth century. Such folk traditions alerted the early antiquarians to the astronomical elements of certain ancient monuments. In 1740 William Stukeley noted that the axis of Stonehenge and its earthen avenue align to the northeast 'where abouts the sun rises when the days are longest'. In 1901 scientist Sir Norman Lockyer attempted to date Stonehenge by calculating back to when the first gleam of the midsummer rising sun would have been dead in line with the axis of the monument. Lockyer furthermore noted that this midsummer axis could effectively be extended as a landscape line many miles long linking Stonehenge with Sidbury Hill in one direction and Grovely Castle and Castle Ditches (all hilltops earthworked in the Iron Age) in the other. Of course, this is perilously close to geomancy, and was resisted by archaeologists not only at the time, but even to the present. They complain that the earthworks on these hills are far more recent than Stonehenge, but this misses the point – it was the hills that mattered. As the perceptive prehistorian Aubrey Burl points out: 'the midsummer sun never rose farther north than the landmark of Sidbury Hill eight miles away nor the midwinter sun farther south than the seven-mile distant Battery Hill. It would have been easy to set up a stone or post in line with these natural features.'[5]

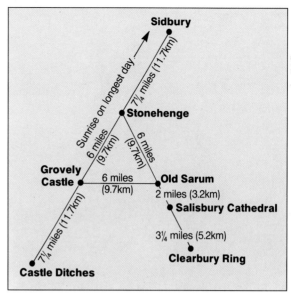

The triangle of alignments linking Stonehenge with landmark hills containing prehistoric earthworks, as noted by Sir Norman Lockyer.

Lockyer also suggested that a diagonal across the Station Stones rectangle gave certain cross-quarter day (such as May Day) sunrises and sunsets. Lockyer's work started the first development of archaeoastronomy as a scientific discipline, and Stonehenge has marked its progress throughout this century.

Some of the best archaeoastronomical work at Stonehenge had to wait until the 1960s, when careful measurements by C. A. Newham confirmed earlier claims that the alignment of Station Stones 92 with 91 gave the summer solstice sunrise, and 94 to 93 indicated the setting midwinter sun. He went on to find more astronomical lines indicated by the megalithic

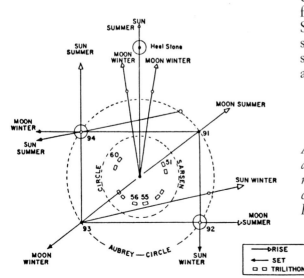

A schematic diagram of the astronomical alignments indicated by the Station Stone rectangle, which lies outside the later sarsen circles but within the henge ditch. (After Gerald Hawkins)

A rather annoyed-looking Heel Stone, viewed from the west.

rectangle. One related to the Heel Stone. This stands to one side of Stonehenge's present axis, and in megalithic times the sun would not have risen over it, as is popularly supposed, but to the left of it as viewed from the centre of the sarsen circle. But in 1979 a stone hole to the left (west) of the Heel Stone was uncovered, and this is now catalogued as stone 97. It seems that the scheme at Stonehenge was to have the midsummer sun rising between the Heel Stone and its now lost companion. The two uprights would have framed the first gleam of the sun precisely and the rising disc would then have grazed the tip of the Heel Stone. Newham also noticed that the Heel Stone would mark the equinox moonrise viewed from Station Stone 94 (this alignment is not shown in the diagram on page 129).

Apart from this astonishing display of astronomical significance, the very fact that the Station Stone rectangle is rectangular is itself remarkable! The French architect G. Charrière noted in 1961, as did Newham and Gerald Hawkins independently in 1963, that the astronomical alignments marked at Stonehenge cross at right angles, and thus generate the rectangle, because of the latitude at which Stonehenge is located. This virtually regular figure could not be produced if Stonehenge were situated much further north or south, if the ground level were different or the horizon altitude other than it is around the site. The implications of this are that the builders of Stonehenge *had a knowledge of the global nature of the Earth.*

Newham felt that, in its earliest stage, Stonehenge 'was essentially a site for the investigation of lunar phenomena'. He felt that the post holes found in the entrance causeway (see page 126) were made by poles used to mark the moon's movements over a century, as the Stonehenge skywatchers worked out the skyline positions of key times in the complex lunar cycle of 18.61 years. He also noted that one of the 30 uprights of the outer sarsen circle was half the size of the others, and suggested that 29½ might have related to the days of a lunar month (literally 'moonth').

In 1963 Gerald Hawkins, an astrophysicist at America's Smithsonian Insitution, published a paper in *Nature*, the journal Lockyer used to edit, in which he described his work using a computer to assess the astronomical lines at Stonehenge. He proposed alignments not only for the earlier phases of Stonehenge but also for the Phase III sarsen structure. In this he suggested that the narrow gaps between the great trilithons allowed narrow viewing angles like gunsights to solar and lunar rise and set positions through the wider gaps between the uprights in the outer sarsen circle. Hawkins suggested that certain hollows in the trilithon uprights had actually been carved to allow for the slight sideways squint required for some of the sight-lines. Nevertheless, despite the narrowness of the trilithon gaps, Hawkins' sarsen stones lines were still fairly wide, so pinpoint accuracy could not be claimed. Hawkins felt that scientific accuracy as we require it was not a priority of the Stonehenge designers, but rather that a more ceremonial usage of astronomical orientation was wanted. In a second paper in 1964 Hawkins went further to suggest that the 56 Aubrey Holes had been a lunar eclipse calculator, which may have employed a

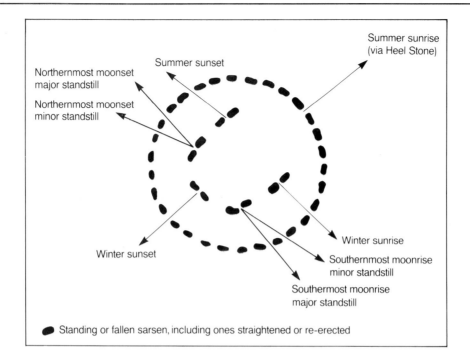

Summer sunrise
(via Heel Stone)

Summer sunset

Northernmost moonset
major standstill

Northernmost moonset
minor standstill

Winter sunrise

Winter sunset

Southernmost moonrise
minor standstill

Southermost moonrise
major standstill

● Standing or fallen sarsen, including ones straightened or re-erected

Astronomical alignments using the spaces between the uprights of the inner trilithon stones and the uprights in the outer sarsen circle at Stonehenge. These sight-lines would have been general and ceremonial, rather than scientifically precise. (After Gerald Hawkins)

One of Gerald Hawkins' sight-lines using the gap between trilithon uprights (nearest camera) in conjunction with space between uprights in the outer sarsen circle.

set of black and white marker stones. By using 56 positions (18.61 × 3 = 55.83) the stone-age computer could have been used for calculations covering many years. Hawkins' published his work in 1965 in a book, *Stonehenge Decoded* (written with John B. White), which captured public imagination and made ancient astronomy a popular area, taking it out of its former obscurity. Much uproar greeted Hawkins' findings in archaeological circles, and he had to mend and modify some of his calculations, but his basic claims remain intact.

Working quietly in the background was the retired Oxford engineering professor, Alexander Thom. He had spent decades surveying hundreds of British megalithic sites, publishing his findings piecemeal in scientific journals. His 1967 book, *Megalithic Sites in Britain*, was so detailed and mathematical that it took a while to make its impact on archaeologists. It was, said one, like a 'well constructed parcel-bomb'. It was so meticulous that it could not be disregarded, and it is still a bone of contention today. At Stonehenge Thom made a new, accurate survey. He finally came to the conclusion that outlying landmarks in the landscape around Stonehenge were used, in conjunction with sighting posts, to mark key lunar rise and set positions. As Earth Mysteries writer and researcher John Michell put it: 'Stonehenge was no longer an isolated monument, but the centre of a vast system of astronomically placed stations extending far across the Wessex landscape. . . .'[6]

Aubrey Burl also noted that the original axis of Phase I Stonehenge had actually been directed at the rising of the major standstill midwinter full moon, thus making the fundamental cosmological line at the site originally lunar, not solar. Later, when the axis was altered almost five degrees, a solar orientation was created: Burl sees this as possibly expressing a shift in cultural archetype from the feminine to the masculine; matriarchy to patriarchy.

Lockyer noted the now famous alignment that runs south from the henge monument through Old Sarum, an Iron Age earthworked hill topped by a medieval settlement and cathedral, Salisbury Cathedral and Clearbury Ring, another hilltop Iron Age earthwork, covered by a clump of trees (see righthand line in the illustration on page 129). Actually, this line had been noticed by an earlier researcher,

Colonel Johnston, director of the British Ordnance Survey in the 1890s, and it was independently rediscovered by other geomantic researchers including the arch ley hunter himself, Alfred Watkins, in the 1920s. It is said of this line that it assisted in improving the accuracy of the Ordnance Survey.

It is an interesting alignment. In 1979, Ian Thomson and this author published a slightly modified version of the alignment,[7] which extended it beyond Clearbury Ring to Frankenbury Camp. In 1989, Nigel Pennick published research[8] showing that this line, which passes through Salisbury Cathedral, fitted *precisely* with the angular arrangement of Salisbury's street grid, laid out in the thirteenth century. It is beyond belief that this could be accidental. There has been much criticism of the Old Sarum line in the past, with sceptics complaining that a medieval site like the cathedral could not have been part of a prehistoric scheme, and, moreover, that Stonehenge is much older than the Iron Age earthworks at Old Sarum, Clearbury and Frankenbury. There can be no doubt now that the surveyors who laid out Salisbury were aware of the cathedral's position on this (largely visible) alignment, which they literally built into the city ground plan. Further, legend states that the site of the cathedral was found by bowshot or as the result of a vision (both versions of folkloric shorthand for forms of divination), and it stands on an important Anglo-Saxon mark point known as a *trifinium*. As to the age difference between Neolithic Stonehenge and the Iron Age earthworks, the matter is obvious: the hillforts are first and foremost *hills* – landmarks – quite probably holy hills of the Neolithic period. They are evolved points in the landscape. (Relatively little excavation has been undertaken on Iron Age hill earthworks, but there are known cases where earlier, even Neolithic, remains have been found.) Finally, John Michell has found that specific measures were used between the points on the Stonehenge to Clearbury length of the line.[9]

Apart from contentious leys, however, the Stonehenge landscape contains a line of unquestionable reality – the Stonehenge Cursus (see Chapter 1 for more on cursuses), which is older even than Stonehenge itself. It lies about ½ mile (800m) north of the henge, and can be accessed by a lane which runs past the west end of the car park. It is well signed by the National Trust and its whole length can be walked.

The western end of the cursus, in Fargo Plantation, has been shown by excavation to be a pseudo long barrow, mimicking a real one which stood at the other, eastern terminus, nearly 2 miles (3km) away. The northern ditch-and-bank runs straight for almost this whole distance. The southern boundary of the cursus was probably ranged out from this, accounting for the discrepancies that occur in its width. The banks were more prominent in the eighteenth century when William Stukeley discovered them: they have since suffered the depradations of the plough and forestry and are in parts now quite invisible.

This monumental earthen line is totally mysterious, but like most cursuses it links long barrows in alignment. Cursuses are related to the dead, or to the spirits of the dead, in some way.

In 1947 an archaeologist noted that the line or axis of the Stonehenge Cursus could be extended to the east through the Cuckoo Stone and on to the centre of Woodhenge, another Neolithic site in the ritual landscape surrounding Stonehenge. This forms an alignment 2½ miles (4km) in total length and is in every way a ley. The course of the alignment can be extended about 3 miles (5km) further east, beyond Woodhenge, to pass over Beacon Hill,

The Stonehenge Cursus, with the line of the northern ditch-and-bank extended eastwards through the Cuckoo Stone and Woodhenge.

visible on the skyline from the western end of the cursus. Watkins felt that beacon hills were major sighting points on his leys.

The cursus is not very well known to the general public, and is one of Stonehenge's 'secrets'. An even more esoteric aspect of the site is the sacred measure and number encoded in the very stones of the site's structure. John Michell, with exhaustive scholarship, has studied the measures of Stonehenge and shown that the lintel circuit of the outer sarsen ring encodes geodetic information, such as the Earth's polar radius and meridian circumference, as well as all the principle units of measure in the ancient world.[10,11] The lintel ring was constructed to a high precision, using only stone tools. Each lintel, fixed by mortice and tenon to its upright, curves slightly so that the whole formed a complete, carefully levelled ring of stone. Michell has also found the basic sacred or canonical numbers incorporated in sites like Stonehenge and the Great Pyramid to occur in the dimensions of the New Jerusalem given in the *Revelations* of St John. St John's visionary celestial city is thus a microcosm of the Earth, derived from the archetypal proportional system that was the corpus of geodetic and other knowledge among the ancients. This information is distributed through time and encoded in many modes, from sacred architecture to sacred scriptures, by many hands. The secret workings behind the public face of history.

The gaunt ruin of Stonehenge has always been a focus for human wonderment. The medieval historian Geoffrey of Monmouth maintained that Merlin had used magical art to bring the blue stones from Ireland, whence they

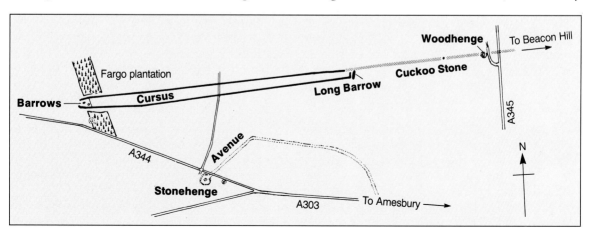

Telephotograph pointing south along the Stonehenge–Clearbury alignment. The ruined medieval walls atop Old Sarum are in the foreground, Salisbury Cathedral is in the middle distance (the line goes through the eastern altar end) and the tree-covered Clearbury Ring earthwork is on the skyline.

had been taken in the first place by giants from Africa. There may be a deep memory encoded in this tradition. The orthodox view is that the stones originated in the Preseli Hills in south-west Wales, but the present author has recently heard from both geologists and archaeologists who have some doubts about this. Whatever their source, the stones, Geoffrey's Merlin further proclaimed, had healing virtue. Water splashed on them accrued this healing power. This seems to hint at some power or energy in the stones, but the Dragon Project Trust[12] has monitored all the blue stones for both magnetic and radiation anomalies and found none.

There are a few anecdotal snippets that tell of unusual natural forces at Stonehenge, however. In the 1940s, a ball of light was seen to dive out of a clear sky and strike the ground near the stones.[13] It was the day before the summer solstice, and, remarkably, coincident with a partially eclipsed sun rising over the Heel Stone. In another incident, in 1983, Gabriele Wilson, a niece of the poet and writer the late Robert Graves, heard a 'ringing' sound emanating from a blue stone in the north east sector of Stonehenge at the time of sunrise.[14,15]

But to be sure, Stonehenge today, with its bustle of visitors and clutter of cars and shanty buildings, is hardly a place where subtle manifestations of power are readily perceived. The august grandeur of the Avebury complex to the north now better guards that indefinable *genius loci*, spirit of place. Nevertheless, Stonehenge still exercises a fascination over us and still bears witness: midsummer games have given way to midsummer battles between riot police and so-called 'hippies', disapproved of by modern society. Worldviews clash here, in all sorts of ways.

CHAPTER 15

CHARTRES CATHEDRAL

FRANCE

WORLD HERITAGE LIST NUMBER 102
ASTRONOMY, ENERGIES(?), EVOLVED, SACRED GEOMETRY, SACRED MEASURE

EVEN FROM GREAT DISTANCES, the soaring profile of Chartres Cathedral dominates the flat landscape of La Beauce. It also rises over the small town of Chartres itself, being built on a modest rise of ground.

Chartres, the epitome of Gothic cathedrals, was designed by an unknown master. Building commenced in 1194 and was virtually completed by 1220; the west towers had been built a little earlier. There had been churches on the site since at least the fourth century. There is little doubt that this location had been a major Druidic centre, on which the Romans subsequently erected a pagan shrine. The student of Chartres Cathedral, Louis Charpentier, argued persuasively that there was originally a Neolithic mound containing a dolmen or a cave which ultimately became the site for a crypt which pre-dated the Gothic structure.[1]

A well, 108 feet (33m) deep, opens in the crypt at Chartres which today houses a copy of a wooden effigy of the Blessed Virgin and Child, a Black Virgin, destroyed in the French Revolution. This Subterranean Lady, *Notre Dame de Sous-Terre*, was surely a representation of the Earth Mother. Charpentier writes:

The statue, carved in the hollowed-out trunk of a pear tree and very ancient, represented the Holy Virgin, seated with the Infant God on her knees. Age had blackened it, for it was made, not by Christians but before the birth of the Saviour by Druids, pagan priests to whom a prophetic angel announced that a Virgin would give birth to a God; and it was thus that they portrayed her, as she was to be, with great devotion and on the pedestal they wrote, in fine Roman lettering, the words '*Virigini pariturae*', meaning, 'The Virgin who will give birth to a child.'

When the first Christians came to Chartres they found this statue and were amazed. They conceived a deep reverence for this prophetic Virgin . . . they called the well on one side of it 'The Well of the Strong', a name it has kept through the ages.

. . . Generations and generations before them came to meditate in the grotto where a Virgin Mother reigned, a Black Virgin who was named Isis perhaps, or Demeter, or Bélisama.[2]

The region was inhabited by the Carnutes, the 'Guardians of the Stone'. Their holy place, Charpentier maintained, 'where the stone was to be seen, was *Carnute-Is*, now Chartres, in Beauce, l' *Is of the Carnutes*.' Suchet, the historian of Chartres, wrote that the cathedral stands 'on an elevation where according to our ancient records, there was once a sacred wood in which the Druids gathered to make their sacrifices and devotions'. Another scholar,

Bulteau, claimed that at the spot was 'the Druids' sanctuary of sanctuaries and the seat of the sovereign tribunal . . . it was the centre of Druidism.'

With regard to the name 'The Well of the Strong', Charpentier noted that the 'rising ground on which Chartres stands was called Place of the strong Saints; but earlier, simply Place of the Strong, which has the particular meaning of "Initiates"'.

A Celtic well is depicted at the foot of the statue of Saint Modeste at the North Door of the cathedral. This door is also called 'The Door of the Initiates', and another carving there depicts the Ark of the Covenant as a chest on wheels, with the inscription *Archa cederis* – 'you are to work through the Ark'. Adjacent to this, another scene includes a man attempting to lift the Ark with his hands covered by a cloth.

The Ark was a mysterious object recorded in the Old Testament. It was said to be a wooden coffer, plated internally as well as externally with gold, which contained the Tables of the Law received by Moses, manna and the rod of Aaron. It seems to have acted as an electrical condenser, because it could give shocks, even fatal ones, to those who touched it. 'God was a sound electrician,' Charpentier observed. It had other formidable energetic properties. After many travels and adventures, it was eventually secreted in Solomon's Temple at Jerusalem. Thereafter, its fate becomes obscure. In his *The Cult of the Black Virgin*, Ean Begg, who admits that the 'original Black Virgins of Chartres and Longpont probably started life as Celtic fertility idols', suggests that when Our Lady

> appears in her black form . . . we should meditate on the title given her in the Litany of Loreto, *Arca foederis*, Ark of the Covenant. . . . Finally, we might do well to cast a sideways glance, since riddlers and puzzlers delight in the subtle word-play, sometimes called green language, or the language of birds, at Arcas, the bear, doubly constellated in the heavens, attribute of Artemis, Arthur and Dagobert II, a fabulous beast, evocative of Arcadia and its sacred mysteries.[3]

Charpentier felt that was a link between the Ark and Chartres forged by the mysterious Order of the Knights Templar. He questioned the immediacy with which Gothic architecture appeared, particularly Chartres, and how it was concurrent with the Romanesque style, not deriving from it. How could it spring up so readily? There must have been a *school* from which the master builders emerged, Charpentier reasoned. The awesome logistics involved in the building of Gothic Chartres, and the curious fact that monarchs from all over Europe contributed to its costs, led him to ask: 'Was Chartres the "Golden Book" of the West in which sages wrote the message of their wisdom?' The first Gothic buildings began to appear 11 years after the return from the Crusades of the original Knights Templar in 1128. The choir at Chartres is a double square; 'the ratio 2 to 1 is exactly that of the Egyptian and Greek temples,' Charpentier observed; 'likewise of Solomon's Temple as far as the Holy of Holies'. A channel for the entry of ancient, occult (that is, secret) knowledge into the scholarship of Europe was certainly provided by the Crusades, and, particularly, the Knights Templar, who ostensibly were supposed to guard pilgrims on their way to Jerusalem. The Western Christians ('Franks') came in contact with Arabic traditions, and the secret wisdom teachings of the Middle East filtered back into Europe. The Knights Templar were doubtlessly instrumental in this, and many believe them to have been an occult order whose job in Jerusalem was quite other than their exoteric role, being more concerned with finding out the secrets of the Temple of Solomon, where they were housed and from which their Order obtained its name – perhaps even unearthing the Ark of the Covenant itself. It is all fascinating speculation, and not without its evidence.

There are many images of the Virgin at Chartres, including another, 'official', Black Virgin – *Notre Dame du Pilier* – in the nave, the current one replacing a thirteenth-century gilt version. There is also a curious 'alter-ego' of the Black Virgin – the window of St Anne, the mother of the Blessed Virgin, which is also black. This is the largest image in the cathedral and is known to have been black when it was made in the thirteenth century. Begg notes that the 'Roman goddess Anna Perenna was considered to be the sister of Belus the father of Danaus and Lamia, though Beli (Belen) was also said to be the son of Anna, "Empress of

The west front of Chartres Cathedral. Note the difference in the heights of the two towers. (Editions Houvet)

Rome". It is at St Anne that this potent symbol persists in Christianity. To the Bretons, according to Saillens, she largely replaces the Black Virgin. . . .'[4] Jean Markale felt that 'surely she is the reflection of the goddess of ancient, pre-patriarchal societies . . . who haunts every corner of life, but reveals herself only very reluctantly, sometimes even as a Black Virgin'.

Gothic architecure developed within the milieu provided by the esoteric traditions in Europe, including that of alchemy, so it is perhaps not surprising that the Gothic cathedrals, the 'books of stone', should contain references to alchemical philosophy. The master builders were certainly involved in the arcane traditions, and Chartres, particularly, may have been a deliberate attempt to record the mystery tradition that had so recently been re-invigorated by contact with the Middle East. Students of the arcane have found alchemical symbolism in some of the windows at Chartres, and the west towers at Chartres (which, remember, were built first) display the sun-moon, masculine-feminine, principles so central to alchemical thought and that of other esoteric traditions.

Facing the west front, the lefthand tower rises 365 feet (111m) – the same height as St Paul's Cathedral in London – and the righthand tower is 28 feet (8.5m) shorter. The lefthand tower therefore represents the number of days in the solar year, the 28-foot (8.5m) shortfall of the righthand tower representing the number of days in a lunar month, 13 of which make the solar year's tally of days to the nearest whole number.[5] The solar and lunar symbolism of the

An old print showing people walking on the labyrinth at Chartres.

towers is further reinforced in that each tower has the appropriate sun or moon symbol on its weather vane!

Another mystery at Chartres is the 42-foot (12.8m) diameter, thirteenth-century labyrinth design laid out on the nave floor (usually covered by chairs nowadays). Geometer Keith Critchlow has noted that if the elevation of the west front of the cathedral is 'hinged down' onto the ground plan, the great West Rose window 'not only conforms basically in size to the maze, but . . . covers it almost exactly.'[6] Nothing was done at Chartres without purpose and planning. The basic labyrinth design goes back to remotest prehistory, but it enjoyed a Christian revival in medieval Europe, and several cathedrals had versions of the pattern, although the one at Chartres is arguably the most famous. It was called 'La Lieue', The League, although the length of its path is considerably shorter than a league (6,850 feet/ 2,088m) at approximately 450 feet (140m). It is believed that the Christian usage of such designs was as penance paths, and there are hints in names for Christian labyrinths that suggest their perambulation could be used in lieu of a physical pilgrimage to Jerusalem. But they are also cosmographic images, and this is indicated by the Chartres design. It is based on a curious 114-fold division of the circle, indicated by the 'spikes' that surround the outer circumference. Actually, there are 112 of these, because the entrance to the labyrinth path cuts out two of them. Researcher Nigel Pennick has written:

> The number 112 is notable as part of the ancient systems of weights and measures used in Europe before the imposition of the Metric System. It survives in the Imperial System of

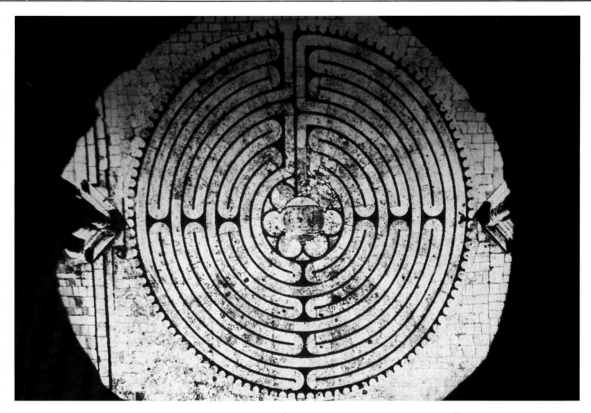

Looking down on the pavement labyrinth in the nave. (Editions Houvet)

weights as the hundredweight, 112 pounds, which is composed of 8 stone of 14 pounds, or 4 quarters of 28. This ancient eightfold division of weight, length, area and time, is part of the overall conceptual framework that underlies geomancy, sacred geography, sacred geometry and weights and measures. ... Little is known of the system which incorporates a 114-fold division of the circle, but it is certain that there is more to this than mere capriciousness, a concept absent from ancient canonical sacred architecture, which is represented par excellence by Chartres Cathedral. At the centre of the labyrinth was the now-removed plaque, surrounded by a six-petalled pattern, which in fact was laid out on a thirteenfold geometry. This 13 may be emblematical of the 13 lunar months of the year, which with the centre makes 14, one eighth of the number of spikes around the perimeter.[7]

Critchlow was, in fact, the first modern researcher to record the 13-fold geometry underlying the labyrinth's central motif, finding by geometric analysis a 13-pointed star polygon controlling several aspects of the design. Speculating on the symbolism of 13 in the design, Critchlow also remarked that one is reminded of the 13 months in the lunar year, but added

> to be practical, if a path is to be made into a twleve-fold system without initially occupying and thus biasing one of the twelve houses, the design must open up to allow in the traveller. Further, the connotations of thirteen with the earthly life of Christ must not be overlooked. He was both the cause and leader of a group of thirteen men. ... The thirteen-pointed star is the hidden, non-visible aspect of the proportions of the maze and we would propose it represents the second type of sacred measure, co-ordinating proportion to number.[8]

Charpentier saw the feature as a ritual contact-ground with the earth ('telluric') currents he considered were strong and anciently recognized at Chartres:

We are now in a place that was chosen for human utilisation of a telluric current that surfaces and must have close analogies with currents that are magnetic. Now, it is a well-known effect of an electric current that all bodies in movement through its field acquire peculiar properties. This is in fact the way electricity is made, by causing a rotor to revolve in a magnetic field, natural or artificial.[9]

He provided evidence to show that the old Celtic word *wouivre* was used to refer to these sinuous, serpentine telluric energies, some of which 'spring from the movement of subterranean waters; others from faults which have brought soils of different kinds into contact, which develop differences of potential according to changes of temperature; some, again, flow from the depths of the terrestrial magma. These currents are a manifestation of a life that goes on deep in Earth herself. . . .'[10] He felt that the labyrinth path was meant to be traversed barefoot, so the body could best receive these energies – reminiscent of the idea of the king standing barefoot on a king stone in the entry on Westminster Abbey.

Both the present author and Nigel Pennick have noted the arresting coincidence of the labyrinth-like forms of some of the energy patterns studied by J. Cecil Maby and T. Bedford Franklin during their excellent scientific research into dowsing during the 1930s (see the illustration above, for example).

To add anecdotal evidence, when this author was at Chartres, close to the spring equinox, he saw a visitor suddenly 'go mad', exhibiting wild behaviour as he walked over the labyrinth segment of the nave (of which the man seemed totally unaware). Further, the author and two of his three companions felt extraordinarily mentally disoriented when coming out of the cathedral, a very real sensation which was by no means subtle, felt independently by each person without comment initially, and which persisted for about 30 minutes. This could, of course, be simply subjective.

One of the more dramatic enigmas at Chartres reveals itself just once a year – on 21 June. When the sun is at the highest point of its journey through the sky, about 12.45 pm local

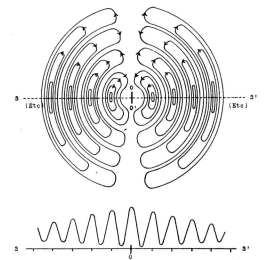

Electric field around a dipolar Hertzian oscillator, showing instantaneous distribution of waves and corresponding field strength as measured by radio receiver. (After Pohl)

The second figure is a graph of field strength along the section of field SS'. OO' is the dipole oscillator

A figure and caption from The Physics of the Divining Rod *by J. Cecil Maby and T. Bedford Franklin, Bell, 1939. The similarity between the labyrinth pattern and this Hertzian field are obvious. Maby and Franklin compared such measurable fields with dowsing responses in them. Their research proved human beings could directly sense such energies.*

time, a beam of sunlight shafts through a small area of clear glass in the window dedicated to St Appollinaire on the western side of the south transept. The beam strikes a flagstone in the south transept's western aisle. This slab is larger than those around it, a slightly different hue, and set at an angle. Moreover, there is a small, round metal tenon set into it. The solstitial sunbeam moves over this metal marker. Charpentier realized that such an event required co-operation between architect, glazier and mason, all working to astronomical information. It bears repeating: nothing occurs by chance at Chartres.

There are more mysteries at this great cathedral than space here allows to be itemized. Its measurements, proportions, patterns, images, resonance properties, subterranean waters, siting and astronomy provide a whole library of ancient, secret knowledge.

CHAPTER 16

DELPHI

GREECE

WORLD HERITAGE LIST NUMBER 157
ARCHAEOLOGY, CONSCIOUSNESS, ENERGIES, GEOMANCY, MYTH

IN THE COURSE OF THIS BOOK we have encountered the core geomantic concept of the omphalos several times. This is the site from which the term originally derives: in myth, Delphi is the sacred centre, the navel of the world. Plutarch, the famous priest of Apollo at Delphi, recorded that the legend was that Zeus sent out two eagles (the birds associated with Zeus) from each extremity of the Earth . Where their flight paths crossed, at Delphi, was the centre of the world. In other versions, it is swans or ravens (Apollo's birds) that are sent out to find the geomantic centre. This legend is the reason archaic depictions of omphaloi often have two birds perched on them facing in opposite directions (although Robert K. G. Temple has argued that they refer to a pigeon-carrier message system between chief oracles of the ancient world[1]).

In another legend, the Oracle of Delphi was discovered accidently by a herdsman, Koretas. He and his goats came across a 'chasm' or fissure in the earth which issued fumes causing the man and his beasts to behave oddly. In the trance-like condition produced, Koretas saw visions of the future. Once alerted to the spot, other people came and were similarly affected.

From about 500 BC the tradition was that the first oracle house at Delphi was timber-built and dedicated to Ge or Gaia, the Earth Mother Goddess. When Apollo came across the place, then called Pytho, he encountered and killed the she-dragon, the Python, that dwelt there. As H. J. Rose observes, because Delphi was formerly 'an oracle of Earth, and as the serpent is a chthonian animal, we may connect this slaying with the taking over of the shrine.'[2] The ancient goddess was usurped by a young god.

The Oracle of Delphi is given numerous titles nowadays, such as the Pythian Sanctuary or the Temenos of Apollo. The ruins, in their dramatic physical setting on the southern slopes of Mount Parnassos, are widely considered among the most evocative in all Greece. On the way up to the sanctuary from Marmaria, where are the ruins of a sanctuary to Athena Pronoia (of Forethought, or Precognition), is the Castalian spring, created, legend tells us, by the hooves of

Drawing of a fifth-century BC votive relief from Sparta showing Apollo (on the left with lyre) and Artemis. An omphalos stone is shown between them. Two birds are shown on either side, their heads turned in opposite directions. (After W. H. Roscher)

The Castalian spring, in the cleft of rocks at Delphi. (John Decopoulos, Athens)

the winged horse Pegasus. The spring or fountain is situated at the opening of the ravine between the twin cliffs of the Phaedriades ('Shining Rocks'). These sacred waters were where the old Bronze Age goddess cult is likely to have been centred, as finds from that epoch have been found in the area. It is said that Apollo planted a cutting of laurel at the spring. The fountain seen today dates from Roman or Hellenistic times.

Within the precinct of the sanctuary itself are the remnants of many shrines and temples, a theatre and other buildings, with a Sacred Way winding through them. There were thousands of statues along the Way and in the shrines. Finds have included an almost life-sized head of Apollo carved out of ivory and with hair fashioned from sheet gold.

The key feature of the site is, of course, the

Temple of Apollo. There were, in all probability, a succession of wooden oracle houses, but the first archaeological remains are of a stone temple of around the seventh century BC. This was destroyed by fire shortly before 550 BC and was replaced by a larger building, which was in turn destroyed by an earthquake in 373 BC. The temple which left the foundations that can be seen today was built in the fourth century BC. The adyton or inner sanctum of the temple was once fed by a spring called Kerna (now Delphousa), rising above the precinct. It reached the temple via the Fountain of Kassotis, northeast of the theatre. It was in the temple that the oracular pronouncements took place (see page 144).

The omphalos stone of Delphi was found in the south wall of the temple (it is now in the Delphi Museum). It is an ovoid stone in common with numerous other known omphalos stones of the ancient world. The surface of this rounded cone of stone is carved with a lattice pattern – again in keeping with various

other omphaloi – which some interpret as representing the forces of the Earth and others suggest is a reference to what they propose was a geodetic usage of such features in marking an ancient system of latitude and longitude. Coins from ancient Delphi show the omphalos stone being sat upon by Apollo or being encoiled by Python – a particularly strong hint of the old Earth goddess origins of the site.

A stadium above the precinct testifies that Delphi was a festival centre, too. The Pythian Games were instituted to commemorate Apollo's slaying of the she-dragon. These took place every eight years at the outset, but every four years at a later date. In the third century BC, the Gauls were prevented from attacking the sanctuary because rocks crashed down on them, and the Soteria festival was inaugurated in celebration of the apparently divine act of protection.

The fame of the oracle came to surpass all others in Greece, and pilgrims came from all over the known world, paying a fee to the city of Krisa (or Kira), which had taken on the

The Temple of Apollo at Delphi.

administration of the oracle temple. This fee became extortionate, and Delphi complained to the Amphictyonic Council, a consortium of 12 tribes of the region. (This arrangement of 12 tribes is very ancient and significant, being part of a greater arcane tradition based on the number 12, and it is explored in a work by John Michell and Christine Rhone,[3] forthcoming at the time of this writing.) This league of city-states declared what became known as the First Sacred War (595–586 BC). Krisa was destroyed and its territories confiscated. Delphi came to enjoy autonomy under the wing of the Amphictyonic Council and was the religious centre of the 12-tribe federation.

The oracle at Delphi was active for over a thousand years, proclaiming on matters of state and international affairs as well as on people's personal concerns. During this long period various other 'Sacred Wars' were fought, and sporadic attempts were made to destroy the sanctuary or corrupt the officiants there. The Romans took over in 189 BC, and they generally had less faith in the oracle than those who had gone before, and the temple's fortunes fluctuated. In AD 385 Theodosius abolished it.

The village of Kastri was built over the site of the sanctuary and this proved a problem in the nineteenth century when archaeologists wanted to examine the famous oracle site. International rivalry developed over the excavation rights. France won, but at the expense of rehousing all the villagers of Kastri at another site, New Kastri (now the modern Delphi), just over ½ mile (1km) to the west. French archaeological investigation has gone on to a greater or lesser degree ever since.

The nub of the Delphi phenomenon is, of course, the oracle. What actually was involved in the oracular process, the *mantic session*? Perhaps surprisingly, scholars are by no means agreed on the subject. Although there were various accounts by Greek and Roman writers, it is hard to sort out what was hearsay, what was embellishment, and what might be authentic and from direct sources. Personal preferences have been developed by modern scholars, and these, along with debatable interpretations of some of the words and phrases used by the classical writers, seem to have clouded the issue further.

The first stages of the mantic procedure do seem fairly clear, however. An animal would be sacrified to see if the omens for a consultation were favourable. Some writers say this was done by studying the entrails of the dead animal, while others claim that cold water was thrown on the living creature and its shiverings were 'read'. If the omens were favourable, the client would go into a room adjoining the adyton, which was probably the oracle chamber, though even this is not clear. No women were admitted. Questions were presented written on leaden tablets. The prophetess or *Pythia* gave the prophecies, and was attended by priests and 'holy ones'. The Pythia was a young peasant woman, but after one was abducted and raped, only women over 55 were chosen. Before a mantic session, the prophetess would bathe and drink from the Castalian spring, and drink the waters of the Kassotis that were channelled into the temple. The great traveller of the Graeco-Roman world, Pausanias, wrote that it was thought she obtained her inspiration from these waters. The Pythia would then burn laurel leaves with barley on an altar, and probably chew a laurel leaf too, before entering the oracle chamber, the *manteion*, where she would mount a tripod – a tall, three-legged metal stool with a bowl-like seat. She held a laurel or bay leaf in one hand, which she occasionally shook. It might have been at this stage when she drank the Kassotis waters.

It has generally been assumed that the Temple of Apollo was built over the fissure (some say a cave) that the goatherd originally discovered, and that the tripod was placed over the point from which the toxic fumes issued. These, it has been said, put the Pythia into trance, in which she uttered mumblings or ravings, perhaps becoming frenzied. The utterings were interpreted by the attendant priests and converted into intelligible language, sometimes in verse. However, all this may be a romantic image which has been built up on assumptions and wishful thinking.

Joseph Fontenrose studied the Delphi phenomenon for 40 years and conducted almost certainly the most thorough appraisal of all the available literature, combined with many site visits. He found a great deal to question in the accepted picture of the mantic session.[4] To begin with, detailed archaeological study of the ground beneath the temple has revealed neither fissure nor cave. (Nevertheless, it should be borne in mind that the site has suffered extensively from earthquake and human damage over the ages, and it is just possible, if somewhat unlikely, that such a feature has disappeared.) The idea that the Pythia descended into a fissure, cave or underground chamber beneath the temple in order to conduct the mantic session has largely hinged on the supposition that the temple was constructed above the feature discovered by the goatherd, and on the ambiguous phraseology of classical writers, some of whom themselves seemed unsure as to the exact situation.

The idea of a toxic vapour seems, from Fontenrose's investigations, to be without foundation, and to stem once more from varied interpretations of the phraseology and meaning of classical writers. Phrases such as *pneuma enthousiastikon*, *spirutus* and *atmos entheos*

were used. As Fontenrose explains, these can, and probably do, relate to abstract concepts of numinosity at the site, an 'Earth spirit' or particularly powerful *genius loci* inhabiting the place and inspiring the prophetess. It is poetic language that has been taken literally, a process that may have begun in the Roman period.

Delphi's omphalos stone, now situated in the museum at Delphi. Note the curious carving which has never been adequately explained.

King Aigeus before the Pythia Themis. From the Vulci Cup, fourth century AD.

Nevertheless, the possibility of an actual toxic emission should not be entirely ruled out. Though such emissions would be most likely to be associated with volcanic country, which Delphi is not, the geology there being limestone and schist, the site is nevertheless subject to seismic activity. This can release emissions of various kinds, including electromagnetic, exo-electron effects, which have been found to affect hormone production in mammals (possibly accounting for the excitation noted in some animals prior to an earthquake).[5,6] Certain hormones can have a 'psychedelic' effect on the brain, and that could, with some stretch of the imagination, account for the Pythian visions. The early writers did comment that the influence of the site grew increasingly sporadic, a decline associated with earthquake action. Fontenrose himself records that in 1936 he heard reports of vapours issuing from clefts in the rocks to the west of the modern village. However, it still seems somewhat unlikely that seismically-generated exo-electron emissions of vapours could account for the many mantic sessions recorded at Delphi, and why would they affect only the Pythia? Perhaps a compromise theory could be that there were originally natural emissions at the place that affected people, but these ceased early on in the life of the temple, and thereafter the prophetic process was continued by rote procedures.

The site awaits the attentions of a modern geomantic researcher equipped with the facilities to monitor geophysically the site and, perhaps more importantly, to analyse the waters of the Castalian and other springs involved in the mantic ritual. It may be that the *waters* had a key part that was not simply ceremonial, as, indeed, Pausanias claimed.

Another source of the supposed intoxication of the Pythia has been her inhalation of the smoke from burning laurel leaves or her eating of them. It is supposed that laurel leaves have a hallucinogenic property, but psychology professor Julian Jaynes has smoked laurel leaves in a pipe for hours on end as well as having chewed them and found no noticeable toxic effect.[7] (However, special preparation for using the relatively mild toxic properties of some plants is called for – a period of fasting, for example. Jaynes does not record that he did this.) Other researchers have suggested that other substances might have been used, such as the hallucinogenics hemp and henbane.[8]

With meticulous scholarship, Fontenrose is in any event able to demolish the idea that the Pythia behaved in a frenzied fashion in any way. The exceedingly rare references to such behaviour by the classical writers are presented in the context of it being an exception to the rule. It seems that the Pythia actually answered the questions put to her with calm clarity, and directly, if sometimes in somewhat of a riddle form. Certainly, the depiction of a Delphic consultation provided by the Greek vase painting shown above endorses such a view.

(It is worth noting in the illustration that the Pythia – her name was Themis in this case – holds a bowl. It is suggested by some scholars that in addition to purely verbal oracular utterances, the Pythia also made use of a divinatory system, such as marked pebbles being randomly selected from a container like a bowl, especially for yes/no answers.)

From an 'energies' point of view, the environment of Delphi cannot be ignored. As archaeologist Alan W. Johnston puts it: 'The brooding physical power of the site must be considered in any account of its [Delphi's] history. Thunderstorms, earthquakes and avalanches are common.[9]

CHAPTER 17

EPIDAURUS

GREECE

WORLD HERITAGE LIST NUMBER 158
CONSCIOUSNESS, EVOLVED, GEOMANCY, MYTH

THE RUINED SITE of the Sanctuary of Aesculapius (Asklepios), or the Hieron of Epidaurus (Epidavros), is situated in an isolated valley between Mount Velanidhia (the ancient Titthion) to the northeast and Mount Kharani (the old Kynortion) to the southeast, in the vicinity of Ligourio on the Peloponnese Peninsula across the Saronic Gulf from Piraeus and Athens.

The cult of the healing god Aesculapius seems to have had its origins in Thessaly, northern Greece, where Homer refers to a remarkable doctor and which was known from ancient times as a region steeped in sorcery and populated with witches who could cure by means of herbs. There may also have been Egyptian influence by a circuitous route. The cult was introduced into Athens after a plague in 429 BC and was installed on the south slope of the Acropolis. By the fourth century BC, the Aesculapian facilities at Athens were enlarged, and the cult came to supplant that of Apollo. By then, Epidaurus, where the worship of Aesculapius had been active from the fifth or even sixth century BC, had become popularly established as the birthplace of the god and was his major shrine.

In Greek myth, Aesculapius was the result of Apollo's union with Coronis, daughter of Phlegyas. She was, however, unfaithful to Apollo, news of which was passed to the god by his faithful messenger, the crow or raven. Although he loved her, Apollo killed Coronis. In remorse he turned the formerly white-plumed crow into the black bird it now is, and saved the unborn child, Aesculapius, who was suckled by a goat and guarded by a dog. His upbringing was entrusted to Chiron, the good centaur, who taught him the art of medicine, which the young son of Apollo brought to perfection. Chiron showed Aesculapius the use of the snake in finding the healing herbs, and this and a rod, and sometimes a dog, became the god's symbols. In some depictions the snake and rod have been combined into the *caduceus* – the snake (or snakes) wound around the rod.

Of the snake symbol, Vincent Scully (see page 148) commented that it indicated 'that Asklepios had close contacts with the old goddess', that is, the Neolithic Great Earth Mother Goddess. We have already noted (see the Chartres entry) how in Celtic times, the same period as we are dealing with here, the powers of the earth were seen as the serpentine *wouivre*. (It was also mentioned in the previous entry on Delphi, how a serpent was depicted as coiling around the omphalos stone.) Wavy lines quite possibly representing some similar idea have been noted from the Neolithic period – three snake-like markings squirm up a stone from beneath ground level in the chambered mound of Gavrinis, Brittany, for example.[1,2]

Although Epidaurus was the chief Aesculapian temple, there were about 300 other such centres of healing in Greece, and many more elsewhere, either dedicated to Aesculapius or to another deity with similar attributes – the Ptolemaic Greeks, for instance, identified Aesculapius with Imhotep, the deified Egyptian architect of the third millenium BC, around whose tomb at Sakkara a healing centre arose. At Abusir in Egypt, on the fringe of the western desert south of Cairo, a tenth-century AD account exists of an oracular dream cavern dedicated to Imhotep. Even in far-flung regions such as Britain, a Romano-British healing temple along Aesculapian lines was active in the fourth century AD at Lydney, Gloucestershire, dedicated to the local god Nodens.

The key element in the healing of Aesculapius was the practice of 'temple sleep' or *dream incubation* (from the Latin *incubare* – to lie down upon). The Greeks called it *psychomanteia*. The idea of sleeping at ancient holy places for cure, prophecy or Otherworld knowledge is, of course, much older than ancient Greece, probably going back to the remotest Paleolithic times in some parts of the world. It continued well into the historic era, too, in Europe and elsewhere, and is today still carried out at certain Indian temples,[3] for instance. In the Aesculapian system, a person could not seek an incubation without first being advised to do so in a prior dream.[4] When attending the temple, the applicant would go through various purifications – bathing, drinking copious amounts of water, refraining from sex, avoiding meat or fish. He or she would have been surrounded by imagery and symbolism relating to Aesculapius – for instance there might have been (non-poisonous) snakes kept within the temple. Finally, infusions of special sleep- or vision-inducing herbs might have been taken.

After being so well-prepared, the incubant would eventually be taken to a special cell, an *abaton*, and there fall asleep in the hope of experiencing a meaningful dream. (At one time, the very act of sleeping in the place was in itself considered to have a healing virtue.) An incubant might dream of Aesculapius himself, who would perform a symbolic operation or else diagnose the malady and prescribe treatment to be carried out after waking. Again, one of Aesculapius' symbols might present itself to the dreamer. For example, as Vincent Scully put it, the serpent of Aesculapius 'might touch his tongue to their afflicted parts or communicate the method of their cure to them by nuzzling their ears'. Temple assistants, *therapeutes* (from which we get our word 'therapists'), would help the incubant interpret a dream or carry out the dream-inspired treatment.

Successfully treated incubants would leave votive offerings, showing the body-part that had been healed or symbolizing some element of the deity, and make gifts to the temple. Many votive items have been uncovered at Epidaurus.

The worship of Aesculapius supplanted that of Apollo at Epidaurus, and the healing god's sanctuary there was partly a religious centre and partly a fashionable spa. Apart from the theatre (see page 150), the site is now rather ruinous. The core of the complex was the Temple of Aesculapius. This is considered a good example of fourth century BC Doric style, and it was built on what was, apparently, a previously unused

The central part of the sanctuary site at Epidaurus. The site of the Christian church is to the north, the theatre to the southeast and the stadium to the southwest.

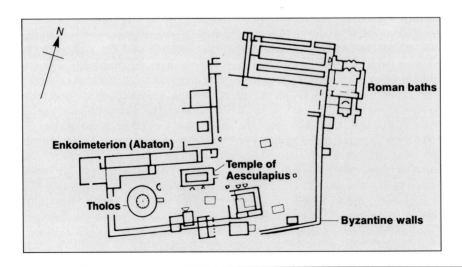

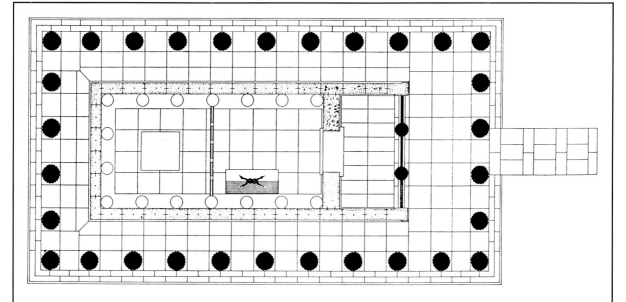

site[5] around 370 BC by an architect called Theodotus. It was fairly small, measuring approximately 80 by 40 feet (24 × 12m). Although little now remains, a stele found last century, and now in the site museum, gave considerable details about the temple. It contained a gold and ivory statue of Aesculapius, and there were paintings of masks on some of the ceiling coffers. There were sculptures and marble reliefs, some of which are now in Athens. Pausanias described the statue of Aesculapius as depicting the god seated on a throne, with a staff in one hand and the other held over the head of his serpent. A dog was by his side.

Southwest of the temple are the remains of a curious rotunda-like building known as the Tholos, also described on the stele. This was built very shortly after the temple, perhaps in 360. It stood on a platform three steps high, had 26 Doric columns around its outer side and 14 beautiful marble columns forming an interior colonnade. The foundations of three inner walls seem to have formed a labyrinth, above which was a chequered pavement arranged in a spiral. The purpose of the building is unknown, but reasonable suggestions have been made that it housed a sacred well or snake pit.

North of the Tholos are the foundations of two long buildings (stoas) that had been built end-to-end forming a construction some 230

Plan of the temple of Aesculapius at Epidaurus. (After E. de Boccard)

A nineteenth-century reconstruction of the east front of the temple of Aesculapius at Epidaurus. (After A. Defrasse and H. Lechat)

feet (71m) long overall. Here was where the actual dream incubation took place – the abaton of Enkoimeterion (though an original abaton may have been sited just to the southeast of the temple). The building was two-storeyed, and in its southeast corner is an ancient well, much older than the Enkoimeterion itself. In the southwest corner is an underground passage.

The Byzantines (see the Istanbul entry) enclosed these core buildings with walls. Close by this enclosure are the remains of Roman baths and a sanctuary of Egyptian gods. To the south of the area are a stadium, an ancient Greek hotel for the patrons of the sanctuary, a theatre and other buildings. The theatre is well preserved. Its fan-shaped auditorium forms an amphitheatre, and its acoustics are perfect. It could seat some 1,200 people, and a 'coin dropped from knee height' on the base of the altar to Dionysius in the orchestra 'can clearly be heard from the top seats'.[6]

Every four years, an athletic and dramatic festival, the *Asculapieia*, was held at the sanctuary. Steles recovered from the sanctuary itemize 44 temple cures. It is also recorded by classical writers that when a serious epidemic afflicted Rome in 293 BC, the sacred serpent of Epidaurus was sent for.

The sanctuary was pillaged in 86 BC and its contents dispersed. A large basilican church was eventually erected by the site, showing the Christian prediliction for adopting pagan holy places.

There are two main aspects to the geomancy of the place. The first is rather obscure, but undoubtedly of great significance: the presence of water. Writer Francis Hitching has noted that the 300 Aesculapian centres in Greece were 'placed at water sources where elaborate rituals took place invoking its magical (or nowadays we might say chemical) properties'.[7] Certainly, the use of water for bathing and drinking was pronounced at these places, and we might also recall the use of the local springs by the prophetess at Delphi. Water is a unique and strange substance, with many mysterious properties. Recent controversy has surrounded scientific findings that it can 'memorize' molecules that have been diluted out of solution, something homeopathists have always maintained; technologists have found that it can also apparently 'memorize' electrical frequencies to which it has been exposed, and numerous researchers have found evidence that certain kinds of water, especially when subjected to vigorous motion (also part of the homeopathy process) seem to have life-enhancing properties.[8] At any event, water locations were important to this cult and to many pagan religions. The waters at another major Aesculapian temple, at Corinth, were piped in several miles distant.

Those waters are mildly radioactive.

The other aspect of the geomancy of the Sanctuary of Aesculapius at Epidaurus relates more recognizably to the topography of the area – at least when it is pointed out. Art historian Vincent Scully, already referred to, wrote a fascinating work in 1962 called *The Earth, the Temple and the Gods*,[9] In it he perceptively described the placing of sacred architecture, particularly Greek temples, within a topography invested with significance. Essentially, he recognized that to the archaic mind the Earth was alive, an actual living being, the Earth Mother, and she was represented by the very contours of the land. Selected peaks were her breasts, and skyline clefts and valleys were her *mons Veneris*, or pubis. Ridges or mountain tops displaying peaks like horns, thus with a saddle or cleft between them, combined both

symbols in one skyline feature, and in ancient Crete, Scully suggested, this was echoed in the use of the bull's horns symbol, both configurations expressing ideas of fertility.

Scully felt that the Aesculapian site at Epidaurus 'speaks of the power of the goddess'. He identified two topographically significant approaches to the place. There is space here to give just one of these in full:

> The way to it from the Argolid is marked by mounded hills, and just before the site itself is reached two rounded ridges open to frame a pyramidical peak between them. This . . . may be Titthion, the 'teat', mentioned by Pausanias as the mountain upon which the infant Asklepios was suckled by a goat and guarded by the goatherd's dog. To the south the valley opens, and a cleft and semi-horned

The ruined site of Epidaurus, nestling beneath the bulk of Mount Velanidhia, the ancient Titthion, where in myth the god of healing sleep, Aesculapius, was said to have been suckled. The remnants of the temple of Aesculapius are in the centre of this picture.

> ridge . . . swings round to enclose it in a full and embracing sweep. Farther along the enclosing hills begin to angle towards the east, and the theatre can be seen lying within their folds. The pyramidical peak now lies directly ahead above the temple of Asklepios himself.[13]

The other 'even more expressive' approach was found by Scully to be from the north, from the sea and old town of Epidaurus. It reveals the architectural organization of the site to be 'a virtuoso performance in the use of landscape'.

151

CHAPTER 18

HISTORIC AREAS OF ISTANBUL

TURKEY

WORLD HERITAGE LIST NUMBER 174
EVOLVED, GEOMANCY

LITTLE MODERN RESEARCH seems to have been done (or, at least, published) with regard to the ancient geomancy of the Islamic world. We note the occurrence of mosques on a much older alignment in ancient Thebes later in this book, and a dramatic alignment of mosques and tombs in medieval Cairo has been recorded,[1] but greater contemporary appraisal of Middle Eastern geomantic patterns needs to be carried out. The alignment in Istanbul described here was initiated as a result of preliminary observations made by architect Patrick Horsbrugh,[2] and it is presented merely in the spirit of experimental research, to bring previously unconsidered material to the reader's attention.

The Old City of Istanbul was the ancient Byzantium and Constantinople. There were fishing villages in the first millenium BC on Saray Point, now occupied by Topkapi Palace. Between 657 BC and 330 AD, Byzantium, a Greek city-state, existed on the Point. This was said to have been founded by Byzas on the somewhat obscure advice of the oracle at Delphi. Byzantium became subservient to Rome, but was partially destroyed by Septimius Severus in 196 AD when it backed the losing side during a civil war. The city was repaired and named Augusta Antonia. Christianity rose under the relatively peaceful Roman rule, and by the middle of the second century it was becoming a force to be reckoned with. As the Roman Empire was beginning to lose its total authority, nervous emperors started a persecution of the Christians, but when Constantine became emperor in 324 he declared religious freedom and called the first ecumenical council at Nicaea in 325. He laid out a new city at Byzantium and called it the 'New Rome'. This was the real Constantinople, and the emperor inaugurated it in 330 AD. Rome fell in 476, leaving Constantinople as the capital of the later, Byzantine, Roman Empire, which lasted for almost a thousand years but reached its height under Justinian in the sixth century. The Prophet Muhammed was born shortly after Justinian's death, and by the seventh century the armies of Islam had conquered vast areas, even threatening Constantinople itself. During the series of Crusades, the city was outrageously pillaged by the supposedly friendly Crusaders at the beginning of the thirteenth century. The weakening Byzantine Empire lingered on, but Constantinople finally fell to the Islamic Ottoman Turks under Mehmet the Conqueror in 1453. Mehmet saw himself as a successor to the great emperors like Constantine and Justinian, and made Istanbul the administrative and commercial centre of his expanding empire. He repaired the walls, built a mosque – the Fatih Camii – on one of Istanbul's seven hills and converted churches to mosques. From the time

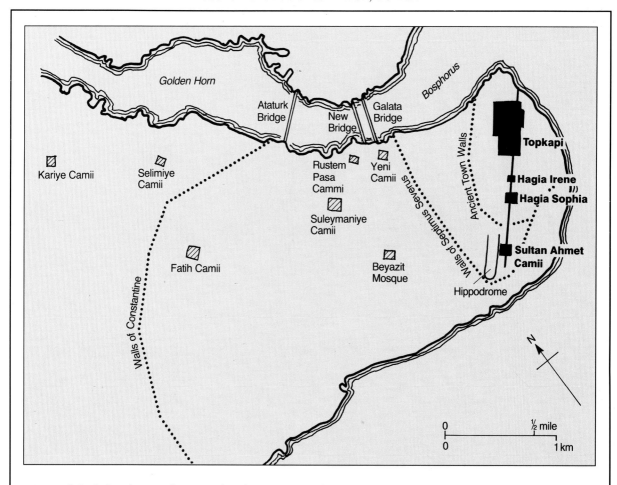

A simplified sketch map showing the alignment in Istanbul plus the old wall of the city at various periods and a few key mosques.

of Mehmet to the sixteenth-century reign of Suleyman the Magnificent, the Ottoman Empire saw its greatest flowering. Suleyman was patron of Mimar Sinan, Turkey's greatest architect. But the Ottoman era gradually declined from Suleyman's time onwards, ultimately giving way to the Turkish Republic early in the twentieth century.

Istanbul is therefore built on deep layers of history. Indeed, when construction work takes place in the city, old foundations frequently come to light. The alignment presented in the illustration above, largely within the most ancient of the various city walls, covers several of the city's key periods and demonstrates the evolution of sites.

The line, barely a mile in length, links four key sites. The southernmost one is Sultan Ahmet Camii (the Blue Mosque, so called because of the colour of the wall tiles used in parts of the interior). Now partially a museum, this magnificent Ottoman holy place stands on the site of Byzantine palaces, and was built in 1609-19 by Muhammed Aga ibn Abd al-Mu'in, who may have been a pupil of Sinan. It is the only mosque in Turkey with six minarets, and its many domes rise tier upon tier heavenward. The mosque contains a piece of the Ka'aba, the (probably meteroic) black stone which is the omphalos of the Muslim faith in Mecca.

The next site on the alignment is Hagia Sophia (Sancta Sophia), over a thousand years older than Sultan Ahmet Camii. It is not dedicated to a saint – *sofia* means wisdom. This Church of the Divine Wisdom was the greatest church in Christendom for 900 years. It was built in 532–7 by the architects Anthemius of Tralles and Isidorus of Miletus (who were to so inspire Sinan a millenium later), at the order of

Hagia Sophia. (EFI/Patrick Horsbrugh)

the Emperor Justinian, on the site of an even earlier church. Using a labour force of 10,000 men, they constructed a basilica in the proportions 2:1 and raised over it a vast dome, the summit of a series of vaults and two semi-domes. Because the pillars supporting the great dome are incorporated into the interior walls and tiers of arches, it seems to float and soar as if weightless. It is a stunning achievement, and it is said that when Justinian first walked beneath the dome he exclaimed: 'Solomon, I have triumphed over you!' However, we do not see this original dome today, for it was destroyed by a quake in 559 – Hagia Sophia, like so many major sacred places of the ancient world, is located in an earthquake zone. It was rebuilt in 588 by a nephew of Isidorus, and again in 989. When Mehmet the Conqueror claimed this supreme church for Islam, he cast soil on his head as an act of humility before entering. As a

Sultan Ahmet Camii, the Blue Mosque. (EFI/ Patrick Horsbrugh)

mosque, various additions were made to the structure. Aware that both Christians and Muslims could claim this holy place, the Turkish government proclaimed it a museum in 1935.

Next in line is Hagia Irene (Aya Irini Kilisesi, Church of the Divine Peace). This also was built by Justinian. An older church preceded it, as at Hagia Sophia, and before that the site was occupied by a pagan temple. It is many centuries since the Justinian church was used for worship, largely because it came within the precincts of Topkapi Palace which Mehmet the Conqueror had built. It now stands in Topkapi's Court of the Janissaries.

Topkapi, now a museum, is composed of four courts, and many buildings. Here were the Sultan's private rooms, harem, administrative and state quarters, small mosques and the holy of holies, the Hirka-i Saadet, Suite of the Felicitous Cloak, which held (and holds) relics

Plan of Hagia Sophia.

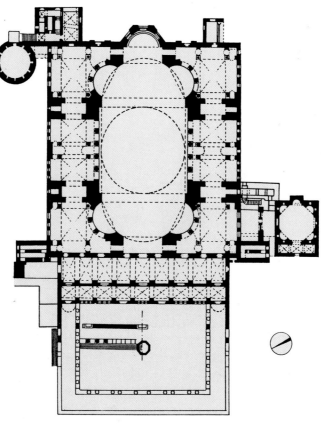

of the Prophet. Although commenced by Mehmet, many additions and developments took place over the years. Much was added during Suleyman's time – including the Sultan's private chamber, built by Sinan. The outer walls of the palace align approximately along the axis of the alignment being described.

This line linked the major sites that developed on the tip of land that butts into the Bosphorus and that saw all the development of Istanbul from prehistory to the Ottoman Empire. The subtle axis of this alignment was therefore respected over at least a 1,500-year period.

A perfunctory check reveals that virtually all Istanbul's ancient holy places may be on alignments, some possibly involving up to six aligned sites at a time. How these relate to various street grid patterns, and what periods *they* belong to, is geomantic analysis waiting to be carried out. Also, a study of Sinan's work in Istanbul and elsewhere in Turkey may reveal a conscious knowledge of sacred geography. But all this is future work.

CHAPTER 19

GGANTIJA
TEMPLES

MALTA

WORLD HERITAGE LIST NUMBER 185
ARCHAEOLOGY, EVOLVED, GEOMANCY, MYTH

THE GGANTIJA TEMPLES are situated near Xaghra on Gozo, a Mediterranean island a few miles northwest of its larger neighbour, Malta. Although the combined surface area of these two islands adds up to merely 125 square miles (320 square km), the importance of the megalithic architecture which has survived there is 'out of all proportion to the islands' size'.[1]

Ggantija belongs to a phase of the temple-building period on Malta and Gozo which lasted from the early fourth millenium BC to about 2500 BC. Colonists from Sicily arrived on the islands about 5000 BC. These were simple peasant farmers, and it was the second set of Sicilian immigrants a thousand years later who started a megalithic tradition. Initially, they dug shafts and hollowed out subterranean rock-cut tombs. These became more complex, incorporating three-lobed forms, and gave rise to surface-level megalithic edifices, which in turn evolved into temples rather than funerary structures. The megalithic building on the Maltese islands is indigenous, for the communities there were self-sufficient, and there is evidence of only minimal trading with other areas. It produced one of the oldest traditions of megalithic architecture we know of. When Imhotep – the so-called 'first architect' – was revolutionizing Egyptian monumental building by introducing stone masonry (at Sakkara), the Maltese temple-building period was already well-established. There are even small terracotta and limestone models of buildings which have been uncovered at Maltese sites, showing the temples to have been planned – truly architecture. There is even one of these models that depicts an arrangement of rectilinear structures which seems never to have been built, for no site like it has yet been uncovered on the islands!

Although the megalithic temples are ruinous now, we have a pretty good idea what they looked like in their prime, because some sites included subterranea – rock-cut tombs that mimicked the surface temples. The best example of this kind of feature is the hypogeum at Hal Saflieni. This had 20 chambers crammed with the skeletal remains of some 7,000 people. The main chamber has pseudo-columns and lintels cut into the rock and was decorated with red paintings of abstract designs and oxen.

Fragments of relief carving and painting survive in some of the surface temples, too. And at many sites figurines and statue fragments of women were found, notably of obese forms that are assumed to be female (though specific sexual characteristics are lacking in some cases): the religion of the Maltese temple builders seems to have related to the Mother Earth Goddess. The most dramatic of this type of image is at Tarxien, where the lower half of a skirted figure survives. Originally this must have

Part of the Ggantija complex. Note the dome of Xewkija Church in the middle distance. (Malta National Tourist Office)

stood 9 feet (2.7m) tall. Carved phalli also occur at this temple site.

The Neolithic communities of Malta and Gozo seem to have been sophisticated and peaceful. For reasons unknown, the temple building came to an end suddenly. David Trump comments that 'the collapse seems to have been sudden and complete, as if the whole population of Malta and Gozo had abandoned everything and fled the islands. So far, none of the many possible explanations, singly or collectively, is clearly preferred by the recovered evidence.'[2] A few hundred years later, around 2300 BC, newcomers arrived on the islands, but these people had metal – they were a Bronze Age society. They also produced megalithic structures, but of a type quite distinct from the earlier temple architecture. Sixteen dolmens from this period have so far been identified on the islands. The temples were re-used, but not for their original purposes: these new people cremated their dead and placed them in urns which were then deposited in the old temples. So although the old beliefs and rituals had been forgotten or were unknown, the Neolithic temples were obviously still considered as sacred places by the Bronze Age immigrants – an important point to remember, as we shall shortly see.

Ggantija is composed of two five-lobed temples, one larger than the other, contained within a common outer wall. The form of both temples is basically a passage with two 'apses' or transepts on either side and ending in a rounded chamber. The limestone for the outer wall is not local. Stones up to 18 feet (5.5m) high and weighing up to 50 tons can be found at the site. Excavations began there in 1827, and drawings of the place at that time show stones and details which have since disappeared. There are a number of carved reliefs on some of the stones (mainly in a transept of the southern temple) though most have become eroded. The designs show spirallic and serpentine forms. It was discovered from small fragments of evidence that the interior had been plastered and painted with a red pigment.

It has been suggested by a number of researchers that the ground plan shape of Maltese temples such as Ggantija may represent the corpulent form of the Great Goddess. Certainly the general idea of emphasized breasts and hips, symbolic of fertility and common to 'Goddess' figurines found on the Maltese islands and elsewhere, back into even the remotest Palaeolithic times, can be read into the temple plans. (This idea of representing the particular deity being worshipped at a temple by the form of its ground plan is common in

many ancient cultures around the world, and we encounter it elsewhere in this book. Christian churches, for instance, added transepts to the rectangular basilica shape to give a ground plan representing the cross of Christ, and by implication the figure of Christ, the cosmic anthropomorph.)

Ggantija's relationship with certain other sites on Gozo is interesting. For example, David Olmen, writing in *The Ley Hunter*,[3] noted that the site falls into line with the church at Xewkija and the Ta'Cenc megalithic complex.

Ta'Cenc is on the south coast of Gozo, in an elevated position commanding extensive views of the island's interior. Other alignments commence at the site too. The complex contains dolmens, a jumble of stones of various structures, possibly a ruined temple and examples of the mysterious 'cart ruts' which occur at points on the Maltese islands – curious grooves in rock surfaces as if the wheels of a vehicle had left their track. But how?

Visible from both Ta'Cenc and Ggantija is the great dome of the church at Xewkija which

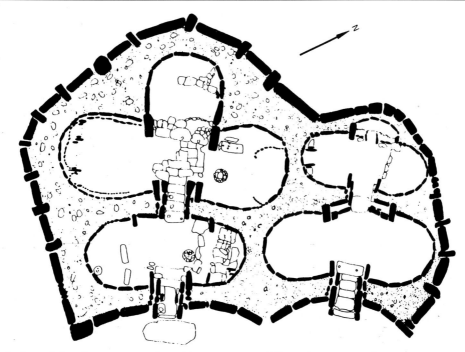

Ground plan of the Ggantija temples, Gozo.
(After J. D. Evans)

The island of Gozo with the position of Ggantija marked, and the two other sites aligned with it.

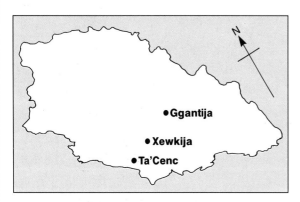

lies on the line between them. The dome is said to be the third largest in Christendom. The building is modern, but earlier churches have stood on the site, which up to the seventeenth century was occupied by a dolmen. This had a 15-foot-square (4.6m square) capstone and four uprights a little under 6 feet (1.8m) tall. Stones from it were used in the present church's foundations, as was a 25 foot (7.6m) standing stone.

The alignment thus incorporates features from the Neolithic temple period and the Bronze Age period on Gozo. We have, however, already noted that the Bronze Age peoples were aware of the old temples as being sacred sites: they were adopted parts of their sacred landscape. And the line provides yet another illustration of Alfred Watkins' claim that earlier pagan sites were sometimes Christianized, thus implying that a church on a ley does not necessarily deny the prehistoric origins of the line.

There is a fascinating relic of folk memory which effectively preserves this alignment in legend. It states that a 'giant woman' brought the stones for Ggantija (which means 'giant's bower') from Ta'Cenc. She nursed a baby and ate beans while she carried the stones. These are all images of fertility, and this bean-eating giant woman figures in other legends on the island relating to other sites (also involved with alignments from Ta'Cenc). One describes how, when a drought came and the bean crop failed, the giantess crept away and disappeared beneath the hills of the island. All these clues seem to indicate that this is a folk memory of the Earth Mother Goddess so repeatedly depicted at the temple sites. In myth, in the deepest recesses of the psyche, she still walks the leys of Gozo.

CHAPTER 20

ANCIENT THEBES & ITS NECROPOLIS

EGYPT

WORLD HERITAGE LIST NUMBER 208
ASTRONOMY, ENERGIES(?), EVOLVED, GEOMANCY, MYTH, SACRED MEASURE

THEBES IS THE GREEK NAME given to what was an ancient capital of Egypt, now most simply identified as Luxor, on the east side of the Nile about 370 miles (600km) south of Cairo. On the opposite side of the river is the great necropolis that includes the famed Valley of the Kings.

Prior to the Middle Kingdom (2040–1786 BC) Thebes was not an especially important town, but it did become home to a local cult of the god Amon (Amun). This god was a fairly shadowy element in the early Egyptian pantheon, but at Thebes he began a rise to power that ultimately was to make him the King of Gods (*Amen-Re-Nesu-Neteru*) through all Egypt. The name of Amon means 'Hidden' or the 'Invisible One'. A god of the air, Amon was symbolic of fertility when represented in ithyphallic mode (Min-Amon), and his symbol was the ram. His other attributes also included the governing of the foundation of temples, the land survey and measure – a god of geomancy!

It was when the throne of Egypt passed to a Theban dynasty in the Middle Kingdom that Thebes began to develop in importance, and Amon became the state god. Amon's existing temple was enlarged and embellished and became the leading cult-centre of Egypt. The Great Temple of Amon is usually referred to today as Karnak, a name taken from the village on the northern edge of Luxor. No one knows when the first temple stood on the site, but there were Old Kingdom (2686–2181 BC) tombs on the west bank of the Nile and Old Kingdom statues have been uncovered at Karnak. In fact, only a few remnants of even the Middle Kingdom temple developments now remain. Much of the visible temple complex today is the work of New Kingdom (1567–1085 BC) kings, but additions and use of the site went on into the early centuries AD. 'Karnak was in a perpetual state of building ferment. Buildings were erected, torn down, reincorporated into new temples and torn down again,' John Anthony West observes, in essence describing the ancient Egyptian habit of re-using sites.[1]

The Karnak complex is composed of the Great Temple of Amon plus other temples and a whole range of incorporated shrines and chapels, contained within a mud-brick wall enclosing an area ½ mile square (130ha) – the Precinct of Amon. Entrance is from the north-west, from the direction of the Nile, along a causeway flanked by ram-headed sphinxes, representing the merging of Amon with the solar symbol of the lion, a significant factor at this site, as we shall see.

The dominating feature of the Great Temple of Amon is the main axis – it runs through the various pylons, halls and shrines and through the sanctuary (the oldest part of the temple, although most of it was rebuilt in the fourth

The sphinx-lined entrance causeway to the Great Temple of Amon, Karnak. Note the dramatic line of the axis right through the temple – this indicated the midwinter sunrise.

century BC). In whatever period additions and changes were made to the Great Temple, they respected this line. In the closing years of the nineteenth century, Sir Norman Lockyer, the 'father of archaeoastronomy', conducted astronomical investigations at Egyptian temples and concluded that they had been oriented to key solar or stellar positions, a view supported by surviving temple wall inscriptions. At Karnak, he deduced that the temple axis was oriented to the northwest – across the Nile and over the necropolis on the other side – towards midsummer sunset around 4000 BC. He felt the dying rays of the sun would have reached into the darkened interior of some earlier temple on the site, perhaps to light up the image of the god kept in the Holy of Holies. He also claimed that another temple within the Precinct of Amon was likewise oriented to the summer solstice sunset, and the easternmost temple block, built back-to-back with the Great Temple, comprised the temples of the Hearing Ear and Ra-Hor-Akhty (roughly 'Sun-Rising, Sun-Brilliant on the Horizon'), pointed to midwinter sunrise.

There are problems with this, however. In 1891, a British Army engineer, P. Wakefield, observed the midsummer sunset from the Great Temple and found the view of the setting sun was in fact blocked by the Theban Hills forming the skyline beyond the Nile: even if Lockyer's line was right in theory, it did not work in practice. The axis was examined in great detail in 1921 by F. S. Richards, who concluded that it was, in any case, directed too far north for midsummer sunset in 4000 BC. For the line to have been accurate, the sunset indicated by the axis would have happened in 11,700 BC according to W. R. Fix (sunrise and set positions on a given day vary over very long periods of time because of the Earth's rotational 'wobble').[2] Either the original antiquity of the site greatly

Looking northwest along the axis from within the temple. Sir Norman Lockyer felt this line indicated midsummer sunset.

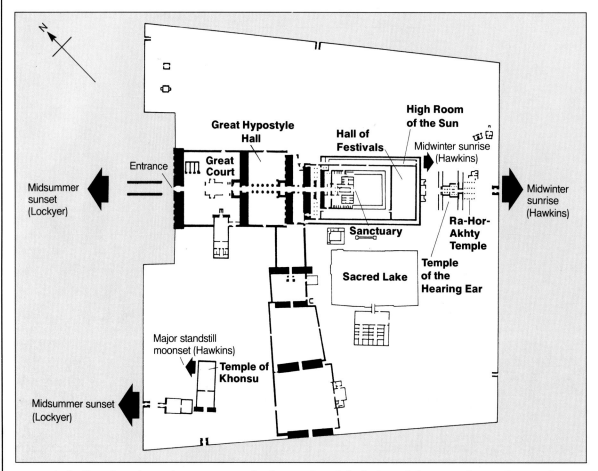

High Room of the Sun

Great Hypostyle Hall

Hall of Festivals

Midwinter sunrise (Hawkins)

Entrance

Great Court

Midsummer sunset (Lockyer)

Midwinter sunrise (Hawkins)

Ra-Hor-Akhty Temple

Sanctuary

Temple of the Hearing Ear

Sacred Lake

Major standstill moonset (Hawkins)

Temple of Khonsu

Midsummer sunset (Lockyer)

Simplified plan of the Karnak temple complex, showing astronomical orientations that have been suggested.

exceeded all archaeological opinion, or the line was never meant to indicate the solar event. However, Fix cautioned against dismissing it out of hand, pointing out that there was in any case uncertainty of plus or minus 3,000 years in the astronomical data, and that if the sunset was viewed from a high position within the temple, thus visually lowering the horizon, the date would be brought forward.

The latest twist in the story of the temple's axis came at the hands of the Smithsonian Institution's archaeoastronomical hero, Gerald Hawkins (of *Stonehenge Decoded* fame, see the Avebury and Stonehenge entry). Hawkins was clear in his own mind: 'something was wrong with Lockyer's survey'.[3] He felt that the Great Temple of Amon was actually oriented *away* from the Nile. When he looked at the Hall of Festivals built by Thutmose II in 1480 BC at the eastern end of the sanctuary complex he acknowledged that he 'could see why Lockyer had calculated for a western orientation' because

the Hall blocked the line of sight eastwards, but he found 'astronomical clues beyond the Hall of Festivals'. The Temple of the Hearing Ear contained 'hymns of praise to that god that appears at dawn', and the temple of Ra-Hor-Akhty suggested a solar skyline link in the meaning of its name (see page 162). Hawkins noted that an archaeologist had found in the ruins a group statue of four monkeys – 'it was a tradition in ancient Egypt that monkeys greeted the dawn'. The Ra-Hor-Akhty temple

was on the same long line of the main axis, a line which began at the Nile, ran along the centre avenue of the sphinxes, through the opening of the six pylons, and through the altar of the earliest temple. . . .[4]

He found that the line continued on through a huge gateway in the perimeter mud-brick wall of the Precinct beyond the eastern temples. With the aid of space-age technology, Hawkins was able to determine that the axial line in fact indicated the midwinter sunrise between about 2000–1000 BC. Lockyer had been looking the wrong way, figuratively speaking, when he assumed the temple's orientation had been towards the Nile and ascribed the main astronomical function of the axis to midsummer sunset. But the problem of the visual obstruction created by the Hall of Festivals remained. No one looking along the axis from northwest of the Hall would have been able to see the sunrise after 1480 BC. Hawkins felt the answer lay with an upper chamber of the sanctuary complex called the High Room of the Sun:

> There was a square altar of alabaster in front of a rectangular aperture in the wall. This roof temple was dedicated to Ra-Hor-Akhty, the sun-god rising on the horizon. The wall carried a picture of the pharaoh, facing the aperture, one knee to the ground, making a gesture of greeting to the rising sun. . . .
> The platform was elevated, the view clear

of obstruction. Here the priest-astronomer could make his observations to check the sun was on course.[5]

Within the temple were battle scenes, and Hawkins saw these as symbolic of the 'battle' at the dark turning of the year, when winter reaches its darkest point, and then the year begins to get lighter – the victory or rebirth of the sun god.

Of course, Hawkins had accepted the principle of the sunrise being seen from an elevated position in the temple, and this does raise Fix's point about a possible similar arrangement for viewing the midsummer sunset.

Hawkins crossed the Nile to the necropolis. This complex of mortuary temples and tombs hewn out of the living rock served many periods of ancient Egypt and covers a large area. The whole landscape is dominated by a remarkably regular pyramidical mountain. Atop it are the remains of a prehistoric mound, pre-dating dynastic Egypt. It is difficult for a

The strikingly regular pyramidical peak that dominates the Valley of the Kings and the whole necropolis on the west bank of the Nile.

geomantic researcher not to consider that the shape of this peak was an important factor determining the Egyptians' initial choice of this area as a major necropolis.

Of the many monuments there are two giant sandstone statues, 60 feet (18m) tall, which the Greeks called the 'Colossi of Memnon'. In fact, they are depictions of Amenhotep III. They stand isolated now, but they once flanked the entrance to the king's mortuary temple. The northernmost figure was famous in Graeco-Romano times as an oracle. As the sun rose it issued a sound that was variously described as a musical note, a trumpet blast or a cord snapping.[6] This effect manifested in the statue after an earthquake in 27 BC. It is possible to

speculate that the sandstone had been giving off ultrasound (high frequency pressure waves such as those used in dog whistles or given off by bats) like the sandstone megaliths of the Rollright circle where the Dragon Project had picked up apparent ultrasonic signals (see Chapter 1). Perhaps the earthquake damage had lowered the frequency range into audible sound? However that might be, Septimius Severus had the monument repaired (rather clumsily) around the beginning of the third century AD and the oracular sounds, 'the voice of Memnon', ceased. Lockyer had claimed that the dawn to which the statues were most accurately oriented was, in fact, that at midwinter. Hawkins noted that the mortuary temple

Looking northwards along the surviving section of the ceremonial avenue that once linked the Temple of Luxor with Karnak. Note the mosque on the line.

The so-called Colossi of Memnon. The statue furthest from the camera was an oracle in Graeco-Romano times.

that existed behind the Colossi in 1400 BC was also dedicated to Ra-Hor-Akhty. Estimating the axis from the orientation of the statues, Hawkins this time agreed with Lockyer: 'The temple and the statues pointed in 1400 BC to that "place of combat" of the sun, the turning point on Midwinter's Day.'[7]

The element of sound turns up in the temple at Karnak as well as at the Colossi of Memnon – but in a different way. Within the complex various obelisks stand or lie fallen. It appears very likely that these features, here and elsewhere in Egypt, were used as great gnomons, like sundials. The edges of the obelisks are very slightly out of square, even though precisely formed. Expert researcher Lucie Lamy con-

siders that this factor, plus the dimensions of the obelisk and the angles of the pyramidion (the pyramid-shaped top) could have given geodetic information – the latitude and longitude where the obelisk was placed. The obelisks were arranged in pairs, one taller than the other, and could have given the astronomer-priests detailed calendrical information and data on the size of the Earth. One of queen Hatshepsut's (1473–1458 BC) great granite obelisks at Karnak is still standing, 97 feet (29.6m) tall and weighing 320 tons. Its companion has fallen. John Anthony West has noted that if one put one's ear next to the pyramidion of this recumbent and broken obelisk and strikes the stone with the heel of the hand, the 'entire enormous block resonates like a tuning fork'.[8] While accepting that this is probably a fortuitous characteristic of cut granite, he wonders if size and cut of stone for obelisks and certain other features were calculated to produce specific sonic resonances.

Nor is that all. The very materials used for the obelisks, and all the sacred architecture of ancient Egypt, were carefully selected. It most certainly was not a case of using whatever stone was to hand: some materials were shipped hundreds of miles along the Nile. The eminent 'alternative' Egyptologist, R. A. Schwaller de Lubicz, made a deep study of the selective use of stone in ancient Egypt. He pointed out that the

choice of the veins running through the stone, of faultless masses for blocks which are often enormous and ... fragile, certainly implies a profound knowledge of the life of rock. The stones are never taken by attacking the mountain from without, but only in interior masses which have never undergone erosion, and immense caverns hollowed in the mountains by Pharaonic quarrymen can still be seen today.[9]

A stone of key symbolic meaning, and used for the most important and sacred parts of a temple site, was granite (and other stones of igneous origin). *Mat* was the heiroglyph for granite, de Lubicz observed, and, significantly, this same word 'determined by a man holding his hand to his mouth' could also mean 'dream, discover, imagine, conceive'. It is possible that there were more than symbolic affiliations with granite. We have noted elsewhere in this book (see Machu Picchu, West Penwith and also Chapter 1) that enhanced natural radioactivity, which is one of the properties of granite, may be able to trigger altered states of consciousness in certain people. John Anthony West pointed out with regard to the granite obelisks that their pyramidions were originally plated with electrum (an alloy of gold and silver). He wondered if today's instruments could have detected energy effects at them when they were in their prime condition.

About 1¼ miles (2km) south of the temple of Karnak is the Temple of Luxor, now surrounded by the modern town. Much smaller than the Karnak complex, it is nevertheless a major site; some consider it the most important in Egypt. It is certainly the most architecturally distinctive. Luxor Temple was dedicated to Amon in his ithyphallic, fertility form. Once a year the cult statue of Amon was carried in its barque in a procession from Karnak to spend time at the Luxor Temple to celebrate his union with Mut. The two temples were linked by a processional way, a few hundred yards of which are still visible today connecting with the northerly entrance of Luxor Temple. This surviving segment of the straight ritual road is lined with small sphinxes sporting the face of Amenhotep III, erected by Nectanebo I in the fourth century BC. Looking along the avenue from the Temple of Luxor end, a mosque can be seen standing on the alignment. Ley hunter Alfred Watkins would have smiled knowingly.

The temple we see today was begun by Amenhotep III in the fourteenth century BC on

the site of an older and smaller temple. The reign of Ramesses II saw more major work. But a millenium after this further additions were still being made – a process that went on even into Roman times. The strange feature of Luxor Temple is that it has three different, distinctive axes, and all the building work down the ages respected these lines. Why the temple should have three axial directions remains a mystery, but after years of detailed work on the site with his stepdaughter Lucie Lamy, Schwaller de Lubicz concluded that 'the figuration of Man' was 'the basis of the architecture of this temple'. In other words, it was the image in sacred architecture of Man the Microcosm. 'The outline of a human skeleton – traced according to anthropometrical methods and very carefully constructed, bone by bone – was superimposed on the general plan of the temple,' de Lubicz wrote.[10] The various body parts fell on specific architectural features of the temple: 'all the proportions of the skeleton may be checked

Sunset glow on the Temple of Luxor.

against the actual measurements of the temple.'¹¹ Some of these correspondences seem to have been quite detailed. John Anthony West notes, for instance, that in the Hypostyle Hall, which corresponds to the position of the lungs in the image presented by Schwaller de Lubicz, there are phases of the moon cut into the bases of the columns there. He points out that in traditional astrology, the lungs come under the influence of the moon. Certainly, the idea of a temple ground plan representing the form of the deity being worshipped is common to many forms of sacred architecture the world over and from many ages, as we have already noted (see the Ggantija entry, for example)

So there are many levels of the symbolism apparently subtly expressed in the architecture of this temple, and, indeed, Schwaller de Lubicz discovered a great many more remarkable things about the building.

The Temple of Luxor is an example *par excellence* of an evolved site. The Romans built

a pagan shrine there. Later, a Christian basilica intruded upon the place. Then, in the thirteenth century AD, as a result of a vision, a mosque was built, dedicated to the great pilgrim to Mecca, Abu el-Haggag. During the annual feast of this saint, determined by the lunar calendar, a boat which is kept in the mosque is dragged in procession around the town. Here is a startling example of the persistence of ancient rites, those being in this case, of course, the procession of Amon's barque from Karnak to the Temple of Luxor.

Finally, we note that these temples are in a sporadically violent seismic zone. There was the great quake of 27 BC that damaged the Colossi of Memnon (and toppled the 1000-ton statue of Ramesses II at the Ramesseum), and in 1899 an earthquake caused the collapse of 11 columns in the great Hypostyle Hall in Amon's temple at Karnak.

CHAPTER 21

MOUNT TAISHAN

CHINA

WORLD HERITAGE LIST NUMBER 302
GEOMANCY, ENERGIES, MYTH

MOUNT TAISHAN (WU T'AI SHAN) is one of the Nine Sacred Mountains of China. It is situated some hundred miles south-west of Beijing. It has five main peaks which rise over a central plateau, itself about 8,000 feet (2,440m) above the North China Plain: the name Wu T'ai means Five Peaks or Terraces.

It is one of the relatively few World Heritage sites that is both a place of natural significance and a cultural site, for scattered across the plateau, perched on ridges and high up the five peaks themselves, are some 300 temples. Wu T'ai is, or was, sacred not only to the Chinese but also to the Tibetans and Mongolians. The temples originated from all three traditions of Buddhism and also Taoism, coloured with hints of earlier nature religions and their deities. The culmination of the journey for many of the pilgrims was to offer homage as they walked 1,080 times around the *chorten* on the mountain supposedly containing a relic of the Buddha. (It may just be an interesting coincidence, but 1,080 is one of the key numbers of various ancient, arcane traditions of numerological knowledge.)

Wu T'ai was considered the main Earthly *locus* of Manjusri Bodhisattva, symbolizing Divine Wisdom. (This is reminiscent of that other World Heritage site, Hagia Sophia in Istanbul, similarly dedicated to Divine Wisdom.) The region became a battlefield between the invading Japanese and the Chinese, and a little later between the Communists and the former regime in China, and the temples were pillaged. We are fortunate, therefore, that the English Buddhist John Blofeld has left us a wonderful record of his visit to the sacred mountain in the late 1930s, shortly before the winds of change blew so fiercely. His book containing the description, *The Wheel of Life*,[1] is highly recommended.

Blofeld was dazzled by his first view of the plateau as he and his travelling companions crossed over the mountain pass above it. It was, he recalled, 'a sight which might have inspired the original conception of Shangri-La'. In addition to the shrines and brightly coloured monasteries scattered on the slopes and clinging to vertiginous rocks, a veritable carpet of flowers bedecked the whole scene, growing in 'extraordinary profusion'. Despite its altitude, the plateau was well sheltered, and was lush

Mount Taishan (Wu T'ai Shan) from afar.
(Patricia Aithie)

Temples cling precariously to the rugged heights of Mount Taishan. (Patricia Aithie)

with vegetation. 'Never . . . had I seen a sight so lovely,' Blofeld admitted.

As he settled in on the mountain, he found the spiritual aspect of his nature to be 'daily refreshed by the winds which blew across the plateau carrying the perfume of incense and wood-fires to the nostrils, and singing of the great Central Asian plains beyond, where the world was either very old or very fresh and young'.

Numerous fascinating experiences were in store for Blofeld during his stay on Wu T'ai. Apart from those that related to his personal spiritual quest, he was shown some strange natural phenomena. In a cave behind the small Mani Bhadra Monastery, for example, he was shown a depression in the ground holding a shallow pool of crystal-clear water. This water was sacred to Samandabhadra Bodhisattva (P'u Hsien, the personification of Divine Action) and countless pilgrims took away bottles of it, as it has supposed healing properties. Though the pool was fed by neither spring nor any inlet, Blofeld himself watched 'several scores' of pilgrims take their fill at the pool without the water level decreasing.

But, as the Englishman observed, 'Eastern places of pilgrimage abound in such small mysteries'. Eventually, he was allowed to witness something else, which was 'much harder to explain' – the Bodhisattva Lights.

Blofeld and a small group of companions toured the five peaks of Wu T'ai, visiting the temples on them as a form of pilgrimage. They left the South Peak till last: it was there, they were told, that the Bodhisattva of Divine Wisdom, the very spirit the mountain was dedicated to, actually manifested in the form of the lights. The small party, accompanied by guides, reached the highest temple on the South Peak by late afternoon. They observed with interest a small tower built on the highest pinnacle of the peak, about 100 feet (30m) above the temple. One of the monks pointed out to the visitors that the windows in the tower overlooked a veritable abyss, as it was positioned at a higher level than any of the surrounding mountains. The Lights always appeared between midnight and two o'clock in the morning, so the pilgrims went to bed in the temple in a state of great anticipation.

Shortly after midnight, a monk with a lantern awoke them with the cry: 'The Bodhisattva has appeared!' They threw on their clothes, their teeth chattering with the cold, the excitement, or both, and they scrambled across the temple courtyard and mounted to the tower. As they entered they found themselves facing one of the windows looking out on the vastness of the space beyond. Everyone gasped in surprise – none of them was prepared for what they saw. Numerous orange spheres of light where floating 'majestically' through the darkness of the mountain night beyond the window. They seemed to be no more than one or two hundred yards (90–180m) away, but because their exact distance could not be judged, their size could not be properly determined. They appeared like the fluffy woollen balls that babies play with seen close up. They seemed to be moving at the stately pace of a large, well-fed fish aimlessly cleaving its way through the water. ... Where they came from, what they were, and where they went after fading from sight in the West, nobody could tell. Fluffy balls of orange-coloured fire, moving through space, unhurried and majestic – truly a fitting manifestation of divinity![2]

The present writer checked with Blofeld that the tower associated with the temple had been specifically built for observing the Bodhisattva Lights. He affirmed that that was the case. We can thus see its positioning as being geomantic: its function was related to the sacred geography of the place.

Blofeld did not think that the nature of the lights could be prosaic. How could it be marsh gas, for instance 'right out in space, a thousand or more feet above the nearest horizontal surface and some hundreds of feet from the vertical surface of a cold, rocky mountain innocent of water?' But was it a trick perpetrated by the monks? 'Yes, if you first suppose two or three hundred men all clothed in black and able to swim slowly through space.' Some form of glowing nocturnal insect, like a firefly? 'Even supposing they were really much closer than they seemed, fireflies almost the size of small footballs?' Blofeld asked rhetorically: 'What remains? Silence, perhaps, is best.'

He was not to know, as we here on our pilgrimage of the world's secret heritage now do, that locations that attract such typical light phenomena are not that uncommon. We have already noted the lightforms of Hessdalen and various sacred sites associated with rumours of mystery lights, and we have discussed the matter of 'earth lights' in Chapter 1. Here it is enough to point out that the peaks of mountains and hills are particularly prone to such phenomena, which are sometimes referred to as 'mountain peak discharge' or MPD.[3] That there is some tectonic association is indicated by such phenomena as the 'Andes Light', a glow fairly common to the South American mountain range, situated as it is on a profoundly seismically disturbed part of the Earth's crust. It has been noted particularly strongly after earthquakes. And, of course, mountain ranges can be expected to abound with faulting and thus manifest tectonic pressure.

Certain peaks that have been seen to produce lights (glows and beams rather than discrete spheroids in some cases) have become holy, like Wu T'ai. Mount Athos in Greece, another World Heritage site, has produced lightforms that are interpreted there as manifestations of the Blessed Virgin Mary rather than of a Bodhisattva. Cader Idris in Wales, which has many legendary Celtic associations, is said to produce lights at certain times of the Celtic year, and this author has, in fact, seen a ball of light erupt from the mountainside there. In England, Pendle Hill, the Lancashire peak that was the focus of the famous Pendle Witches and where George Fox, founder of the Quaker movement, had his great vision in 1652, is known to have produced lights for centuries at least. The sacred mount of Glastonbury Tor, also in England, has had light phenomena seen around it sporadically – again one manifestation was witnessed by the present writer in 1967, when three balls of orange light partially encircled the summit. The hill of Changkat Asah, near Tanjong Malim in Malaysia, attracts lightforms very much like those described by Blofeld, and they are said in local legend to be the spectral heads of women who died in childbirth. Mount Omberg in Sweden had a monastery on it at one time, and quite recently lights, both as globes and as beams, have been witnessed on its bare, rocky peak. Mount Shasta in California, sacred to the Wintu Indians, has produced lights and other prodigies over the years.[4] Sorte Mountain in Venezuela is sacred, especially to members of the Maria Lionza religion, 'a syncretism of many traditions, including old Jaguar cults of Amerindian origin, Haitian voodoo, Yoruba and other African traditions and Christianity'.[5] The focus for shamanic healing pilgrimages, the mountain is thought to be specially favourable to the rites if the 'spirits' appear on it, 'which are evidenced by strange lights seen near the peak toward sunset'.[6] John Blofeld was 'not much interested' in 'scientific' explanations of the Bodhisattva Lights. He need not have worried: the *full* understanding of these lights lies well beyond the current status of scientific knowledge. The science that finally encompasses them will be of another order to that prevailing today.

PART 3

SEEKING THE
SECRET HERITAGE

One of Cornwall's Neolithic dolmens, dreaming it's ancient dreams . . .

CHAPTER 22

WEST PENWITH (LAND'S END)

CORNWALL, UK

A PROPOSED WORLD HERITAGE LIST LANDSCAPE
ASTRONOMY, GEOMANCY, ENERGIES, MYTH, CONSCIOUSNESS

THE SECRET HERITAGE we have been uncovering in this book is not a dead thing; it is not some museum item. The sites we have discussed may belong to lost cultures and societies, but the geomantic realities they express are perennial. The movement of the heavens, the forces of the Earth, and the silent shimmer of human consciousness go on, even if now rarely synchronized with one another. West Penwith, the tiny tip of land forming the southwestern extremity of England, provides one example that demonstrates this living geomantic heritage. It does this in two ways: as a potential landscape for inclusion on the World Heritage List, and for the research and association with ancient sites that is going on there.

In Chapter 2 it was pointed out that the compilation of the World Heritage List is an ongoing process. Sites and areas are proposed to the World Heritage Committee on a continuing basis. Whether they obtain acceptance depends on the stringent requirements already discussed. For example, an American group

nominated West Penwith – Land's End, as it is usually known, and among the more westerly reaches of Europe – as a possible landscape for inclusion on the List. At the time of this writing (February 1991), the proposal is still under consideration. The area has both natural and cultural features of exceptional interest, yet it is this 'mixed' characteristic, which may hinder its acceptance (although as we have seen there are already 'mixed' World Heritage sites, such as Mount Taishan).

Whether or not it finally gets accepted is in one sense unimportant: it is a prime *type* of landscape that exemplifies our planetary heritage. It has already been officially designated as an 'area of outstanding natural beauty, great scientific and historic value'. We will use the landscape here to provide a final and dynamic look at some of the themes pursued in this book – dynamic because in West Penwith they are being actively acknowledged.

West Penwith – the Land's End Peninsula – is the western extreme of Cornwall (Kernow); its 'capital' is the lively town of Penzance. The peninsula is barely 90 square miles (23,310ha) in area, and is connected to the bulk of Cornwall by an isthmus less than 5 miles (8km) across. The central part of the region is composed of granite hills and moorland, and that is surrounded by a coastal shelf punctuated by small valleys. The coastline is rugged, with small, sandy coves and picturesque harbours. This, and the area's balmy climate and clear light, have made the region a magnet for artists.

West Penwith has a complex, interesting geology and has enjoyed considerable mineral wealth. It was a great source of tin for Bronze Age cultures from the Baltic to the Mediterranean, and was 'the first place in Britain to be described in documentary record, following the visit of the geographer Pytheas of Massilia (Marseilles), c.325 BC, whose observations formed the basis of works by scholars like Diodorus Siculus of the first century BC'.[1] To the classical writers the peninsula was known as Belerion.

Mining for tin continued to be a key feature of the area through historical times, and today, as examples of industrial archaeology, the ruins of old tin mines with their distinctive chimneys punctuate the landscape. It is not for nothing that there is the old saying 'at the bottom of many a mine around the world you will find a Cornishman'.

Cornwall shares many characteristics with Brittany, across the English Channel. The Cornish language is Brythonic Celt, as is Breton (and Welsh). Both areas have a similar topography, and place-names echo one another – Finistère in Brittany is of course the equivalent of Land's End in Cornwall, for example. Both places share the legend of a sunken land offshore – Lyonesse in the case of Cornwall, Ynys in Brittany. Both areas have a linked Celtic tradition, with some of the same Celtic Christian saints featuring in it. And both have rich remains of a much older megalithic culture still dotting the land.

West Penwith's 90 square miles (23,310ha) has around 800 visible archaeological sites and about half as many again known sites which are no longer extant. It is arguably the most concentrated area of ancient sites in all Britain. These sites range from a variety of Neolithic stone monuments, through Iron Age villages and underground chambers (or 'fogous' as they were called in Cornwall) to Celtic chapels, crosses and holy wells (doubtlessly Christianized sacred waters from pre-Christian times). As local archaeologist and writer Craig Weatherhill puts it, the Land's End district is 'a living museum'.[2]

The ancient landscape of West Penwith contains examples of virtually all the themes we have been tracing through the world in previous pages. Here the secret heritage is being particularly well served because it has come under the scrutiny of Earth Mysteries researchers, modern geomants, in recent years, and for various other reasons. For instance, it happens to be where the Dragon Project Trust (see Chapter 1) has its office. (This part-time research effort exists outside the mainstream of science and survives only by dint of donated time, expertise and funding; those wishing to support it can contact the Trust at PO Box 92, Penzance, Cornwall TR18 2XL, UK. Donations by British tax payers are tax deductible.) The oldest and premier specialist journal of geomancy and Earth Mysteries, *The Ley Hunter*, is also based in Cornwall and can be contacted at the same address as the Dragon Project. Furthermore, Cornwall has its own pagan-oriented Earth Mysteries magazine, *Meyn Mamvro* (51, Carn Bosavern, St Just-in-Penwith, Cornwall, UK). There is active neo-pagan activity involving sacred sites in the area, and there are several local researchers who span the gap between archaeology and the broader scope of Earth Mysteries. Several of the mainstream archaeologists active in the region are aware of, and occasionally sympathetic with, the geomantic approach.

Because of this happy confluence of factors, an entire book could be written on the Earth Mysteries topics of this tiny portion of the Earth's surface, but there is space here to touch only very lightly on a few of them, linked by just a handful of sites as examples. In the cases outlined below, the reader will note how a given site (Chûn Quoit, for instance) can be involved with several themes – this is often a feature of ancient sacred places.[3]

The themes we have traced through the many sites described in this book are the subject of contemporary research in West Penwith: an ongoing revelation of the World's secret heritage.

ASTRONOMY

When he was developing his work on archaeoastronomy around the turn of the century, Sir Norman Lockyer chose the megaliths of West Penwith as one of his study areas. One of his observations was that from the Tregeseal stone circle, an early Bronze Age monument 72 feet (22m) in diameter, the May Day sun could be seen rising behind a tall standing stone called the Longstone, whose tip is visible jutting up behind the ridge to the northeast of the site. Another of Lockyer's several astronomical claims was that the Pleiades rose above the Merry Maidens circle in 1960 BC when viewed from the outlying monolith, Goon Rith. Apparently, this would have given warning of May Day sunrise.

In recent times Earth Mysteries researchers have directly witnessed hitherto unsuspected astronomical events at Penwith sites. The peninsula's best preserved stone circle,

Boscawen-un, has a leaning pillar stone set off-centre within the ring. It points to the northeast, and observation by Earth Mysteries artist Chris Castle in the 1970s confirmed that it indicates the rising midsummer sun when viewed from its base. Faint axe-head carvings on the stone are thrown into strongest relief by the oblique lighting at this time. Boscawen-un has 19 stones – 18 granite and one pure quartz, which may be a 'moon stone' in that it shines out very prominently in moonlight. Whether a lunar alignment is indicated by it still has to be ascertained.

Another example of modern astronomical discovery involves the Neolithic stone chamber

The Longstone on Boswens Common. This monolith is on an astronomical sight-line from Tregeseal circle and also on a ley alignment. See 'Astronomy' and 'Geomancy' sections.

A view over the quartz 'moon stone' to the leaning central pillar which indicates midsummer sunrise at Boscawen-un circle.

or dolmen of Chûn Quoit, an isolated monument in a broad expanse of high moorland. Cheryl Straffon, editress of *Meyn Mamvro* magazine (above), noted that it is situated in exactly the right position for the midwinter sun to appear to set in a notch on the natural outcrop called Kenidjack, which stands prominently on the southwestern skyline as viewed from the dolmen. The name of this outcrop means 'Hooting Cairn', which might indicate ancient oracular connotations. It was certainly a holy peak in prehistory, for many monuments are arranged around it.

A third instance of recently perceived ancient astronomy is provided by the careful fieldwork of local artist Ian Cooke, who confirmed that the northeastern ends of virtually all West Penwith's fogous are directed at the rising midsummer sun.[4]

The midwinter sun sets behind the capstone of Chûn Quoit and into a notch in Carn Kenidjack on the skyline beyond the dolmen, out of sight in this view.

GEOMANCY

In 1974, John Michell published one of the best regional studies of ley-type alignments – *The Old Stones of Land's End*.[5] He took Lockyer's original Penwith astronomical sight-lines, the 6-inch (1 :10 000) Ordnance Survey of the peninsula, and the best archaeological catalogue of sites available at that time, and checked for alignments, especially extended versions of Lockyer's astronomical lines. Checking 'only . . . menhirs, stone circles and dolmens' he found that 'virtually every one stands on one or more alignments with at least two others . . . these alignments were always perfectly accurate . . .'. Some were astronomical, as Lockyer had noted (though much of Lockyer's work in West Penwith was marred by various inaccuracies), but as most were not, Michell concluded that the 'system of alignments . . . in the West Penwith district . . . has some further meaning'. In tracing the lines in the field, Michell noted that 'each site in line is visible from the next provided one knows exactly the direction to look, for a stone was often placed at the extreme limit of visibility so that only its tip showed above the horizon'. Of course, with modern obstructions to lines-of-sight, and fallen or destroyed stones, this aspect of the alignment network was impaired. One example that still functions in this manner, however, is the line-of-sight from the Tregeseal circle to the Longstone (see page 176) on Boswens Common. As one walks from the circle to the standing stone, the monolith becomes more visible, increment by increment. Further, Michell discovered that in addition to being a May Day sunrise line, the alignment continued on through the ruins of West Lanyon Quoit, an Iron Age settlement and other possible stones. At Boscawen-un, he discerned a very accurate line of five standing stones, three standing and two fallen, running southeast from the circle for a little over 3 miles (5km). Lockyer had noted only one of these stones from the circle, and calculated that it indicated the November sunrise.

The Michell ley survey has caused considerable controversy. There were statistical findings for and against some of the lines, and arguments about which sites were or were not admissible. But it remains an intriguing study, and by 1990 archaeologists too were claiming strong evidence for intervisibility between the standing stones of West Penwith.[6] Archaeologist Frances Peters conducted highly detailed field work at all the identifiable menhir sites in the district and concluded that the stones 'were purposely positioned along contours . . . and that they were placed so that they tend to be fairly easy to see, particularly from other menhirs. None of this would exclude a ritual function. The standing stones . . . appear to have been positioned with a view to visibility over some distance . . .'.

Other workers have claimed further instances of alignments and intervisibility among sites at Land's End over recent years.

The menhir at Trelew, one of the stones on the remarkable ley alignment John Michell found running from the Boscawen-un circle. A curious feature about this stone is that the narrowest end was set into the ground. A pit containing bone, flint, wood and clay fragments was found alongside it.

ENERGIES

Lights without the fairy connotations are still seen in modern Penwith. In the dark interior of the Boleigh fogou, Jo May, a former university research psychologist, saw 'tiny pricks of light, like stars' and 'thin spirallic filaments' moving over the interior granite surfaces of the subterranean chamber. The 'stars' would sometimes 'streak' across the rock. Inside the granitic Chûn Quoit dolmen, archaeologist John Barnatt and photographer Brian Larkman saw 'periodic short bursts of ... light' flashing across the underside of the capstone.[8]

West Penwith is primarily granite country, and so background radiation levels are relatively high. Inside enclosed granite structures like dolmens and fogous, the ambient radioactivity is, of course, heightened. Interestingly, Boleigh and Chûn Quoit had among the highest read-ings obtained by this writer at any of the sites in the area when he conducted geiger readings as part of the Dragon Project. They were directly comparable with readings obtained by him inside the granite-clad King's Chamber in the Great Pyramid at Giza.[9] The highest readings, however, were found on the water surface at Sancreed holy well, where the waters rise into a roughly hewn stone reservoir in a subterranean stone chamber. Many people have noted a sense of languor at this truly sacred spot, and it has been suggested that heightened natural radiation can perhaps engender this feeling. If this is so, it is possible that the factor was used to help promote ritual sleep at such sites.

The entrance to Boleigh fogou, an Iron Age subterranean chamber. This site has produced strange lights and visions.

MYTH

The Penwith Peninsula abounds in legend and lore, and only a few examples can be given here. Many of the circle sites are called 'maidens' – Merry Maidens, Nine Maidens. This is almost certainly a corruption of an earlier version of the Cornish *meyn*, *maen* or *mên*, meaning 'stone'. The Merry Maidens are also known as 'Dawns Mên', which is Cornish for 'a dance of stones'. This may be inchoate folk memory of ritual at such sites. The same idea, albeit with Christian filtering, may be contained in the legend attached to the site: the Merry Maidens were young lasses who danced on the Sabbath and were petrified for their transgression. So were the musicians – the pair of great monoliths called the Piper Stones a short distance away, and the Blind Fiddler menhir further off.

Numerous sites have healing traditions. Men-an-Tol, Cornwall's famed holed stone, could cure children afflicted with rickets if they were passed through the hole three or nine times, and dragged counterclockwise around the stone a similar number of times. (This stone also had an oracle tradition.) Many of the area's ancient holy wells have healing virtue too, according to local lore. The well at Madron, for example, can boast some famous cases of healing in recent centuries, and in addition, its waters can bestow the power of prophecy. It still attracts devotees, and the bushes around it can be seen festooned with votive rags.

'Giant' associations are made in folklore with a number of sites in the area. Trencrom Hill, which has an Iron Age site on its summit, is said to have been built by giants, and their treasure is still buried there. The legends say that the giant Cormoran was responsible for piling up St Michael's Mount, the startling pinnacle in Mounts Bay at Penzance, and within 'sight of Trencrom Hill. Lanyon Quoit, one of Penwith's most famous monuments, was also called the Giant's Quoit or Table.

Cornwall is famous for its brand of fairyfolk, the piskies, and Cornish miners had a range of elemental sprites such as spriggans, which they saw – or, more usually, heard – down in the mine levels. An incident in the late nineteenth century at the Neolithic site of Carn Gluze on the coastal cliffs near St Just, on the western extremity of the peninsula, has been handed

The Merry Maidens stone circle. Does their legend and Cornish name contain a folk memory?

down into local lore. Miners returning from work in the mines adjacent to Carn Gluze saw 'burning lights' and 'fairies' bedecking the monument. The site is situated over faulting and tin and copper deposits (this may have been where Britain's indigenous Bronze Age began), a classic kind of environment for 'earth lights' appearances. It has been found that strange lights were typically classed as 'fairies' by rural folk.[7]

The sun setting over Lanyon Quoit, one of West Penwith's most famous dolmens.

The dreaming stones . . . Chûn Quoit is one of the sites chosen for the Dragon Project's Dream Programme.

CONSCIOUSNESS

That certain geophysical conditions might affect the mind is just one possibility being tested in a research programme going on under the auspices if the Dragon Project Trust. A limited set of ancient sacred sites throughout Britain have been selected for their noteworthy geophysical properties such as concentrated background radiation, magnetic stones or reported light phenomena. At these places, a core team of some 20 volunteers, plus 'random guests' are conducting a long-term dream incubation experiment (see the Epidaurus entry for more on dream incubation). The volunteer gets comfortable at the selected site, and, hopefully, falls asleep. He or she is watched over by a helper, who would have been the *therapeute* in the Greek temples. When Rapid Eye Movements (REMs) are noted beneath the volunteer's closed lids, dreaming is indicated and the sleeper is awoken so that dream recall can be fairly well assured. The dream or dreams are then audio recorded directly. These are later keyed into a computer database. The participants in the experiments do not know who else is doing dreaming on the programme.

When a large number of such dream records at the selected sites have been collected, they will be sent to researchers in California for cross-referencing. What is to be checked is not the personal aspect of the dreams (that is the private affair of the individuals concerned) but rather the *transpersonal* elements that may (or may not!) appear. The aim is to see if certain motifs, symbols, images or themes recur at *specific sites*, irrespective of who the dreamer is. Is there a *geography of the mind?* Do sites have some kind of memory field? Can geophysical areas somehow influence the subconscious mind? Is consciousness generated within the brain or merely modulated by it – is it a field effect? No one expects there to be identical dreams at given sites, but if cross-referencing does show some site-specific elements recurring to some extent, then the implications, however debatable, may be important and more intensive and detailed work will be called for.

The practical part of the experiment com-

German anthropologist Christian Rätsch prepares for a dream incubation session at Chûn Quoit dolmen.

menced in the summer of 1990 and is likely to run for two or three years. Three of the selected 'dream sites' are in West Penwith: a dolmen (Chûn Quoit), a fogou and a holy well have been chosen. The experiment is, of course, something of a 'long shot'. But the very act of sleeping at these ancient guardians of the World's secret heritage may be of value in itself. It is certainly an exciting experience, and it is surely time that the Dream of the Earth was resumed – let it lead where it will.

Red light is used for illumination on a dreaming session inside Chûn Quoit giving an eerie effect.

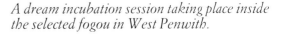

A dream incubation session taking place inside the selected fogou in West Penwith.

Dreamwork at a Celtic holy well.

REFERENCES

1 SACRED GEOGRAPHY

1. Observations by Bronislaw Malinowski and Lévy-Bruhl, quoted in *Primitive Mythology* (1935), L. Levy-Bruhl, University of Queensland Press edition, 1983

2. *Dreamtime and Inner Space* (1984), Holger Kalweit, Shambhala edition, 1988

3. 'Beyond the Brain' by Stanislav Grof, in *Gateway to Inner Space*, Christian Ratsch (ed), Prism Press, 1989

4. *The Old Straight Track* (1925), Alfred Watkins, Garnstone Press edition, 1970

5. *Lines on the Landscape*, Nigel Pennick and Paul Devereux, Robert Hale, 1989

6. Barrett and Gifford, 1933, cited in *Chaco Roads Project – Phase 1*, Chris Kincaid (ed), US Dept. of the Interior, 1983

7. *Mystery on the Desert*, Maria Reiche, Heinrich Fink, 1968

8. *Lines to the Mountain Gods*, Evan Hadingham, Random House, 1987

9. *Pathways to the Gods*, Tony Morrison, Michael Russell, 1978

10. *The Etruscans* (1956), Raymond Bloch, Thames & Hudson edition, 1958

11. *The Penguin Book of Lost Worlds* (1962), Leonard Cottrell, Penguin edition, 1966

12. *Etruscan Italy*, Nigel Spivey and Simon Stoddart, Batsford, 1990

13. *The Canon* (1897), William Stirling, Garnstone Press edition, 1974

14. *The Gate of Remembrance* (1918), Frederick Bligh Bond; Thorsons edition, 1978

15. See, for example, 'Psychic Archaeology in Ireland' by Chris Walker, in *The Ley Hunter*, 90, 1981

16. *Psychic Archaeology* (1977), Jeffrey Goodman, Wildwood House edition, 1978

17. Watkins 1925/1970 *op. cit.*

18. *Shamanism and the Mystery Lines*, Paul Devereux, Foulsham (in preparation)

19. *The Stars and the Stones*, Martin Brennan, Thames & Hudson, 1983

20. *Time Stands Still*, Keith Critchlow, Gordon Fraser, 1979

21. *The Middle Kingdom* (1959), Dermot Mac Manus, Colin Smythe edition, 1973

22. *Places of Power* Paul Devereux, Blandford Press, 1990

23. *The Body Electric*, Robert O. Becker, Quill, 1985

24. *The Electric Shock Book*, Michael Shallis, Souvenir Press, 1988

25. *Cross Currents*, Robert O. Becker, Tarcher, 1990

26. *Electromagnetic Bio-Information*, Fritz-Albert Popp (ed), Urban & Schwarzenberg, 1989

27. For further deliberations on such ideas see: *Earthmind*, Paul Devereux and John Steele, David Kubrin, Harper & Row, 1989; and *Earth Memory*, Paul Devereux, Quantum, 1991

28. *Carnac – une porte vers l'inconnu*, Pierre Méreaux, Robert Laffont, 1981

29. *Earth Lights Revelation*, Paul Devereux, Blandford Press, 1989

30. 'Luminous phenomena and their relationship to rock fracture', John S. Derr, in *Nature*, 29 May 1986

31. *The Temple Tiger*, Jim Corbett, OUP, 1934

32. Marco Bischof, pers. comm.

33. *Earth Memory, op. cit.*

2 THE WORLD HERITAGE

1. *The World Heritage*, UNESCO, 1989

2. *ibid.*

3. *ibid.*

3 CHACO NATIONAL HISTORICAL PARK, USA

1. *Chaco Canyon*, R.H. Lister and F. Lister, University of New Mexico Press, 1981

2. *Chaco Roads Project – Phase 1*, Chris Kincaid (ed), US Dept. of the Interior, 1983

3. *People of Chaco*, Kendrick Frazier, Norton, 1986

4. Kincaid *et al.* 1983, *op. cit.*

5. Frazier, 1986, *op. cit.*

6. *Living the Sky*, Ray A. Williamson, University of Oklahoma Press, 1984

7. *Lines on the Landscape*, Nigel Pennick and Paul Devereux, Robert Hale, 1989

8. 'Remote sensing applications in archaeological research: tracing prehistoric human impact upon the environment', Thomas L. Sever, doctoral dissertation, University of Colorado, University Microfilms, Ann Arbor, Michigan, 1990

9. 'A unique solar marking construct', Anna Sofaer, Volker Zinser, Rolf M. Sinclair, in *Science*, 19 October 1979

10. Frazier, 1986, *op. cit.*

11. *The New Mexican*, 25 November 1990

4   CAHOKIA MOUNDS, USA

1. *The Cahokia Atlas*, Melvin Fowler, Illinois Historical Preservation Agency, 1989

2. *ibid.*

3. *Mythologies of the Great Hunt*, Joseph Campbell, Harper & Row, 1988

4. Fowler, 1989, *op. cit.*

5. *Echoes of the Ancient Skies*, E. C. Krupp, Harper & Row, 1983

6. *Living the Sky*, Ray A. Williamson, University of Oklahoma Press, 1984

7. Campbell, 1988, *op. cit.*

8. *Primitive Mythology* (1959/1969), Joseph Campbell, Penguin edition, 1976

9. Williamson, 1984, *op. cit.*

10. *Investigations of the New Madrid, Missouri, Earthquake Region*, F. A. McKeown and L. C. Pakiser (eds); Geological Survey Professional Paper 1236, 1982

5   TEOTIHUACAN, MEXICO

1. *Echoes of the Ancient Skies*, E. C. Krupp, Harper & Row, 1983

2. *Mythologies of the Great Hunt*, Joseph Campbell, Harper & Row, 1988

3. Krupp, 1983, *op. cit.*

4. 'America's Ancient Skywatchers', John B. Carlson, in *National Geographic*, March 1990

5. *ibid.*

6. Hugh Harleston, cited in *Mysteries of the Mexican Pyramids*, Peter Tomkins, Harper & Row, 1976

7. Krupp, 1983, *op. cit.*

8. *The Ancient Stones Speak*, David D. Zink, Paddington Press, 1979

6   CHICHEN ITZA, MEXICO

1. Iris Barry, in *The Atlas of Archaeology*, K. Branigan (ed), Macdonald, 1982

2. 'America's Ancient Skywatchers', John B. Carlson, in *National Geographic*, March 1980

3. 'Tropical Astronomy', A. F. Aveni, in *Science*, 10 July 1981

4. 'Political history and the decipherment of Maya glyphs', T. Patrick Culbert, *Antiquity*, March 1988

5. Thomas Gann, cited in *Chaco Roads Project – Phase 1*, Chris Kincaid (ed), US Dept. of the Interior, 1983

7   MACHU PICCHU, PERU

1. *Highway of the Sun*, Victor W. von Hagen, Duell, Sloan & Pearce, 1955

2. Iris Barry in *The Atlas of Archaeology*, K. Branigan (ed), Macdonald, 1982

3. *Beyond Stonehenge*, Gerald S. Hawkins, Hutchinson, 1973

4. *Healing States*, Alberto Villoldo and Stanley Krippner, Simon & Schuster, 1987

5. Hawkins, 1973, *op. cit.*

6. America's Ancient Skywatchers', John B. Carlson, in *National Geographic*, March 1990

7. *The Ancient Stones Speak*, David D. Zink, Paddington Press, 1979

8. *Places of Power*, Paul Devereux, Blandford Press, 1990

9. Villoldo and Krippner, 1987, *op. cit.*

10. *Earth Lights Revelation*, Paul Devereux, Blandford Press, 1989

11. Barry, 1982, *op. cit.*

12. Devereux, 1990, *op. cit.*

13. Villoldo and Krippner, 1987, *op. cit.*

8   CUZCO, PERU

1. *Highway of the Sun*, Victor W. von Hagen, Duell, Sloan & Pearce, 1955

2. *Echoes of the Ancient Skies*, E. C. Krupp, Harper & Row, 1983

3. *Lines to the Mountain Gods*, Evan Hadingham, Random House, 1987

4. Krupp, 1983, *op. cit.*

5. 'Tropical Astronomy', A. F. Aveni, in

Science, 10 July 1981
6. *ibid.*
7. Hadingham, 1987, *op. cit.*
8. *ibid.*

9 RØROS, NORWAY
1. *Earth Lights Revelation*, Paul Devereux, Blandford Press, 1989
2. 'Northern Lights', Hilary Evans, in *Magonia*, 14, 1983
3. *Project Identification*, Harley D. Rutledge, Prentice-Hall, 1981

10 AACHEN CATHEDRAL, GERMANY
1. *The Early Christian and Byzantine World*, Jean Lassus, Hamlyn, 1967
2. *Sacred Geometry*, Nigel Pennick, Turnstone Press, 1980
3. Review by Horst Hartung, in *Archaeoastronomy*, Vol. VII (1-4), 1984
4. *Das Geheimnis Karls des Grossen Astronomie in Stein: Der Aachener Dom*, Hermann Weisweiler, C. Bertelsmann Verlag, 1981
5. Hartung, 1984, *op. cit.*
6. *ibid.*

11 SPEYER CATHEDRAL, GERMANY
1. *Der Dom Zu Speyer*, Clemens Jöckle, Verlag Schnell & Steiner, 1990
2. 'The Speyer Ley', Ulrich Magin, in *The Ley Hunter*, 110, 1989
3. Jöckle, 1990, *op. cit.*
4. *ibid.*
5. Magin, 1989, *op. cit.*
6. John Palmer, pers. comm., 1987
7. *Blue Stones*, John Palmer; unpublished manuscript, 1990
8. John Palmer, pers. comm.
9. *Lines on the Landscape*, Nigel Pennick and Paul Devereux, Robert Hale, 1989
10. *ibid.*
11. *ibid.*
12. Jens Möller, in paper given at Basler Psi-Tage, October, 1990

12 WESTMINSTER PALACE AND ABBEY AND ST MARGARET'S CHURCH, UK
1. 'Legends of London', Nigel Pennick, in *Legendary London*, John Matthews and Chesca Potter (eds), Aquarian Press, 1990
2. *ibid.*

3. *Prehistoric London* (1914), E. O. Gordon, Covenant edition, 1932
4. Quoted in *Old England*, Charles Knight, Sangster, 1860
5. *Westminster Abbey*, Christopher Wilson *et al.*, Bell & Hyman, 1986
6. 'Legends of London', Nigel Pennick, in Matthews and Potter, 1990, *op. cit.*
7. Pennick, 1990, *op. cit.*
8. *Earth Lights Revelation*, Paul Devereux, Blandford Press, 1989
9. *The Xanten Mosaic-Cosmogram*, Josef Heinsch, Fenris-Wolf edition, 1979
10. 'Mapping Roman Southwark', Kieron Heard, Harvey Sheldon & Peter Thomson, in *Antiquity*, September 1990
11. *The Old Straight Track* (1925), Alfred Watkins, Garnstone Press edition, 1970

13 THE TOWER OF LONDON, UK
1. *The Mabinogion*, Gwyn Jones and Thomas Jones translation, Everyman's edition, 1949
2. 'The Guardian Head – Sacred Palladiums of Britain', Caitlin Matthews, in *Legendary London*, John Matthews and Chesca Potter (eds), Aquarian Press, 1990
3. *Prehistoric London* (1914), E. O. Gordon, Covenant edition, 1932
4. *Mysterious Britain*, Janet and Colin Bord, Garnstone Press, 1972
5. *The Archaeology of London*, Ralph Merrifield, Heinemann, 1975
6. Gordon, 1914/1932, *op. cit.*
7. 'Legends of London', Nigel Pennick, in Matthews and Potter, 1990, *op. cit.*
8. Gordon, 1914/1932, *op. cit.*
9. *The London Walkabout*, Andrew Collins, Earthquest, 1984
10. 'The Goddesses of London', Caroline Wise, in Matthews and Potter, 1990, *op. cit.*
11. *Lines on the Landscape*, Nigel Pennick and Paul Devereux, Robert Hale, 1989

14 AVEBURY, STONEHENGE AND RELATED MEGALITHIC SITES, UK
1. *The English Heritage Book of Avebury*, Caroline Malone, Batsford, 1989
2. 'The bank barrows and related monuments of Dorset in the light of recent fieldwork', Richard Bradley, in *Dorset Natural History and Archaeological Society Proc.*, 105, 1983

3. *Places of Power*, Paul Devereux, Blandford Press, 1990

4. Account given by Terence Meaden, in *The Journal of Meteorology*, January 1990

5. *The Stonehenge People*, Aubrey Burl, Barrie & Jenkins, 1987

6. *A Little History of Astro-Archaeology*, John Michell, Thames & Hudson, 1989 edition

7. *The Ley Hunter's Companion*, Paul Devereux and Ian Thomson, Thames & Hudson, 1979 (re-issued in digest form as *The Ley Guide*, Empress, 1987)

8. *Lines on the Landscape*, Nigel Pennick and Paul Devereux, Robert Hale, 1989

9. *The New View Over Atlantis*, John Michell, Thames & Hudson, 1983

10. *Ancient Metrology*, John Michell, Pentacle, 1981

11. 'The dimensions of Stonehenge and the whole world', John Michell, in *The Ley Hunter*, 90, 1981

12. The Dragon Project Trust, PO Box 92, Penzance, Cornwall TR18 2XL, UK

13. *Places of Power*, Paul Devereux, Blandford Press, 1990

14. Gabriele Wilson, pers. comm., and in *Erde und Kosmos*, 1985

15. Devereux, 1990, *op. cit.*

15 CHARTRES CATHEDRAL, FRANCE

1. *The Mysteries of Chartres Cathedral* (1966), Louis Charpentier, Thorsons/RILKO edition, 1972

2. *ibid.*

3. *The Cult of the Black Virgin*, Ean Begg, Arkana, 1985

4. *ibid.*

5. *Chartres Maze – A Model of the Universe?*, Keith Critchlow *et al.* RILKO, 1975

6. *ibid.*

7. *Labyrinths – Their Geomancy and Symbolism*, Nigel Pennick, Runestaff, 1986

8. Critchlow, 1975, *op. cit.*

9. Charpentier, 1966/1972, *op. cit.*

10. *ibid.*

16 DELPHI, GREECE

1. *The Sirius Mystery*, Robert K. G. Temple, BCA edition, 1976

2. *A Handbook of Greek Mythology*, H. J. Rose, Dutton, 1959

3. *Twelve Tribe Nations*, John Michell and Christine Rhone, Thames & Hudson (forthcoming)

4. *The Delphic Oracle*, Joseph Fontenrose, University of California Press, 1978

5. *When the Snakes Awake*, Helmut Tributsch, MIT Press, 1982

6. *Earth Lights Revelation*, Paul Devereux, Blandford Press, 1989

7. *The Origin of Consciousness in the Breakdown of the Bicameral Mind*, Julian Jaynes, Houghton Mifflin, 1976

8. 'Der Rauch von Delphi. Eine ethnopharmakologische Annäherung', Christian Rätsch, in *Curare*, Vol. 10, No. 4, 1987

9. Alan W. Johnston, in *The Atlas of Archaeology*, K. Branigan (ed), Macdonald, 1982

17 EPIDAURUS, GREECE

1. *Megalithic Brittany*, Aubrey Burl, Thames & Hudson, 1985

2. *Places of Power*, Paul Devereux, Blandford Press, 1990

3. Rupert Sheldrake, pers. comm.

4. 'Dream Incubation: a reconstruction of a ritual in contemporary form', Henry Reed, in *Journal of Humanistic Psychology*, Vol. 16, No.4, Fall, 1976

5. *The Archaeology of Greece*, William R. Biers, Cornell University Press, 1980/87

6. *ibid.*

7. *The World Atlas of Mysteries*, Francis Hitching, Collins, 1978

8. For a more detailed discussion of these and other aspects of water, see *Earthmind*, Devereux *et al.*, Harper & Row, 1989, and *Earthworks*, Lyall Watson, Hodder & Stoughton, 1986

9. *The Earth, the Temple and the Gods*, Vincent Scully, Yale University Press, 1962

10. *ibid.*

18 HISTORIC AREAS OF ISTANBUL, TURKEY

1. *Lines on the Landscape*, Nigel Pennick and Paul Devereux, Robert Hale, 1989

2. Pers. comm.

19 GGANTIJA TEMPLES, MALTA

1. 'Megalithic architecture in Malta', David Trump, in *The Megaliths of Western Europe*, Colin Renfrew (ed), Thames & Hudson, 1981 and 1983
2. *ibid.*
3. 'Ley Hunting in Gozo', David Olmen, in *The Ley Hunter*, 113, 1991

20 ANCIENT THEBES AND ITS NECROPOLIS, EYGPT

1. *The Traveler's Key to Ancient Egypt*, John Anthony West, Knopf, 1985
2. *Pyramid Odyssey*, W. R. Fix, Mayflower, 1978
3. *Beyond Stonehenge*, Gerald Hawkins, Hutchinson, 1973
4. *ibid.*
5. *ibid.*
6. *Places of Power*, Paul Devereux, Blandford Press, 1990
7. Hawkins, 1973, *op. cit.*
8. West, 1985, *op. cit.*
9. *Sacred Science* (1961), R. A. Schwaller de Lubicz, Inner Traditions edition, 1982
10. *The Temple in Man* (1949), R. A. Schwaller de Lubicz, Inner Traditions edition, 1977
11. *ibid.*

21 MOUNT TAISHAN, CHINA

1. *The Wheel of Life* (1959), John Blofeld, Rider edition 1972

2. *ibid.*
3. *Handbook of Unsusual Natural Phenomena*, William R. Corliss, The Sourcebook Project, 1977
4. For further information on this and all aspects of earth lights phenomena, see *Earth Lights Revelation*, Paul Devereux, Blandford Press, 1989
5. 'Sacred Places in Nature', Jim Swan, in *Shaman's Path*, Gary Doore (ed), Shambhala, 1988
6. *ibid.*

22 WEST PENWITH, CORNWALL, UK

1. *Belerion*, Craig Weatherhill, Alison Hodge, 1981
2. *ibid.*
3. This is demonstrated in depth in *Earth Memory*, Paul Devereux, Quantum, 1991
4. *Journey to the Stones*, Ian Cooke, Men-an-Tol Studio, 1987
5. *The Old Stones of Land's End*, John Michell, Garnstone Press, 1974
6. 'The possible use of West Penwith menhirs as boundary markers', Frances Peters, in *Cornish Archaeology*, 29, 1990
7. *Earth Lights Revelation*, Paul Devereux, Blandford Press, 1989
8. *Places of Power*, Paul Devereux, Blandford Press, 1990
9. *ibid.*

(If readers encounter problems locating any of these references through their normal bookshop or library, please contact Empress, PO Box 92, Penzance, Cornwall TR18 2XL, UK, which will be able to indicate a source if available anywhere, or, in many cases, actually supply the title.)

INDEX